D0793734

Alternatives
to
College

Miriam Hecht
Lillian Traub

Macmillan Information
A Division of Macmillan Publishing Co., Inc.
New York, N.Y.

Collier Macmillan Canada Ltd.

LB
2322
H37

Copyright © 1974 by Miriam Hecht. Published by Macmillan
Information, A Division of Macmillan Publishing Co., Inc.
New York, N.Y. All Rights Reserved. Manufactured in the
United States of America.

No part of this book may be reproduced or transmitted in any form
or by any means, electronic or mechanical, including photocopying,
recording, or by any information storage and retrieval system, without
pemission in writing from Macmillan Information.

Library of Congress Cataloging in Publication Data

Hecht, Miriam.
    Alternatives to college.

    1. Education, Higher—1965-. 2. Vocational
education. 3. Vocational guidance. I. Traub, Lillian,
joint author. II. Title.

LB2322.H37   378   74-9194
ISBN 0-02-468900-9 (hardbound), 0-02-469290-5 (paperbound)

Macmillan Information

866 Third Avenue
New York, N.Y. 10022

Collier Macmillan Canada Ltd.

Table of Contents

39562

Introduction

Today, in the United States, more than 85 percent of the adult population are not graduates of a four-year college. Of the country's jobs, 80 percent do not require a college degree.

Yet over 50 percent of our high school graduates go on to college; in some communities, the figure is close to 70 percent. Half of them will never graduate; another quarter will stretch out their undergraduate studies beyond the traditional four years. And untold numbers never wanted to go in the first place.

These are bright, energetic young people who could certainly succeed in college if they wanted to. They're simply not sure they want to. After twelve years of sitting still and listening to their teachers' voices, they're ready to try something else. They want to look after themselves, to travel, to meet people. They want to work and—with an open-mindedness their elders might well emulate—they are willing to work at anything. They want to stretch—physically, mentally, and spiritually.

Instead, they go to college.

They go by default because no one offers them anything else. Parents have been conditioned to believe that higher education is something they owe their children. Schools, themselves permeated with university graduates, see education as the one bright spot on the horizon. Employers seize upon the trend to demand college degrees for jobs in which they are completely irrelevant. Whatever the motives, the results are the same: students are channeled into college as if alternatives did not exist.

This is not a book against college. Thousands of young people will go to college and benefit enormously. Some will devote their lives to scholarship and research. Others are pointed toward professions which demand a college degree. Still others enter college with no clear purpose, but find a purpose as they study and mature.

However, there are thousands more for whom college is not the answer. If you are one of them, then no matter how right it may be for someone else, it is wrong for you. You want alternatives, and you deserve them. The United States turns out close to three million high school graduates a year; they cannot be put into a single mold.

The purpose of this book is to explore channels which, for some of these three million, are long- or short-range alternatives to college. There is nothing radical about the channels themselves; they include work, occupational education, the Armed Forces, and the like. What may be radical is the viewpoint that they represent desirable and appropriate courses of action, even for students who could handle college if they wanted to.

The idea of not attending college comes as a shock, particularly to parents who have been preoccupied with the prospect for years. How can they let their children be dropouts, when studies show that college graduates earn more and live better than anyone else? The studies do exist—but they incorporate a major flaw: any study comparing college graduates with their non-college counterparts is also comparing a brighter, more prosperous and more privileged group with one that is slower, poorer and relatively disadvantaged. Of course differences will be found—but who can say whether they're due to college or to all these other factors? Indeed, recent research suggests that students who could hold their own in college can also manage very nicely without it.

Many young people are already thinking along these lines; it is their elders who must catch up. Parents must recognize that as children differ in talents, personality and temperament, so the options open to them must reflect these differences. Guidance counselors, themselves steeped in an academic tradition, have too often equated counseling with college counseling; it is time they enlarged their horizons. Libraries must furnish support in the form of books, pamphlets, and other references; the Occupational Outlook Handbook should be as much a part of the student's home reference library as the dictionary.

Our unthinking commitment to college may be related to another difficulty: our attitude to the subject of work. By and large, work is what *adults* do, yet the word is rarely heard in American classrooms. The Europeans are far ahead of us here: their youngsters learn about the conditions of working life, the structure of industry, the role of trade unions, and basic labor laws as early as the seventh grade. We can benefit from their example. In or out of college, our students would be enriched by an orientation to the adult working world.

Here and there, ideas like these are taking root. On the high school level, more and more students are holding jobs or participating in work-study programs. California children are learning about work as early as grade school. The reports of the Carnegie Commission on Higher Education repeatedly recommend that work and study be interwoven throughout life, instead of being separated as they are now. The publication,

Youth: Transition to Adulthood, prepared by the President's Science Advisory Committee, stresses the same point. Sociologist Blanche Blank has called for legislation eliminating the college degree altogether as a prerequisite for any job; you qualify if you can do the work—with or without a diploma.

However, the ultimate authority rests with the high school graduates themselves. As technological skills loom larger and opportunities narrow in such fields as teaching and the humanities, more and more of them are considering college—and turning it down. Capable and determined as they are, they are applying their gifts elsewhere. If we can see our way clear to liberating our teen-agers from the mindless insistence on college, countless more will follow this example.

Perhaps we should think of these young people, not as drop-outs, but as drop-ins. They are dropping into the world of work and responsibility. They are learning to function among adults, to deliver what they promise, to persuade, to produce—in short, to carry their own weight. They are learning to grow up.

In preparing this book, we were assisted by more individuals than can be named. However, we cannot close without mentioning a few who were particularly helpful. Dr. Ivar Berg of Columbia University generously shared his own insights, and provided sources of additional information. Dean Blanche Blank of Hunter College interrupted her busy schedule more than once to answer questions. We are grateful to the office of Dr. James Coleman for letting us see a copy of *Youth: Transition to Adulthood* in advance of publication. Professor Arthur A. Dole, of the University of Pennsylvania, shared with us the results of his researches, and provided warm encouragement. Saul Traub was invaluable in preparing the chapter on the Armed Forces. Librarian Arthur Goldzweig of Hunter College tracked down references with uncanny skill. Others who were generous with resources or expertise were King Bleimeyer of the Army Times Publishing Company, Clara Clapp of the Carnegie Foundation, Tula Lewnes of the Small Business Administration, Peter Kleinbart of the National Commission on Resources for Youth, and the staff of the New York City Voluntary Action Center.

Above all, however, we are grateful to the many young people—students, clients, children and friends of children—who shared with us their problems and points of view. It is they who provided the impetus for this book, and it is for them that it was written.

Miriam Hecht
Lillian Traub

1

The Need for Alternatives

In 1971 a prophetic story appeared in the inside pages of *The New York Times*. It described a handful of high school graduates—bright, capable young people from prosperous homes—who, with or without their parents' blessing, were not going to college. Some felt they'd probably get there sooner or later, others were less sure; but all agreed that for them, at this point in their lives, attending college was not what they wanted to do.

The very idea smacks of heresy. We are so saturated with the dogma that college is good, that the questions "Good for what?" "For whom?" "Compared with what else?" are rarely heard. In 1939 10 percent of all American high school graduates entered college. By 1955 the figure had reached 35 percent; in 1973 it was over 50 percent.

Today Americans are spending over 12 billion dollars annually on undergraduate college education. Parents cut corners and take second jobs in order to meet the very considerable cost. College admissions has spawned a whole new industry, complete with advisers, cram courses, review books—even computers to match student with institution! At the hub is the high school senior himself, compulsively filling out applications and sweating out the returns.

Yet when we look at the campus, it tells a different story. Parents—the very ones who boasted of all the college acceptances received—complain that the college experience, far from preparing their child for the "real world," seems to be alienating him from it. Faculties valiantly experiment with new content and style, only to be once more rejected by the new breed of student. Above all, the undergraduates themselves affirm in a hundred ways that whatever they are looking for, they are not finding it in the classroom. One top-ranking Dartmouth graduate admitted that he felt absolutely no sense of accomplishment. In his valedictory address he stated, "I have made no plans because I have found no plans worth making."

What happened? Are the new students as dissatisfied as they appear to

1

be, the grown-ups as rigid, the courses as irrelevant? Or has the difficulty resulted from a serious distortion of the old American dream?

COLLEGE: OPTION OR TRAP?

Traditionally, the option of going to college was available only to the well-to-do. Even if tuition and living expenses could be managed, few could afford the luxury of converting their time into learning instead of paid work. As a rule, financial aid—in the form of scholarships, part-time jobs and free public institutions—was directed toward the students of uncommon ability; even then, there wasn't nearly enough to go around. Millions of young people were denied a college education and, with it, the entire range of choices and opportunities which depend on college. In a country whose keystone was opportunity, this was unconscionable. Gradually there arose the conviction that higher education should be made available to every qualified high school graduate.

However, *offering* college to all graduates is one thing; *insisting* that they go is quite another. The first opens a door; the second closes every door but one. J. A. Gengerelli, professor of psychology at the University of California, feels that we have created an "educational tube" leading from kindergarten to the bachelor's degree and shutting off all vistas and alternatives along the way. At one time, teen-agers could choose freely from a whole spectrum of alternatives. College was merely one possibility among many; a youngster could turn it down without a sense of personal, social or economic failure. Over the years, however, college became the only accepted choice. In effect, all the other options—including merely postponing college—were eliminated.

The result has been a mass of students who drag to classes semester after semester, taking notes, writing papers, accumulating credits, with barely a glimpse of why they are there. These are the ones who complain that their studies are not relevant, without facing the question, "Relevant to what?" They "get the required courses out of the way," and simultaneously grumble that the schools deny them a chance to pursue their interests. They reproach the educational system for failing to provide everything from free breakfasts to free abortions, while turning their backs on the learning and scholarship it was meant to provide. So little do they appear to benefit that one wonders why they come. Let's look at a few and find out.

Take Andy Koehler. For three summers, and part-time during the school year, Andy worked for a plant nursery. He liked the job. He liked using his muscles, dealing with people, and—never one for dressing up—he liked working in dungarees. He had a good eye for design, and customers often asked his advice. When the boss offered him a full-time job, Andy wanted to accept. His school counselor, however, was aghast. Andy's grades would admit him to the local branch of State U. If Andy was interested in plants, he could major in science. Mr. Koehler, Andy's father, had never been to college; he assumed the counselor knew what was best.

So Andy's in college now. He's trying; he studies hard. But he misses the feel of the nursery, and he gets fidgety sitting in his required trigonometry and social studies classes. He admits that he's picked up a thing or two in his once-a-week art course, but he could easily have enrolled for that single course. Andy's bound to learn something in college, but he might have learned as much, or more, at the work he wanted to do.

Jennifer has a different story. She's the type whose teachers described her as a "dear child," even when she was eighteen and a high school senior. Docile and soft-spoken, she deferred willingly to authority, rarely argued, and maintained her B average, in part at least, because she was so trouble-free. Privately, Jennifer's parents agreed that she was going to college because there wasn't another thing in the world they could think of for her to do; they hoped vaguely that the experience would "mature" her.

But one month as a freshman made it clear that maturity is a long way off. Nothing in Jennifer's tastes or work habits prepared her for a college level of study. She puts things off, never gets organized; her grades are settling at an uncomfortable C. She's found her friends among a group very much like herself—students who flounder through their lectures, gossip and play records hours on end and, collectively, provide a serious deterrent to the growing up each of them has to do.

It is hard to say why Jennifer's parents believed that relocating her a few hundred miles away, to fend for herself among new people and new problems, would miraculously mature her, but parents make that mistake all the time.

Still, Jennifer and Andy aren't what you'd call "real students." Let's have a look at someone like Fred. Fred is the product of a prestigious private day school. Over the years a whole series of instructors had pumped him with learning. Fred didn't mind; studying was easy for him, and even term papers aren't bad if your father's secretary does the typing.

Fred's announced goal in college is to "discover" himself. He's certainly discovering a lot about everybody else. He's discovered that his current teachers are as impressed by flattery, money and a veneer of pseudo-scholarship as his previous ones. He's discovered that his high school papers, with updated bibliographies and footnotes, earn him decent grades, even here. He's discovered that if he tells people he's still "exploring the curriculum," they stop bothering him. Yet as his record grows—and it's a good record—so does his cynicism about the whole system that brought him here.

Jennifer, Andy, Fred, and the thousands like them attend college for a variety of reasons—to be with friends, to get out of the house, to satisfy the demands of their parents, or merely because they can think of nothing better to do with themselves. Some grumblingly refer to college as a "meal ticket" . . . and with justice: industry has long demanded college degrees for jobs requiring little more than a high school diploma, a bit of poise, and some common sense. Above all, they go because it is expected of them. Their parents, their teachers, their entire world have brought them to a point where the move from high school to college is as mechanical as that from kindergarten to first grade.

THE CASE FOR DROPPING OUT

What is the typical high school senior choosing, when he chooses college? For one thing, he's choosing a period of nonproductivity, of sitting on the sidelines just when he may be aching to get into the thick of things. He is choosing to learn second-hand through words and formal lectures, rather than directly through experience. He is choosing an incredibly sedentary way of life (the amount of sheer sitting demanded by college boggles the mind!) at a time when he is already restless. And this says nothing of the other choices—of companions, courses, field of study—for which he may not be ready.

Let's not paint too bleak a picture. The fact is that thousands of college students soon determine what's expected of them, make the necessary adjustments, and gain a great deal. But American high schools turn out over two million graduates a year. Some are too mature to fit into the structure of college; others are too immature to benefit from it. For thousands the wisest choice may be travel, or working, or marrying and settling down, or joining the Army, or mastering a trade. A recent Carnegie Commission report notes that "maturity of judgment and clarity of goals both gain from nonformal educational experiences." Yet let a "college-material" youngster decide he'd rather use his talents some other way, and the head-shaking begins; he is a "dropout," a "social misfit."

Against this background we can reconsider that handful of high school students whose quiet rebellion was described in *The New York Times*. For 12 years the central experience of these youngsters was school. Now they demanded the right to step off the educational treadmill. One of them —a girl who had served as a teaching aide and as editor of her school paper—felt that college might be a waste of her time and her parents' money. She explained, "Most of the growing up I did in the past four years—the intellectual growth, too—took place outside of school." A young man planned to get a job because he wanted to think more about his future before settling into college. Others chose to travel or study abroad. Whatever their alternatives, these young people expected them to be more rewarding than the continued life of the classroom.

We see signs of the same rebellion on a higher level. A study of Columbia and Harvard seniors reveals that an increasing number have refused to continue with graduate work, or even to go after the kind of jobs for which their degrees qualified them. Instead, they have become cabdrivers, mechanics, cabinetmakers, craftsmen, blacksmiths, or have just drifted awhile. The Dartmouth graduate quoted earlier planned to keep busy at some menial work until he decided what to do with his life. Bartending was a possibility, because "it's something to do with the hands, and it's being with people." For all their education, these young people felt something missing, and they went after it.

The students described above are a highly individualist minority. Yet their grievances are also heard in some eminently respectable places. The American Academy of Arts and Sciences has urged that we eliminate the "involuntary servitude" of those students whose primary reason for attending college is social or economic pressure; it suggests that for some of them, a sophisticated vocational program might make more sense. Along the same lines, Dr. Sidney Marland, Jr., former United States Commissioner of Education, has pointed out that "we have hypnotized ourselves . . . we are so preoccupied with higher education that it has become a national fetish." He asks us to redefine our standards so that "a first-rate artisan who works with his hands is held in as high esteem as the graduate of a liberal arts college." Dr. William McGill, president of Columbia University, suggests that the best system would be one in which a student spent some time at the university, then obtained some job experience, and then returned to school. In its report, *Less Time, More Options,* the Carnegie Commission on Higher Education states even more strongly:

Young people have changed. They reach physiological and social maturity at an earlier age—perhaps by about one year, and yet more of them are kept longer in the dependent status of student. They are more resistant to the seemingly endless academic "grind" that, for more of them, goes on for more and more years without letup, sitting at their desks as recipients of knowledge but without productive contribution. This takes an internal discipline and a fixed concentration . . . which many of them no longer feel . . . Sixteen years of education straight through to a B.A. or 20 to 22 to a Ph.D. . . . does not suit many of them. Many students would like to have productive experience on their way to the degree and to get into regular productive effort earlier in their lives.

THE ROLE OF INDUSTRY

In pinpointing the sources of today's discontent, many critics have singled out industry as a prime offender. *Less Time, More Options* recommends that ". . . essentially, employers should do more of their own screening for talent and rely less on the instrumentalities of the college, which are designed primarily for other purposes."

Now industry is beginning to agree. During the fifties and sixties, corporations took to requiring a bachelor's degree for all sorts of administrative and managerial openings. What benefits did they expect from the degree? Ivar Berg, professor of sociology, Columbia University Graduate School of Business Administration, put the question to a cross-section of personnel executives. In his book, *Education and Jobs: the Great Training Robbery,* he reports on their responses:

> . . . The unifying theme was the diligence and "stick-to-it-iveness" of a young man who can endure four years of college. The college degree was consistently taken as a badge of the holder's stability and was apparently a highly prized characteristic of young recruits. . . . The content of a college program mattered a good deal less than the fact of successful completion of studies. The poise and self-assurance of college graduates received considerable attention.

In recent years industry has been asking whether this description still applies. Several years ago, *Fortune Magazine,* a leading business periodical, reported on attitudes of college and non-college youth in certain areas considered important to employers. Some of their responses are given here:

	Percent Agreeing	
	Non-college	College
Easily accept outward conformity for career advancement	35	14
Easily accept power and authority of the boss at work	71	49
[Believe that] money is very important	40	18
[Believe that] hard work always pays off	79	56
[Believe that] competition encourages excellence	82	72

Since then, a growing number of executives have taken a stand against the mindless insistence on college graduates. Al Birlow, director of college placement for the Chase Manhattan Bank, has noted, "There are a lot of junior military officers coming out of the service now, and they are going to make a terrific impact. . . . We find these young men more mature than the average fellow coming right out of college, more responsible, and with an eagerness to catch up." J. Wasson, chairman of the board of directors of the Pacific Telephone and Telegraph Company, has remarked, "Over the years we seem to have become afflicted with a college-degree syndrome, and this, to me, is unfortunate. For I have always defined a successful man as one who uses his talents to the fullest, regardless of how great or how limited these talents happen to be. The problem is how do we get the right person into the right slot, not how do we get everyone into graduate school."

New college graduates are being particularly hard-hit in the current job market. In part, this is due to the decreased demand for teachers, engineers, and certain other professionals; but it may also reflect a changing attitude on the part of business. Far from presenting himself as the diligent, cooperative individual of Ivar Berg's report, the current graduate may be an awkward, self-centered young person who is deeply troubled to learn that he is there to meet the firm's needs, rather than the other way round.

COLLEGES EXAMINE THEMSELVES

Attacked from all directions, the colleges are doing some soul-searching of their own. If their goal is to enhance a student's understanding of himself, of the world outside him, and of his relation to that world, where have they fallen short? Are the years from 18 to 22 really the best time for higher education, or might the experience be deferred? Why must the work be done in four consecutive years and in a particular place? How can the learning that comes with work, with responsibility, with outside activities of every sort, be given academic recognition? Has the formal classroom outlived its usefulness?

As part of the housecleaning, colleges are taking a closer look at their own students. The findings suggest that there are as many misfits inside college as outside it. Of all the students who begin college, fewer than half graduate; of that number, close to half require more than four years. The campus disruptions of the late 1960's are well-known; but while violent disruption has become the exception, Columbia's president William McGill notes that discontented students, far from being a tiny minority, comprise one-third to one-half of the entire student body. Meanwhile Dr. Dana L. Farnsworth of Harvard University points out that of every 10,000 college students, 1000 will have emotional conflicts severe enough to warrant professional help; 300 to 400 will have feelings of depression deep enough to impair their efficiency; 15 to 25 will require hospital treatment of psychological disorders; 5 to 20 will attempt suicide, and 1 to 3 will succeed. This is offered, not as a condemnation of the campus, but as evidence that college is no insurance against the usual problems, tensions and difficulties of growing up.

But if not college, then what? What are the alternatives? Here we must ask, alternatives for whom? We are talking about an annual crop of three million high school graduates; no single alternative can serve them all. The student who wants to help others has one set of alternatives; the one who wants to leave home has another. We must sort out the graduates who want to play football, become lawyers, get married. Before we can offer our teen-agers alternatives to college, they must know what it is they are looking for, what it is they want. Only then will they know which alternative is right for them.

2

Why They Go to College

Why do people go to college? The answer depends on who's asking the question, and who's answering. Academia has one set of reasons; the students, another. Parents have some off-the-record contributions of their own. And as we will see, there's a substratum of powerful reasons that hardly anyone bothers to mention.

THE COLLEGES' ANSWER

Speaking for the colleges, W. Todd Furniss of the American Council of Education suggests that traditional liberal education has the following overlapping goals:

1. Fostering individual traits beneficial to the student, such as confidence, dignity, aesthetic sensitivity, resourcefulness, adaptability to new conditions, and commitment (characteristics today included in the catch phrases "life style" and "self-awareness");
2. fostering the acceptance of such social values as honesty and integrity in dealing with others, concern with their welfare, and acceptance of responsibility to work for the common good;
3. fostering the kinds of behavior thought to be appropriate to the occupations for which the student is being prepared; and
4. teaching the student the skills and knowledge appropriate for his success in each of these aspects of life, with emphasis on analytic techniques, and ability to generalize and synthesize.

Of these four goals, only the last deals directly with the teaching function of the college. The others address themselves to the student as an individual and in relation to the adult world.

9

THE PARENTS' ANSWER

For parents, things shape up a little differently. In a 1972 Gallup poll of public attitudes toward college, they gave the following reasons for sending children to college:

	Percentage mentioning this reason in some form
To get better jobs	44%
To get along better with people at all levels of society	43%
To make more money, achieve financial success	38%
To attain self-satisfaction	21%
To stimulate their minds	15%
Miscellaneous	11%

It looks like parents put better jobs over self-satisfaction, two to one. And, of course, it's the parents who pay the bills.

THE STUDENTS' ANSWER

But what of the students themselves? Arthur A. Dole, professor of education at the University of Pennsylvania, asked college freshmen to choose, from a list of 78 possible reasons, those which were most important to them. The top ten responses, for men and women, are given below:

Men

1. I feel that a college degree is necessary for the kind of work I want to do.
2. I hope to prepare myself to be a success in life.
3. I want to prepare myself for specialization in some field.
4. A college degree means a great deal to me.
5. Opportunity for advancement. It will help me to get a good job in which I can get ahead in life.
6. Satisfaction from field. I am interested in the kind of thing I plan to study and enjoy it.
7. Aptitude. I feel that I will be able to do well in what I plan to study.
8. Self-improvement. I can help myself become a better person.
9. Independence. It will help me to stand on my own two feet and do things for myself and by myself.
10. Interest in work with ideas, such as planning, analyzing, thinking about things, etc.

Women

1. I feel that a college degree is necessary for the kind of work I want to do.
2. I hope to prepare myself to be a success in life.
3. Satisfaction from field. I am interested in the kind of thing I plan to study and enjoy it.
4. Self-improvement. I can help myself become a better person.
5. A college degree means a great deal to me.
6. Security of employment. I will be sure of getting a job.
7. Chance to serve others. It will help me to be of greater service to people.
8. Most practical thing to do. It will be useful to me later on.
9. I want to prepare myself for specialization in some field.
10. Independence. It will help me to stand on my own two feet and do things for myself and by myself.

This is what students told a university professor, in a college setting. Yet when they talk among themselves, a new note creeps in. We hear comments like, "My boyfriend's going, so I'm going," "My family expects it of me," "I couldn't live in that house another minute," and "What else is there to do?" Reasons like these don't appear on questionnaires, but they could carry more weight than the conventional ones.

To get the complete picture, let's look at a few entering freshmen. At the age of six, Marcia tried in vain to nurse an ailing butterfly back to health. At eight, she had better luck with a pigeon. Since those days Marcia's known that she would be a veterinarian. Her chemistry grades—B one semester, C+ the next—suggest that she may have some trouble; and right now she's worried because the best veterinary schools want a year of calculus. But none of that will stand in her way. She knows why she's going to college, and so does everyone else; there's no problem.

Jerry wishes his reasons were as good. He hadn't planned on attending college; his father has the biggest hardware store around, and everyone knows that Jerry will take it over some day. But there's this girl, Ellie . . . "She's a nice girl," his mother explains, "but he should get out more . . . meet other people." Ellie has her own version. "They've been trying to break it up since out first date!" Jerry? Jerry hardly knows any more. He knows he's in love with Ellie . . . or was . . . or thinks he is. But his parents are okay, too—most of the time. If only he could get away somewhere, by himself, and think things through!

So Jerry's going to college. He leaves in three weeks—rather to the annoyance of his father, who really could use him in the store.

For Warren, things shape up differently. He's the fellow with leadership qualities. He has held a half-dozen important school posts, and has done well at each. Some students claim he's an operator; he uses people. They may be right. But wherever Warren ends up—management, administration, or running his own business—you can be sure he will be giving the orders, not carrying them out. And the passport is a college diploma.

Then there's Barbara. The only tranquil moments at Barbara's house are when they've all stopped talking to one another. Otherwise it's one endless stream of nagging, bickering, whining, and shouts. A year ago things were different; they'll be different again a year hence. But right now, the battling seems to be as inevitable as breathing. However, the end is in sight because, come September, Barbara is going to college. Central State. Of course she'll get in; her average isn't that low. And 130 miles is close enough to come home on weekends—not that they'll insist on it.

Where do these four belong on Dole's list? Marcia is easy: "I feel that a college degree is necessary for the kind of work I want to do." Warren fits neatly into "I hope to prepare myself to be a success in life." What about Jerry? On the questionnaire, he might have checked "Independence . . .," but that's stretching a point. As for Barbara, her reason—*not* included in Dole's list—is simple: she wants out of the house.

In one sense, all these reasons are valid. Each of them recognizes the student's individual needs; each can be, and has been, achieved at college. Yet there is one critical difference among them. Certain goals can be achieved *only* in college; the rest can also be achieved in other ways. This means that a few students have virtually no alternatives; others have a wide range of choices. Let's examine the question of whether or not to attend college from this point of view.

SITUATIONS WITH NO ALTERNATIVE

Consider the student who has already chosen a field requiring college, for example, Marcia. In this country, at this time, the only way she can become a veterinarian is by going to college. The same applies to would-be doctors, teachers, lawyers, social workers, engineers, scientists of every description, and architects, to name only a few.

It wasn't always so. A hundred years ago, grade school was taught by eighteen-year-old girls with rather skimpy educations of their own; as for architecture and law, the standard procedure was to apprentice oneself to someone in the field. In Germany, to this day, entrance to most professions is by examination; you can qualify if you know the material, regardless of where you learned it. But this changes nothing for Marcia right now. For her and the thousands of others with specific professional goals, college is the only answer.

Then there are the students with a natural love of learning. We've all met a few of this type. One is fascinated by history; another tracks down the mythological allusions in *Paradise Lost*. Where their classmates cover an assignment from a single book, they consult a dozen. They simply love to learn.

People like this are few and far between. But it's for them, as much as for our future doctors and engineers, that universities exist. Often, their long-range goals are hazy, although they're apt to think in terms of research or university teaching. But whatever they do, it's sure to require a long, luxurious immersion in pure scholarship.

There may be other, isolated cases in which the student has no real alternative to college, but these two are probably the most important. Let's look at the next category.

SITUATIONS WITH ALTERNATIVES
Economic Goals

Everybody knows, or thinks he knows, that college graduates make more money than their non-college counterparts. How much more is not clear. Even less clear is the question of why they're making it. Is it merely because of the diploma? Or do all the other factors that characterize college students also play a part?

For example, look at Steve. Steve's father is an engineer; his mother does substitute teaching in the local high school. They've always set a high priority on education. They aren't rich, but one way or another, they'll raise the cost of sending Steve to college. He certainly has the grades for it; he may not be at the very top of his class, but he's clearly in the top quarter. His own part-time job will cover extras, not necessities.

However you look at it, Steve has a lot going for him—with or without college. If he goes, he has a good chance of graduating, getting a nice job, and living more comfortably than most. But suppose he doesn't go? He still has the same ability, background and drive. A boy like Steve can start anywhere—a gas station, an office, a hardware store—apply his talents to the work at hand, and end up doing well. The same resources that will enable Steve to get ahead in college will serve him as well outside it, and the rewards may be even greater.

This is why the question of college and money is more confused than it appears. If we take a young person who is bright, vigorous, who comes from a comparatively prosperous family—and who, in addition, goes to college—how can we claim that his later success is due to college and nothing else? To make the case properly, we must compare him with non-college people who are equally bright, vigorous, and well-connected. And when this is done, we find that the dollars-and-cents return from college is a good deal smaller than is generally believed. The details are discussed in Chapter 4; here we can only repeat the warning in a recent Carnegie Commission report, that "higher education as an investment, at least in the United States, does not support widespread, mostly exaggerated notions about its profitability in dollar terms."

Moreover, if by law or custom the best-paying jobs are restricted to college graduates (and this is true in industry, civil service, and the armed forces, as well as in the professions), then it's not surprising that college graduates fill the choicest spots; no one else ever gets a crack at them. Ivar Berg, author of *Education and Jobs: the Great Training Robbery,* has pointed out that for many jobs requiring a diploma, only the diploma is mandated, and not any specific knowledge or skills. Were this to change— and as we will see, vigorous steps are being taken in that direction—the economic benefits of college could be reduced considerably.

Developmental Goals

In the goals we call "developmental," the underlying idea is maturity. Socially, intellectually and personally, the high school senior is not yet mature. He's not ready to assume the responsibilities of adulthood. He needs more time. Students themselves are the first to agree. On Dole's list of reasons for attending college, "I can help myself become a better person" and "It will help me to stand on my own two feet" rank high for both men and women. Wherever adolescents collect, we hear the same theme. They want to remain uncommitted while they come to terms with themselves and the world around them.

How can college be expected to help? For one thing, it certainly gives the student more responsibility for himself. Whether he goes away or continues to live at home, his schoolwork, grades and friendships are in large measure his own affair. His parents accord him a new respect; as a college person, he is assuming new and serious responsibilities. If he goes away to school, his autonomy is even greater. He can, if he wishes, stay up all night, cut classes, eat a half-dozen meals a day, or spend a week's food money on a special date. No one will reproach him; there's a good chance that no one will even know. For better or worse, he's living his own life.

With all this independence we look for a move toward increased self-awareness. Often the real talents, convictions and potential of young people aren't known, even to themselves. They aren't sure where they're going, where they're capable of going. What they want is an atmosphere free of premature pressures and demands, in which they can find a special combination of encouragement and testing, sympathy and challenge. The prevailing view is that college provides such an atmosphere. As they explore the curriculum, meet with others, think and talk, they can develop their strengths and come to terms with their weaknesses.

However, maturity doesn't develop in a vacuum, and one of the great attractions of college is the opportunity to meet new people. Even before they get their programs or learn their way around the halls, the freshmen are already examining each other for the first tentative signs of friendship. Some look for kindred spirits. Others prefer friends from new places, with new contributions and new points of view. The teachers will be a new breed: informed, assured, sometimes world famous. College means people, and people are as much a part of education as the work of the classroom.

College also means learning. Privately, every student suspects that in an important sense, he doesn't know anything about anything. There's a culture gap crying to be filled. If he has read all of Dickens, he's ignorant of science; if science is his main interest, he knows little about history. Cleopatra is a movie, Isaac Newton a name, Dante or Spinoza, less than either. When he reads the papers, he skips the parts on art and music, politics and finance. People he never heard of win Nobel prizes. Somewhere, intellectual wheels are going around that have barely touched his life. College, where culture is packaged and sold three credits at a time, will solve the problem.

Very often, the whole thing works. Developmental goals—autonomy, self-awareness, meeting new people, building up a cultural background—

are realistic; they have been achieved, in greater or lesser degree, a million times over. The graduate who seemed so shy and dependent when he first entered college does in fact, develop new purpose and assurance. He has a better sense of what he wants, and perhaps of what the world wants of him. He's ready to take responsibility, at least for himself. Parents observe the change, congratulate themselves, and decide the money was well spent.

But what do we see when we look at the non-college group? The teen-ager who began as a clerk is now a poised, self-respecting secretary. The former Army recruit has acquired the authority and judgment of a ser-geant. The boy who loved cars is a first-rate auto mechanic; the town couldn't function without him. It isn't college that transforms adolescents into adults; it's experience and time. As of 1971, only 11 percent of the adult population of the United States had graduated from a four-year col-lege; this figure is not expected to rise above 15 percent, even by 1985. Unless we're prepared to write off millions of Americans, we must allow for alternatives.

In Europe, young people operate on a different timetable. Only one in seven ever gets to the university;* the rest choose vocations, locate jobs, and start functioning by the late teens. "Young adults," our current label for the college-age population, has a stricter meaning there. It designates just that—productive, purposeful younger members of the community.

Social Goals

The developmental changes outlined above suggest rather deep personal growth over a long period of time. Naturally, there are outward changes as well. in speech, appearance, interests and choice of friends. Social goals bypass the deeper maturing process and concentrate on these visible signs. They involve the things that show: the way we spend our time, the people we spend it with, how much money we're making and what it's buying us. Among reasons for attending college, social considerations are generally played down. But their force is substantial and in many cases decisive.

For parents, one issue seems settled. "It's not what you know that counts," they'll tell you, "it's who you know." They're sending their chil-dren to college to meet people a notch or two up in the social scale—well-spoken people with firm handshakes and nicely fitted clothes, people more impressive than oneself. Those other children will share classes, dormi-

---

*However, European universities should not be equated with ours. They are in-tended for serious academic work. As a rule, Americans who wish to attend must first complete two years of college over here. On the other hand, Europe offers a great variety of specialized schools which prepare students for such fields as technology, teaching, and architecture. Students entering such schools have presumably decided on their lifework, and need only learn it.

tories and escapades with one's own son or daughter, and everyone will be friends for the rest of their lives. College will serve as a spontaneous finishing school, enabling the next generation to go where we ourselves have never been. It is the classic American dream, too deep and painful to talk over with the children.

Boys and girls are indifferent to firm handshakes and nicely fitted clothes, but they have their own dreams. Above all, they dream of meeting each other. The shyest young men, the most unassuming girls, have fantasies about the very special people they'll meet in college. They don't discuss it with their parents (who often have the same dream, and don't discuss it with *them*!), but for millions of young and not-so-young students, it is never very far from their thoughts.

There's another dream the freshmen don't mention at home. They dream of having a very good time. Whatever the student's idea of fun, he expects to find it in college. For some, it consists of sports, parties and beer-drinking with a few good friends. For others, it's long walks, conversations and wine-drinking with a few good friends. It may be dramatics, politics, sex, music, fraternities, cheerleading, demonstrations, religion—you name it, there's sure to be a supply, and perhaps an oversupply, at college. It's not surprising that parents don't hear much about this reason; they may be unenthusiastic about paying up to five thousand dollars a year so that their children can "have a good time."

However, there's one goal on which everyone's in agreement: success. Parents want success for their children; children want it for themselves. On Dole's list it's the second most important reason for attending college. But success is hard to pin down. Some people succeed without a college degree, others fail with three or four. Does the word have a meaning of its own, apart from the economic, developmental, and other goals already considered? Or is it merely a one-word label for, "I want to be healthy, wealthy and wise, and if I ever decide to do something, I want it to turn out really good." In short, is "success" a reason for going to college, or merely a label for the lack of a reason?

The last social factor is most complex of all. It arises from a whole network of real or imagined pressures, duties, and expectations. Perhaps it can best be understood by seeing it in action.

Mr. Lowell is a real estate broker, and he's doing very well. As it happens, he never got past the sophomore year of college himself; that's when he took his first job in a real estate office, and never bothered to go back. Yet there is no question in anyone's mind that Lowell's son David will go to college. David himself is yielding to the inevitable. His own notion would be to work awhile hauling loads cross-country, and then decide what he wants to do. But it's not worth the trouble of fighting his father's decision.

Marvin Smith's parents watch with interest. Mr. Smith is an electrician;

he's done work at the Lowell home, and the boys are in school together. If Lowell is sending David to college, there must be a good reason for it; shouldn't Marvin be going, too? Smith has friends in the contracting business, and they would surely give Marv a job. But maybe the boy deserves better. He's a good worker, and a lot smarter than Dave Lowell. Don't the Smiths owe their son the same breaks that David gets?

Emma Green is Harriet Smith's cousin. When Mrs. Green hears that Marvin is going to college, every maternal instinct comes into play. Emma loves her daughter Angela just as much as Harriet loves that boy, and she'll prove it. Mr. Green isn't doing too well as a wholesale candy salesman, but Emma has worked before and she can work again. Angela may not be the best of students, but she's going to college.

The motives here are a jumble of love, social pressure, obligation and guilt. What they have in common is this: they all stem from the needs of the parent rather than those of the child. David would rather not go to college; Marvin can take it or leave it; Angela won't last out the year. It doesn't matter; all three will go.

Moreover, there is a danger that the parents' obligation to give becomes the child's obligation to receive. The teen-ager is cornered. How can he refuse to go to college when his parents are giving up so much to send him? The very idea makes him feel guilty. Pressured by his own conscience as well as by school, community, friends, he goes because there's no way out.

Factors like these don't show up in the surveys, and their impact is hard to measure. But they probably account for thousands of college admissions every year.

Tension-Reducing—or "Get Me Out of Here"

Tension-reducing reasons for attending college come in all sizes and shapes, but they all reflect a common state of mind: "Things are rough; get me out of here." The student is preoccupied, not with what he's getting into, but with what he's putting behind. Physically or psychologically, college becomes an escape. In Barbara's case, college was the easiest way to get out of the house. For Jerry, it was a maneuver to put some distance between his parents, his girlfriend and himself. Here and there, someone feels he's made a bad start at home; he wants to try again someplace else. And innumerable students use college as a reprieve from the question, "What will I do with my life?" In some cases, the college may be just across the street, but the escape is no less real.

Of course, young people have always needed escape channels, and have always found them. A century or two ago, they might have headed for the frontier. The girls could marry young and set up households of their own. Later, there were the great migrations to the cities. But today there are no frontiers, marriage is hardly a full-time job, and no one's that far from a city. College has taken their place.

Of the reasons mentioned in this chapter, some may be better than others, but none is categorically "bad." Each must be understood in terms of the individual's own goals. More pertinent, therefore, are questions like these:

Is college the only way to attain this goal?

Is college the best way for this person to attain this goal?

Will college create more serious problems for this person than the ones he wants to solve?

Let's look more closely at these questions.

3

What Do They Find
When They Get There?

The freshmen have arrived. Their eyes scan the campus—it's *their* campus now—and they're overwhelmed by the thought of everything that's going to happen. They plan to grow up here, choose a lifework, fall in love. The fat ones will become thin, the shy ones confident. They expect, not so much to learn, as simply to know; they want to know everything, all at once. They hope to meet great men, and secretly they hope these men will recognize the greatness in them. In routine matters they'll become adept at a single stroke; they'll get part-time jobs, manage their money, and write home twice a week.

Administration and faculty see it differently. Of all these newcomers, approximately one-quarter will graduate on schedule. Others will transfer, often within the first semester; a few transferees will transfer back. Some will drag out their studies, perhaps for years. Of those that stay, about one-third will switch majors, sometimes two or three times. A few will be asked to leave because of grades, but thousands of others will drop out of their own volition, with no plans to return.

What are their reasons? Contrary to expectations, neither money nor grades have much to do with it; in these respects, the ones who voluntarily withdraw closely resemble those who stay. Nearer to the truth is the idea that they are in some way disappointed, unfulfilled; they came to college with needs the college was not prepared to meet.

HOW THE COLLEGE SEES ITSELF

Basically, the typical college sees itself as a place for teaching, for research, and for the preservation of knowledge. Whatever else it may achieve, its primary thrust is academic. It is organized into academic de-

19

partments, offers an academic curriculum, and holds out its greatest rewards to those committed to an academic way of life. Its major obligation to its students is teaching: formal, structured teaching from lectures, laboratories and books.

Nowhere is this more important than in the school's attitude toward grades. A college may condone all sorts of erratic behavior on the part of the student. But let his grades fall below some arbitrary cut-off point, and he is dropped as a matter of course. To fail, from the viewpoint of the college, means to fail academically and little else.

Similarly, the criterion for faculty members is not character, nor charisma, nor ability to deal with the young; it is scholarship. College faculty think of themselves as chemists, historians, mathematicians, classicists, botanists, linguists, economists, musicologists, researchers in every area of human knowledge. The university recognizes their commitment and rewards it; they are hired, retained, and promoted on the basis of scholarly achievement. Even colleges with few academic pretensions look for faculty with Ph.D.s and published articles.

Not that professors are blind to other issues. They know that students are beset by financial and personal problems. They may offer sympathy and concern; occasionally, they steer someone to the guidance department. But it isn't part of the job. Their primary responsibility is simply to provide an opportunity for learning. Interested students are welcome; gifted ones may receive a wealth of time and understanding. As for the others, the professor's standard question is, "Why are they here, if they don't want to learn?"

The question is rhetorical; everyone knows all the non-academic reasons for being on campus. No one even questions them. College staff are the first to admit that maturity, autonomy and poise are more valuable than grades. They delight in watching individual students grow up, get along, and learn to stand on their own feet. But that doesn't mean the college teaches these things. College faculty are not psychiatrists, spiritual leaders, or substitute parents. They have no secrets for inculcating charm, stability, willpower, judgment, or good habits of health and hygiene. They research, they teach—sometimes very well—and there the matter rests. In particular, maturity, if it is acquired at all, is acquired as a by-product; it cannot be considered part of the college curriculum.

THE TRANSITION TO ADULTHOOD

But recently, a more serious question has arisen. Granted that college was not designed to help the student with maturity and other developmental goals, does the danger exist that it might actually be hindering him?

This question was raised in the early 1970's by the Panel on Youth of the President's Science Advisory Committee. The panel, a group of social scientists and educators headed by James S. Coleman, met over a period of time to examine "the period of transition from child to adult and . . . the institutions in which that transition takes place for youth in the United States." In their book, *Youth: Transition to Adulthood,* the panel presents a list of goals essential to the growing-up process. Their conclusion is that college, far from meeting these goals, may not do the job at all.

The first of the panel's goals concerns "cognitive and non-cognitive skills necessary for economic independence and for occupational opportunities"—in short, the acquisition of marketable skills. Whatever else adulthood may imply, it begins with the ability to earn a living.

The second goal is "the capability of effective management of one's own affairs." Schools, it is claimed, provide little serious opportunity for the self-management which must be part of the makeup of every functioning adult.

Another objective is "experience with persons differing in social class, subculture and in age." The point is made that for most young people, this fundamental human experience is "simply unavailable."

But mere interaction is not enough. Young people need "the experience of having others dependent on one's actions." Specifically, opportunities are needed for "caring for others who are younger, sick, old, or otherwise dependent, and to engage in activities that are responsible in the sense that they have significant consequences for others."

Other of the panel's objectives include developing a sensitivity to "the store of cultural achievements, whether art or literature or music or science;" acquiring "capabilities for engaging in intense, concentrated involvement in an activity;" and participating in "interdependent activities directed toward collective goals." A final, and less specific, objective is acquiring "a sense of identity and self-esteem [with which to] form the foundation on which an adult life is built."

Most adults know all this without being told. They support and manage themselves, look after their children, their parents, and each other, and do it all as a matter of course. They work together on the job, maintaining at least a measure of harmony, and subordinating their own egos when necessary. In short, there is nothing lofty, impractical, or idealistic about the panel's objectives; they describe the ordinary, day-in, day-out business of living.

Not that anyone expects all this of college freshmen. For this group they are intended as guideposts, indicating the direction that the training, insight, and experience of young people should take. Many young people, in and out of college, are already on the way. The engineering or pre-med major knows he must function in the adult world, he knows in what capacity he will function, and he is taking the first formal step. The student who's been putting away money to help pay tuition understands exactly what is meant by "interdependent activities directed toward collective goals." The freshman who soaks up mathematics, or history, or Spanish literature is, in his own way, preserving some of the most important achievements of the human race. But the one who's never even dealt with such objectives may find college a notably poor place to begin.

This is the point Coleman makes in his foreword to *Youth: Transition to Adulthood:*

> ... Schooling, as we know it, is not a complete environment giving all the necessary opportunities for becoming adult. School is a certain kind of environment: individualistic, oriented toward cognitive achievement, imposing dependency on and withholding authority and responsibility from those in the role of students. So long as school was short, and merely a supplement to the main activities of growing up, this mattered little. But school has expanded to fill the time that other activities once occupied, without substituting for them ...
>
> ... It appears reasonable now ... to look a little more carefully at the task of becoming adult, to ask not the quantitative question, "How much more schooling?" but the qualitative one: "What are appropriate environments in which youth can best grow into adults?"

The Panel's answers to this question are social in nature. They include such recommendations as work programs, youth communities, projects to promote interaction among different age groups, and the like. However, whatever the answers may be, there are thousands upon thousands of freshmen for whom college is not one of them. These are the students who come looking for maturity, poise and other developmental goals—in short, the ones who want to grow up.

COLLEGE AND MATURITY

Webster's definition of "mature" includes "having or expressing the mental and emotional qualities that are considered normal to an adult, socially adjusted human being." Perhaps the best way to attain these qualities is within the functioning adult world. It is here that the individual learns to deal with things as they are. He learns to compromise among valid but conflicting claims. He sets priorities among his needs; at times, he subordinates all of his needs to those of others. He defines himself through a constant process of testing, succeeding or failing, drawing back, advancing again ... not in isolation but as a participating member of the adult society. Like Coleman, Webster defines maturity within the framework of appropriate adult goals.

What happens to these goals on the campus today? Only a handful of the students oriented to maturity come intent on learning marketable skills; many of them are no more employable when they leave than when they began. Economically, college is a never-never land; even the student who contributes toward his own expenses is being subsidized by parents, private philanthropy, or public funds. In return, he need do nothing but pass courses, and that at a rather low level. He takes minimal responsibility for himself, and none at all for anyone else. Author Michael Novak has described the students' life as one in which "no one and nothing depends on their talent, skill, work, performance. They are socially useless. They often feel guilt and self-hatred, rage and resentment. They *should be* needed by somebody, but they aren't."

Of course, there are plenty of students who are delighted with college, and to whom none of this applies. It is illuminating to see how they differ from the rest. Researchers Alan and Caroline Waterman made a careful study of students most satisfied with college. They found that

[one dimension] associated with satisfaction can be termed *traditionalism*. High levels of satisfaction were found for students who made an early selection of their major field and who perceived their parents as strongly approving of their choice. Satisfaction was also expressed by students describing themselves as having a religious preference and as attending religious services approximately once a week. The strong rejection of the nonconformist orientation was also associated with the expression of high levels of satisfaction.

It appears that students who bring with them a set of values, a sense of self, and some realistic vocational goals will find what they want in college. The others have come for something that isn't there.

The Classroom and Beyond

What they do find is the one staple of college: classes. Since they didn't come to study in the first place, they tend to find their studies irrelevant. Nonetheless, as a group they usually pass. School is one thing they can cope with; they are in the habit of passing. But their work is desultory— without zest, commitment, or a sense of intellectual triumph. Repeatedly, they console themselves that they could do better if they really tried. In that case, why don't they try? The answers are evasive. Perhaps study is too low in their order of priorities; to the extent that their goals are developmental rather than academic, classes are secondary. Their real fulfillment will come about through insight, reflection and contact with other human beings.

Only occasionally is such contact with the faculty. Some faculty members, including the most productive and responsible, simply don't have the time. Others, whatever their intentions, are rather anomalous models for the young. They may themselves be refugees from the world of business or industry, with its impersonal criteria of productivity, efficiency and quality control. If tenured, they are held to virtually no criteria at all. Secure financially and professionally, coming and going pretty much as they please, producing or not, as they see fit, college faculty present a life-style which may work on campus, but which hardly serves as a model for the conventional adult world.

Lacking adult models, or in some cases deliberately rejecting them, the students do the next best thing: they turn to each other. Classmates become friends, mentors, lovers and teachers, all in one. The noted pyschologist Bruno Bettelheim claims that "they want essentially group therapeutic experiences which will help them to become mature, secure, to find themselves. But colleges are not mass therapeutic institutions and hence disappoint the student where the greatest need lies." Meanwhile, far from cultivating "the mental and emotional qualities that are considered normal to an adult, socially adjusted human being," they create a minority subculture of their own.

The problem of the youth culture lies, not in the merits of long hair over short, or jeans over flannels, but in the fact that it is antithetical to the process of growing up. The person who wants maturity must, by definition, be prepared to relinquish his youth. Not that our adult society cannot be improved upon; indeed, the improvements may very well come from the direction of the youth culture. But students who reject adulthood outright are not likely to work at improving it. What was once a natural and desirable transition from "child" to "adult" has become something to be resisted as long as possible.

Meanwhile, whatever else the student is doing, he is accumulating a set of grades. From the first semester, his academic record documents every spurt and every lapse in unmistakeable quantitative terms.

The Issue of Grades

It's fashionable today to dismiss grades. Students have demanded, and in many cases received, alternatives; pass-fails and attendance credit have sprung up everywhere. On the other hand, accepting the college's view that the student is there to learn, and acknowledging that some students do a better job of it than others, the academic community has every right to be concerned about grades. Yielding to fashion in this manner may be unwise and even dangerous; a decade from now, the fashion may change, but the grades will stay the same. Today, students may laugh off their D's in gym, or condone their C's in English or math on the grounds that the instructor was incompetent. In years to come, no one will know whether they were right or wrong, but the C's and D's will stand. The academic record is unique and irrevocable; the student will never have another as long as he lives.

For some purposes, this may not matter one bit. Some students are depressed by poor grades, but others adjust with surprising alacrity. They graduate, find jobs, and do very well indeed. In his book, *Inequality,* Harvard sociologist, Christopher Jencks reports that for at least one group —teachers—there seems to be little or no connection between college grades and on-the-job performance. "The difference between good and bad work seems to be more a matter of habits, values, attitudes, and outlook than of knowing the right answers to written or oral questions."

But there are times when grades matter a great deal. For transfer students, they are critical. If it's a question of getting into graduate schools, grades often outweigh everything else. And they may make the difference between getting or not getting a desired job—particularly in this era of narrowing opportunity.

So the student who knows himself, his plans and his prospects also knows whether he should be worried about grades. Unfortunately, the freshmen we're talking about aren't likely to be in this category. They're the one's who change majors, transfer, pick up courses here and there as non-matriculated students. And wherever they go, their transcripts will follow. In the everyday world, the kid who botches his first couple of jobs need never mention them again; on campus, people in their thirties and forties are routinely tripped up by academic follies committed decades ago. So the undergraduates who seek maturity at the expense of good grades are short-changing themselves in two ways: they may attain neither the one nor the other.

COPING WITH THE NEW ENVIRONMENT

So far, we've considered college only in relation to maturity. Critical as this issue may be, the fact is that thousands of students attend for altogether different reasons. How well do they do?

Self-Management

The answer often lies in something we'll call "self-management." College is a new situation, with new demands and new prerogatives. Self-management is a measure of how well the student can deal with them.

Whatever the freshman's expectations, college is usually something of a shock. The campus is hotter, or colder, or damper, or drier than it has any right to be. Instead of a few cozy buildings, he finds a proliferation of schools, halls, chapels, gyms, dormitories, auditoriums and libraries—all in different directions, for different purposes, and all an impossible distance from where he happens to be. His roommate disapproves of his taste in music; he can't stand his roommate's cigarettes: they glower at each other and wonder how they'll get through the year.

Classes are equally unrecognizable. Up to now, a class meant twenty-five good friends and a teacher who knew him, his sister and probably his parents. Here a class can mean anything at all. Biology is a few hundred kids in a darkened lecture hall; the instructor is so remote that if you saw him in daylight you wouldn't recognize him. Psychology is a self-study affair where—for eighty dollars a credit!—the student gets a text and an outline; the rest is up to him. In high school, the first day or two were pleasantly taken up preparing a seating plan and getting acquainted. Here the instructor uses the first day to distribute an eight-page reading list, and may never get acquainted.

But the hardest adjustment of all, and the one on which all the rest depend, is the adjustment to freedom. Over the years, college students have clamored for independence. Today they have it to an extent undreamed of by their predecessors. Even if they're living at home, they have a new autonomy. Their comings and goings are under their own control. In such matters as choice of courses, class attendance, conferences with teachers and grades, they are treated as responsible human beings. If trouble arises, the college deals directly with the student; the days are gone when Mother was called to school. Socially, the campus may become the center of activity. Friends are drawn from a wider circle and are less often brought home; parents no longer know just where their children are, or with whom.

Campus Freedom

Students living on campus have even more freedom. On a day-to-day basis, they are accountable to no one. They can skip breakfast or skip town. They may subsist on french fries, wear the same clothes all term, drive illegally in borrowed cars, stay up all night, spend the day in bed, or drag around with a fever of 103°. We're not talking now about such dramatic dangers as drugs or sexual or political extremes; most students are well aware of these problems, and have worked out solutions they can live with. We're thinking of all the everyday decisions that define the tenor of life: when to get up and go to bed; what to eat and when and how much; whether to wear a coat, spend money, get off the phone, go to class, consult the guidance office, attend a party, or finish a book. These are the choices that look like nothing at all—until they take the wrong turn.

In class, such choices are even more critical. A college class is like a gold mine: the riches are there, but it's the student's job to get them out. The professor prides himself on not being a policeman. He lectures, makes assignments, answers questions, and there the matter rests. He may go through the entire semester without once taking attendance or checking homework. Tests are infrequent and class participation, if any, limited to volunteers. Reports may be assigned weeks, even months, in advance, and never mentioned until the day they're due.

This is where self-management comes in. Thousands upon thousands of freshmen can deal with their new freedom, at least tolerably well. If they break a rule, they use good sense about when and where. They keep up, more or less, with their assignments; they muster some interest in their work; they even maintain communication with faculty and others on the far side of the generation gap. They bring with them the necessary re-sources of responsibility, self-discipline, and judgment; they can manage.

But others, fresh from the routine of high school, find their freedom more than they can grasp. The one reality appears to be, "I have nothing to do." There's an English paper to hand in six weeks from now, and the social studies reading should be finished by November, and somewhere he'll have to fit in a mess of language labs. But for this glorious moment, he's free as a bird.

Perhaps if college started in the dead of winter, with winds howling across the campus, freshmen might be content to sit in overheated libraries and do their work. But it begins in September. The sun is shining, the air is brisk; surely wisdom dictates that a flawless morning like this be spent outdoors.

Ultimately, of course, there comes a day of reckoning. The professor asks the student for a conference; the life of overeating and undersleeping lands him in the infirmary; with nine days left he's taken only two of the six required tests in his self-study class. Girls discover it's easier to invite a boy into the dorm than to get him out again; parents inquire apologetically about grades. But all that's very remote at the start of the semester, com-pared to the sheer joy of exploring, making friends, or just sleeping late. No wonder educators Lass and Wilson, authors of *The College Student's Handbook,* warn that ". . . freedom is the toughest test freshmen every-where face. It is freedom that destroys more college freshmen than any other factor in the college environment."

Goals that Work

Against this background, we can return to the earlier question: what happens to the thousands of students who attend college for reasons hav-ing nothing to do with maturity? In each case, there are two things to con-sider. First, does this reason correspond to something which can in fact be found on campus; and second, can the student manage himself well enough to take advantage of it?

THE STUDENT WHO LOVES TO LEARN

One type of student is clearly in his element: the one who loves to learn. The school exists to teach; he is there to be taught; there is a perfect mesh-ing of goals. In a study of college "persisters" and "withdrawals" (that is, those who remain in college and those who drop out), researchers Trent and Metzger found that the chance of graduating is highest for those high school seniors who have enjoyed school, who rate college as "very impor-tant," and who regard the primary purpose of education as "the gaining of knowledge and appreciation of ideas." Similarly, Alan and Caroline Water-man note that high satisfaction in college goes with "the earning of a high

39562

gradepoint average, plans to do graduate work, and the intention of pursuing an academic career."

Yet even these students may flounder. They are often younger than average, and may be unprepared for self-management. Some are committed to one subject area, but unable to cope with anything else. A few of the most creative students may be too individualistic for college; in a study of potentially creative students, Heist found that a majority left college before their senior year. Or, confronted for the first time with suitably tempting alternatives, the student may abandon all pretense of scholarship and declare, to the horror of family and friends, that now, at last, he's learning how to live.

But usually these difficulties are worked out right on campus. The fact is that in both satisfaction and persistence, the academically inclined freshman fares better than any of his classmates.

THE FUTURE PROFESSIONALS

Not far behind are the would-be professionals: doctors, teachers, engineers. Scholarly or not, these students know they can't get anywhere without college, and they have every intention of sticking it out. Trent and Metzger found that for male pre-med students, the persistence rate was 75 percent; for male engineering students, it was 72. Among women, 68 percent of the future teachers stayed to graduation. These findings dovetail with those of the Watermans and other researchers; the student who's headed for a profession soon learns to adjust for the sake of the degree.

When such students do drop out, the reasons are often academic. Engineering and medicine are among the most demanding curricula; the students work, and work hard, or they don't stay very long. Moreover, standards are high. The liberal arts majors can get by with B's and C's; pre-meds with those grades will be barred from virtually every medical school in the country, and they know it. Some students shut out distractions, buckle down and do the best they can. Others change majors or quit.

COLLEGE AS FUN

Another large group finds college everything they dreamed of. These are the students who attend to meet people and have fun. One glowing sophomore described school as "like camp, but better . . . and all year round!" Meetings, movies, and get-togethers fill the day and half the night; around every corner, there's a friendly face. Administrators may groan and professors tear their hair; the students know what they want, and as long as they maintain their grades and keep out of trouble, they get it. A comprehensive survey of college seniors conducted by educators Alexander Austin and Robert J. Panos reports that over 70 percent found "just the right amount" of social life at college (only 7.1 percent of the men and 4.2 percent of the women reported too much); over 80 percent found "just the right amount" of personal contacts with classmates. The same study reveals that 34.0 percent of the men students and 43.2 percent of the women fell in love during their senior year; about one in five of the seniors got married. Of course, the miracle is not limited to college. College provides a concentration of lonely, receptive young people. Inevitably, boys and girls pair off—as they do all over the face of the earth. When it comes to courtship, the campus has no monopoly.

Moreover, all this sociability takes a while; one-third of the students admitted that when they first came to college, they felt "lost." (The survey dealt with seniors, who remained in school; the most dissatisfied students may have dropped out and not been represented at all.) Today, students on hundreds of campuses claim that their schools provide no sense of community or identification. In one Midwestern university, students fight their isolation by wearing bright orange buttons, signifying to friends and strangers alike, "I'd be glad if you came over to talk with me."

Indeed, the very shyest and most reticent student may be worse off on campus than at home. In his own community, he has the reassuring presence of family, neighbors, and former schoolmates, providing at least a toehold on some form of human relations. At school, as his classmates get acquainted and form their own circles, he may be caught up in an unbearable anonymity. Literally no one knows him; no one knows he exists. On one California campus, a student committed suicide in his room and was not found for 18 days.

But such cases are extreme. Usually the sheer number of human beings on campus guarantees that whatever a person's outlook and idiosyncrasies, he'll find a few like-minded friends. Even the students who complain of isolation protest in bands of ten or twelve.

COLLEGE AND CULTURE

Finally, there is one more type of student who is in his element at college. Like many others, he's there to find maturity. But unlike them, he looks for it, not in rap sessions or encounter groups, but within and through the content of the class. What he wants is nothing less than to study the intellectual achievements of the human race. He sees himself in historical perspective, the recipient of a tradition ten thousand years old. Not only has he heard of men like Aeschylus, Newton, and Spinoza, but he knows that they have something to say to him.

Faculty greet these students as one of their own. To the extent that they can help anyone mature, their help takes precisely this form. Professors maintain—often against objections—that one of their responsibilities is the transmission of the world's cultural heritage. It is to students like these that they transmit it.

Nonetheless, such students do well to identify in advance the courses they should take; otherwise, they may never get on the right track. Time was when every liberal arts student was exposed at least to a required history sequence and the standard literature course—*Beowulf* through Yeats. Today, many schools have abolished requirements altogether. Others have defined them so loosely that they carry little weight. "Humanities" may mean a choice of Plato or stagecraft; "literature" is satisfied equally by Shakespeare or Hermann Hesse. In one college, and one which prides itself on its mandatory "prescription" courses, a student can graduate with no knowledge of any event—historical, cultural, or aesthetic—occurring before 1832. Under these circumstances, the student who arrives with a topographic map in his head, showing the mountains, plateaus, and valleys of human achievement, can fill in the details as he goes along. Otherwise he may think he's discovering the wisdom of the ages, when in truth he's merely picking up a smattering of fads.

Failing to Cope

If college poses this many difficulties, how do the students manage? The answer is simple: they don't.

It's an old story that the majority of college freshmen never finish at all. Nearly half leave within, or directly after, the first year; in two-year colleges, the typical stay is seven months. Ten percent of all students withdraw, reenroll, and withdraw again, all within a four-year period. Whatever the reason for these comings and goings, it's neither money nor grades. When a group of "withdrawals" were asked for their reasons, only 12 percent mentioned finances; 16 percent cited poor grades. Another study found that 20 percent of college dropouts have I.Q.s of over 135. Clearly, these students could manage the classwork as well as the next one. What they couldn't manage was finding a reason to stay.

Those who remain in college show the same uncertainty. Close to one-third transfer to another school, and the figure keeps rising. Change of major is another preoccupation. A study of Auburn University students found that 32 percent of the students had changed their majors "at least once; in a number of cases, the second or third change carried them back to their initial choice." At Pennsylvania State University, the figure was even higher: 43 percent. We don't know whether all these changes made the students any happier, but one thing is sure: it wasted a lot of time. Perhaps this is why, of those students who do finish college, only about half graduate in the traditional four years.

What this adds up to is a lot of young men and women who don't know what they want, and who, in the sheltered environment of the campus, don't have much chance of finding out. A recent survey of 1961 graduates —people who had time to think it over!—showed that more than 60 percent believed there should be an interruption in formal education, either between high school and college or during college. No wonder Brown University, one of the most selective in the country, offers the following suggestion to its incoming freshmen:

> If it has occurred to you to "take a year off" between school and college, you should contact the Director of Admission. . . . Such a decision should be made in light of the fact that maturity is at a premium when it comes to making the best of a demanding college—especially one which, like Brown, lays so much responsibility on the individual. You might well enrich your college experience through the broadened perspective gained from a leave of absence from what has unfortunately become for some a kind of ritualistic merry-go-round. You might travel, work, study abroad, join VISTA. There are a great number of possibilities and combinations . . .

Finally, what of the students who see college as an escape? If all they want is to get away from parent, boyfriend, or whatever the current irritant may be, they can't help succeeding; they succeed in the very act of leaving town. But escaping their problems is something else again. Situations like these are not, as a rule, externally imposed. They represent subtle interactions in which the most important role is played by the student himself. Back home, he could blame his problems on parents, teachers, or a hostile environment. Now he finds his problems are following him; whatever hangups he had at home yesterday, he has on campus today. The boy who sees college as an escape from one entangling alliance may, within a few weeks, be caught up in another. The girl who strikes out against the imagined tyranny of home comes up against the imagined tyranny of school. Or an old problem may reappear in new form. The boy who fled his mother's nagging suddenly finds he misses it; freedom doesn't amount to much when it means only that nobody gives a damn. Details vary, but one thing is sure: to the precise extent that the student's problems arise from his own disposition and mode of attack, to that extent will they reappear anywhere he goes.

Over and above all this, college adds its own measure of problems. Classes continue, grades accumulate; a whole new set of tensions arises alongside the old. The student who was unable to deal with one difficulty back home is even less equipped to handle a battery of them at school.

Granted, there are students for whom a change of scenery is accompanied by a change of outlook and habits. There are even cases in which running away, if not the ideal solution, remains the most expedient one. But more often, it suggests nothing so much as a bad case of immaturity; a condition for which college does not have the cure.

THE PARENTS . . .

So far, we've been looking at college from the students' point of view. Let's turn our attention to the parents.

If there's one factor motivating parents, it's using college to maneuver their children upward in the socioeconomic scale. However, not many undergraduates feel bound by their parents' sense of the social order. They're not attuned to social ups and downs; it's hard even to tell rich from poor when everyone wears the same clothes, listens to the same music and lives in the same miserable dorm.

Morever, even accepting the idea of social strata, parents should be warned that in the nature of the thing, every move upward must be countered by a move down. The coin can fall either way; Susie may snare the son of an oil tycoon, but by the same token, the son of the town drunkard may snare her. In any case, most students turn their backs on these niceties. They form friendships on the basis of temperament, interests, outlook, charm—criteria that have prevailed for centuries.

Parents have another hurdle to contend with. On today's campus, experimentation is the order of the day. Religious and racial distinctions have gone by the board. Sexual mores are taking a new turn. The Gay Liberation crowd sets up a table admonishing passers-by: "Don't knock it till you've tried it." Other organizations extol the virtues of anarchy, yoga, chanting, Young Republicanism, atheism, macrobiotic diets, Bible-reading and meditation. To bewildered freshmen in search of values, any of these may appear to be—or may actually be—the answer. But whatever the merits of such solutions, they probably aren't what Mom and Dad had in mind.

Of course, the conflict of old and new values is hardly a novelty, and parents must cope with it, as they always have, in terms of their own children's maturity and goals. On the other hand, parents who expect their tuition money to buy upward social mobility should be alerted to the things it may buy instead.

One factor remains: financial security. Even more than their offspring, parents have faith in the well-paying job at the end of the college rainbow. What happens to the students who attend college in the hope of ultimately getting some undefined "good job"? This is what we'll explore in the next chapter.

4

Education and Jobs

As we have seen, the reasons for attending college are many and varied. One person may gain a lifelong interest in literature or art; another gains a lifelong circle of friends. In tallying the advantages of college, we must keep in mind the possibility of living better, doing more absorbing work, and all the other intangibles that accrue, or are said to accrue, from college.

Nonetheless, economic returns loom very large in the overall college picture. More parents mention "better jobs" as a reason for sending their children to college than any other factor; not far behind is the pressure to achieve financial success. Among students, financial considerations seem less imperative, but even among this group, such considerations as "I hope to prepare myself to be a success in life," and "It will help me get a good job" rank high. That college graduates make more money is part of American folklore. Who makes it, how much more, and under what circumstances, are less clearly defined. So let's look at two important questions. First, just how much extra money does a college education bring? And second, how much longer is this state of affairs likely to continue?

DIFFERENCES IN EARNINGS: WHY?

On the surface, determining the difference in earnings between college and non-college people looks easy. Find the average earnings per year for graduates and for non-graduates, and compare the two amounts.

Unfortunately, it's not that simple. Traditionally, college students represented only part of the high school crop. Academically, they were the ones who met college standards. Economically, they had the money—not only to cover college costs, but to compensate for the four-years' income they were forgoing. Socially, they came from families that felt college was worth it. In short, college graduates were not merely those who went through the four-year mill; they were also the ones who started with better grades, more money, and better-educated parents. When we compare col-

33

lege and non-college students, we are also comparing the brighter with the less bright, the wealthier with the poorer, the well-connected with the less prominent. To study their incomes requires a meticulous sorting-out process. If graduates are making more money, how much of the difference is due to college, and how much to all these other factors?

To answer this question, we would have to earmark two groups of high school graduates, equal in mental ability, family background, health, and any other attributes which could conceivably be relevant. Of these two groups, one would go on to college, and the other, for whatever reasons, would not. We keep track of both groups, and over the years we are ready to report on who's making more money, how much, and why.

But here we come to another problem. When we talk of the money earned by college graduates, we don't necessarily mean in the first year or so after college; what we're talking about is the "long run." So we must not only find our subjects, but we must keep track of them for a number of years—ten, fifteen, or even more. Such a project is known as a longitudinal study; it follows the same people over a considerable period of time, noting all the changes along the way. This means that the results filtering down to us today are based on students who entered college in the fifties—and it's hardly news that colleges have changed since then. By the same token, if we start such a study with today's high school graduates, our questions won't be answered for another fifteen years—by which time colleges will have metamorphised into something else again.

This does not mean that such studies should not be attempted. On the contrary, they should be encouraged; we need all the information we can get. What it does mean is that they must be interpreted carefully, in the light of changing individual and social circumstances.

DIFFERENCES IN EARNINGS: HOW MUCH?

Meanwhile, one more point must be made. College may bring in money, but it also costs money. Today, the bill at a state university may run anywhere from $2500 to $3000 a year; at private schools, it can easily amount to $5000 or more. During this time the typical student earns relatively little. So we must add to the cost of college the value of forgone earnings—the money the student didn't make because he was using his time at school. These calculations—and they are accepted by most economists today—can bring the actual cost of a college degree to thirty or forty thousand dollars. Even at these prices, higher education isn't self-supporting; it depends heavily on government and private subsidies. And the current opinion is that middle-class families should be paying even more of the actual costs involved. What are they getting for their money?

This, too, is a complicated subject. It involves estimates of income for thirty or forty years ahead, including such factors as taxes, interest rates, and inflation. But let's see what economists have to say. A Carnegie Commission study reports on "recent estimates of the Bureau of the Census (1970) based on 1968 data. Using a discount rate of 5 percent,* expected lifetime income for male, year-round, full-time workers is estimated at $128,000 for high school graduates and at $187,000 for college graduates (four years or more), resulting in an excess for the latter of $59,000."

If we figure the working life of a college graduate at forty years, this comes to less than $1500 a year; a definite gain, to be sure, but hardly a spectacular one. And of course, it includes such well-paid groups as doctors and lawyers along with the less affluent teachers, librarians, and engineers. Furthermore, the Carnegie report reminds us that these payoffs "ought to be compared with the costs of education consisting of tuition and income forgone because of college attendance." In short, even this $59,000 isn't free and clear; somewhere, we must take into account the $30,000 or $40,000 required to get the degree in the first place.

Now, everybody knows that money brings a return, whether in the form of bank interest, stock dividends, or whatever. This is what we mean by the "return on the investment." The rate of return on bank deposits is usually five to six percent or more; the rate of return on stocks may be somewhat more or less, and so on. If we think of college as an investment, what is the rate of return?

This question is examined by sociologist Christopher Jencks in his book, *Inequality:*

Suppose that we define the "cost of education" as the student's out-of-pocket expenditures plus the earnings he loses by not working while in school. Suppose we define the "benefits" as his additional earnings that result from extra schooling. In addition, let us assume that the entire income difference between the well educated and the poorly educated is due to schooling. On these simplified assumptions, the "rate of return" on an individual's "investment" in schooling . . . [for college] averages 7 to 12 percent for white males. Taking differences in family background and cognitive skill into account would probably lower these estimates to . . . 4 to 7 percent for college. The rates of return appear to be appreciably higher for white middle-class males and somewhat lower for white working-class males, black males, and females of all classes and colors.

Economists Paul Taubman and Terence Wales report similar results. Their information is based on the records of some 5000 World War II Air Force veterans who were exhaustively tested at the time of the war, and interviewed again in 1955 and 1969. Data was available in at least four essential areas: ability, family background, education and earnings. Using sophisticated statistical techniques, Taubman and Wales were able to separate the returns due to college from the money the men could have earned anyway, because of their natural ability, family connections, or whatever. They found that the economic return to the holder of a B.A. degree (ex-

*Discount rate is a way to adjust for expected inflation.

cluding holders of higher degrees) is in the neighborhood of nine percent.

Incidentally, the authors discovered that for graduate work, the return is even smaller. Holders of a Ph.D. (other than doctors and lawyers) realize an average four percent return, while those who stop at the Master's Degree achieve about seven percent. One reason for these low returns is that many holders of advanced degrees go into the notoriously low-paying profession of teaching. In fact, throughout their study Taubman and Wales found it necessary to incorporate a "bonus" to teachers for the presumed personal satisfaction of their work; otherwise the percents would have been even lower.

Now, there is nothing wrong with a seven to nine percent return, particularly when it may be accompanied by other, less tangible benefits. But from an economic point of view, it is hardly awe-inspiring. In fact, it about matches the interest being paid by financial institutions and certain bonds. Whatever the advantages of a college degree, cold cash does not appear to be one of them.

But even this situation may not prevail much longer. Already, it is under attack from another point of view.

COLLEGE AS A SCREENING DEVICE

In one vocational area after another, the person without a college degree will not even be considered. The non-graduate is simply out of the running. And in being barred from the job, he is automatically barred from whatever opportunities it offers and, in particular, from opportunities for financial betterment.

Of course, if the job opening is one requiring specific skills normally acquired in college, the employer is within his right. The same is true if the graduate can deliver increased productivity, better performance, or some other job-related benefit. However, studies have shown that only occasionally is this the case. In a great many situations, personnel managers have used the degree simply as a cheap screening device for cutting down on numbers of job applicants.

This is the central issue of Ivar Berg's book, *Education and Jobs: the Great Training Robbery*. Berg actually examined job performance in one industry after another, to determine whether college graduates surpassed their co-workers. Summarizing his findings in an article for the Journal of Higher Education, he writes: "In none of the many thousands of jobs examined by the writer was it revealed that less-educated employees performed less adequately than better-educated workers doing the same tasks. Indeed . . . we found educational achievement to be either uncorrelated or negatively correlated with performance."*

*Negative correlation is a statistical term. As used here, it signifies that the more highly educated workers were *less* effective on the job than their colleagues.

Many employers are unaware of this. They hire college graduates and pay them more in the sincere, if unsupported, belief that somehow, these men will be better for the firm. But others use the degree quite deliberately as a device for weeding out applicants, at no cost to the company. And some have adopted it, consciously or unconsciously, to maintain class and ethnic barriers. Even today, 93 percent of all college graduates come from middle to upper-class homes. In demanding the diploma, the employer is shying away from the problem of blacks, Mexicans, Puerto Ricans, foreign accents, complicated backgrounds, and the threat of the unfamiliar. Whatever the reason, the effect is the same: college graduates earn more money, not because of any special knowledge or skill, but because personnel officers have given them an automatic and often unwarranted priority. So marked is this effect that Taubman and Wales attribute to it a full half of the nine percent "economic return" mentioned earlier.

Only recently has the built-in injustice of this situation become apparent. Berg's studies, published in 1971, brought the issue to general attention. In 1972, Professor Blanche Blank, Dean of Social Sciences at Hunter College, proposed that "Congress should be urged to add to our civil rights legislation a section that would outlaw employment discrimination based on college degrees . . . Note, please, that we are talking about *degrees,* not education, content, or skills." In New York, State Senator Joseph R. Pisani has already proposed such legislation. Joining in the battle are minority groups, sociologists, and even educators who are tired of seeing their institutions become, in Blank's words, "servants of big business and big government."

Of course, we are talking without reference to the actual skills and information required to do the job. If a particular job requires, say, statistics, well and good. And if the usual place to learn this material is college, that's well and good, too. But what's needed is *statistics*—not a degree. Any individual who manages to learn it, by whatever means (for example, by taking the college courses without going for the degree) deserves the same chance at the job. As for the cost and responsibility of "credentialing" (determining who is qualified to do the work and who is not), they revert to the employer—a rather reasonable shift, since it is he who receives the benefits.

JOBS AND THE "COLLEGE TYPE"

The fact is that college has no monopoly on teaching, on learning, or on bright and ambitious human beings. There are a good number of able young people in college; there are a good number outside it. College by itself is no guarantee of drive, competence, reliability, poise, or any of the other qualities normally sought by employers—as they themselves are beginning to find out. For years, employers have been paying a premium for college-trained personnel. Now they are beginning to ask what they've been getting for the money.

One thing they've been seeking is a so-called "college type." Ivar Berg's interviews with business management brought out an interest in the graduate's "personal commitment to 'good middle-class values,' industriousness, and seriousness of purpose, as well as salutory personal habits and styles."

For good or bad, college students have hardly been moving in this direction. The evidence of the *Fortune* survey mentioned earlier (Chapter 1) suggests that the college student is apt to be a strongly individualist, youth-oriented person who distrusts his employers and puts his own interests ahead of theirs. John Folger, executive director of the Tennessee Higher Education Commission, notes,

The job opportunities for college graduates outside the traditional professions are going to be concentrated in government administrative and management fields, business management, and sales, advertising, and similar service industries. Most of these will be conventional bureaucratic positions, which require the ability to work in an organization. In most of these jobs expressiveness and individuality are not valued as much as a conformity and dedication to the work ethic. The youth culture and the college experience may thus be cultivating values and goals in youth which are inconsistent with the requirements and expectations of the major employers in the next decade. In the past, college graduates have been sought for many jobs because college graduation was an indication of intelligence and motivation, as well as the development of interpersonal skills and contacts which would facilitate job performance. In the future, employers may search more carefully to find those students who have the right attitudes and motivation for work; this process of selection may favor the upwardly mobile student from a working class or lower middle class family background in spite of his more limited connections and less prestigious alma mater.

Evidence is accumulating to support this point of view. Franklin W. Gilchrist, president of Aptitude Testing for Industry, reports that as far back as 1963, a study of 97 star salesmen showed that 59 percent either did not finish college or did not attend at all. The director of personnel for a major drug chain, with over 300 stores, chooses management trainees for such qualities as ambition, drive and ability to work within the organization; education beyond high school is completely irrelevant. (Incidentally, this is a firm in which every executive, up to and including the president, started as a management trainee!)

LEARNING FROM EXPERIENCE

On a more sophisticated level, J. Sterling Livingston of the Harvard Business School suggests that "managers are not taught in formal educational programs what they most need to know to build successful careers in management. Unless they acquire through their own experience the knowledge and skills that are vital to their effectiveness, they are not likely to advance far." Livingston distinguishes between two types of behavior: the first enables a person to get high grades and otherwise do well in school, but the second and more critical one consists of "finding problems and opportunities, initiating action, and following through . . . [and which] can be developed only by doing what needs to be done."

Right now, the prospect of hiring other than college graduates may seem very attractive to American business. The graduate commands more in additional salary than he returns in higher productivity or skill. If his job is routine or "low-level," he is apt to suffer from feelings of inferiority and dissatisfaction. And when he finally does become useful to the firm, there's a good chance that he'll leave. Moreover, the businessman who eschews college graduates can not only save money, but he can do so in the name of good citizenship and social concern: his action is likely to favor such groups as women and blacks.

WHERE ARE THE JOBS?

But while we deliberate on who should get the jobs, there's a compelling challenge from still another direction. The real question may be, "What jobs?"

Job forecasting is based on variables that no one can predict exactly; it has always been a risky business. The current surplus of teachers is well known, but a Federal program supporting nursery schools, smaller classes, or training of the handicapped can change the picture overnight. Military realignments can turn a surplus of engineers into a shortage. If, as a nation, we calculate our health needs one way, there will be a critical need for medical personnel; if we calculate it another, supply and demand will be in balance.

It is therefore not surprising that the job picture for college graduates during the next decade is clouded. Yet, if the experts can be believed, prospects range from poor to terrible; no one, anywhere, is optimistic. The heyday of the 1960's, when recruiters crowded the campus and graduates could choose from a half-dozen offers, is over, and it is not expected to return. A special report issued by the U.S. Department of Labor in 1973 points out that of the 1.1 million men and women who received degrees in 1970 and 1971 and were available for work in October, 1971, 7.4 percent were unemployed. Of those employed, more than half were in jobs not directly related to their fields of study; and of these, 56 percent took the jobs because they could find nothing else. In 1972, *Business Week* predicted that "by 1977, every recognized profession will have an oversupply of new graduates. Even the perennial shortage of doctors will end by 1978." The report goes on to say that "by 1980, the surplus of college graduates—including the jobless and those working at jobs below their educational levels—could reach a staggering 1.5 million." John Folger, taking a less extreme position, nonethless warns that "considerable frustration of college graduates' ambitions is likely from the doubling of the number of college graduates in a decade when the increase in jobs where college training is directly related to job performance will be on the order of 50 percent."

By putting together the figures from various sources, we can roughly pinpoint the trouble spots. By 1980, we will see between 105,000 and 128,000 graduates in biological sciences and health professions,* competing for about 75,000 jobs. In other sciences, including engineering, there will be about 130,000 graduates and at best 70,000 openings. With an anticipated 114,000 to 135,000 graduates in education, the total number of vacancies in all teaching levels below college will be 90,000. Even in the field of business we find between 122,000 and 183,000 graduates scrambling for at best 120,000 jobs—of which nearly a third are in sales.

The picture appears to be much the same throughout the country. A 1973 report from eight California colleges notes that "liberal arts and social science majors have been hard hit; in the teaching field, only about 50% of those seeking jobs found them, with some seven applicants to every opening." The report's advice to students has a depression-years ring: gain work experience; diversify; achieve ("More than ever before, the 'average' student will have great difficulty landing the job he wants— grades, recommendations, etc., are of prime importance."); be mobile; don't count on a job merely because you have a degree. A study of Illinois degree recipients predicts that by 1980 the total surplus of college graduates will be 20 percent, ranging from 19 percent surplus in education to 38 percent surplus in communications.

Even where jobs exist, they may not dovetail with the needs of available graduates. The graduate in communications may lack training even for a related field like speech therapy. Similarly, the librarian with an affinity for literature cannot take over the duties of a medical records librarian. So even when we count up graduates and jobs, the question remains: which graduates for which jobs?

The problem may be particularly acute for women. Women's Liberation has left its mark; in the next few years the prospects for women graduates should be better than ever. But this assumes the availability of trained women in fields where vacancies exist. Until now, two-fifths of all women professionals have been in teaching. Now this field is drying up; if women hope to find careers, they must redirect their interests to such traditionally masculine areas as engineering, accounting, or dentistry. So far, there are

---

*Estimates vary according to the statistical and sociological techniques used.

few signs of such a change. Unless it occurs, the clamor of the women's rights movement will avail them nothing; equality with their male counterparts will mean only the equal right to be under-employed, if employed at all.

We close this chapter as we opened it: with the warning that to consider college in exclusively economic terms is artificial and even misleading. Studies by the Carnegie Commission and others have shown that college graduates find great rewards in more gratifying work, more meaningful leisure-time activities, and a heightened sensitivity to the world around them.* The typical university professor wouldn't change places with a businessman making three times as much; the teacher, clergyman or librarian may find deep satisfaction in the lives they lead. To the extent that economic return is a factor in college attendance, it should be given the weight it merits—no more and no less.

*However, one shortcoming of such studies is that—unlike the economic studies mentioned earlier—they do *not* separate the effects of college from those of ability, background, family income, and the like. When they compare college graduates with others, they are comparing two groups that differ in many important respects, quite apart from college.

5

Selection of Alternatives

Until now, we've focussed on the goals students bring to college, and whether these goals can really be attained there. In the rest of this book we ask, "Which of these goals can be attained through alternate channels, and what are the channels?"

But before you start sorting out specific alternatives, you'll want to take an essential first step: developing some sense of yourself. You'll need to understand who you are, what you want, how you relate to your co-workers and surroundings. Chapter 6, **Knowing Yourself,** is designed to help you. Begin by reading it carefully. It won't work miracles, but it may raise a few questions about yourself that you never really asked before.

Thereafter you can skip around. If **Going into Business for Yourself** strikes a responsive chord, by all means begin with that chapter. On the other hand, if you already know that you can't afford a major commitment to volunteer work, or that you have no intention of joining the Armed Forces, don't read those portions unless you want to. Work through the book with an eye to your own needs; evaluate each suggestion in terms of yourself.

At this point many of you may be clearer about your goals than about the channels for attaining them. For example, you may already know that your primary purpose in considering college was to make friends, to move to a new environment or, in the long run, to earn a lot of money. You're reading this book to learn how such goals can be attained.

In that case, Exhibit 5-1 will be of use. At the left of this chart we list some of the objectives mentioned earlier which are achieved through attending college. Across the top are some of the alternatives which will also meet these objectives. A check in the box where the column and row meet indicates that the desired objectives can readily be achieved through that alternative. A dot suggests that the combination is possible, although perhaps not typical. Suppose, for example, that one of your important goals is to move to a new environment. One sure way to achieve it is by joining the

EXHIBIT 5-1

Alternative Choices to Meet these Objectives:

Objectives Normally Achieved Through College:	Work	Occupational Education	Apprenticeship	Starting your own Business	Volunteer Work	Armed Forces	College
Meeting requirements for profession or field of work	✓	✓	✓	✓	●	✓	✓
Learning for its own sake	✓				✓	●	✓
Gaining maturity	✓	●	●	✓	✓	✓	●
Gaining independence	✓	●	●	✓	✓	✓	●
Making new friends*	✓	●	●	●	✓	✓	✓
Meeting influential people	●			●	●	●	●
Filling in cultural background*					●		
Having fun	●			●	●	●	✓
Living in a new environment	●	●			✓	●	✓
Don't know what else to do	✓	✓			✓	✓	●

✓ A good choice for this objective.
● A possible choice for this objective.
*Can be done just as well in your own leisure time.

Armed Forces. Another is by doing volunteer work in another part of the country. So you'll find check marks under these two headings. The dots under "Work" and "Occupational Education" suggest that these alternatives can also be combined with your particular goal. However, if what you want above all is to leave home, you'd better think twice about starting a business of your own. A complicated venture like this is best attempted in a familiar community where you understand the problems and needs.

Paradoxically, college itself appears on the list of alternatives. This book isn't designed to talk you out of college, but to suggest other choices that might serve as well or better, depending on your own purpose and goals. College should remain a possibility—but only one among many.

Obviously, the alternatives considered here are only a sampling; we couldn't begin to examine them all. What we've tried to do is suggest those possibilities which appear realistic and workable for a fair number of young people. Certainly if you want to leave home, one way is to take a six-month tour of Europe and the Near East; another is to become a professional baseball player. Unfortunately, the first takes more money and the second more talent than most of us possess. For similar reasons, the question of marriage is minimized. Undoubtedly, there are some high school graduates for whom marriage is in fact a valid alternative to college. But it's an alternative which will work only for a small group of people under special circumstances. If you never even considered marriage until you read about it in a book, chances are you're not ready.

One alternative does not appear in the chart: simply to pursue your goals by yourself in your own leisure time. For example, if you feel a serious need to learn about the great artistic and literary traditions of the past, there are innumerable books, discussion groups, museums, clubs and classes to help you. If you want to meet people, look into new sports and hobbies, church or political groups, and the like. Such channels are omitted, not because they're unimportant, but because they don't represent a major commitment of your time and energies.

Remember, the chart is intended only as a guide. If you're not sure of what you want to do or why you want to do it, just read along, skimming or slowing down according to your own interests. Perhaps your imagination will be captured by something you never even thought about before.

Finally, don't expect any single alternative to meet all your needs. You'll probably have to weigh the various possibilities, evaluate all considerations and, in the end, arrive at a suitable compromise. This, after all, is how most decisions are made. The critical thing is to define your priorities in terms of your own personality, skills and goals, and work out a solution that's right for you. The rest of this book is designed to help you.

Know Yourself

Before we can talk about alternatives, there are two areas to be examined: the world at large, and the world of you. The world at large offers thousands of variations and choices, but there's only one of you; so this is where we'll start.

By the time you finish high school, certain things are pretty well set; what you like and dislike, what you're interested in, your reactions to certain typical situations. Every decision you make will be governed by these relatively stable factors. Of course, as you encounter new experiences and ways of life, there will be changes. But the place to begin is by assessing where you are right now.

There are four major categories through which you can explore your own inclinations. These are:

- Interests
- Abilities
- Temperament
- Values

We'll look at each in some detail, and see how it ties in with you and what you do.

INTERESTS

Nine out of ten young people seeking vocational counseling want some kind of test to tell them what they're interested in. Interest "tests" list activities—the number may range from several dozen to several hundred—and ask you to check your preferences. The activities may be completely unfamiliar; you can only guess at how you'd feel about them. On the other hand, you've been living with yourself all your life. There's a lot you already know about your own interests. With a little direction, just examining your background can tell you as much as the tests, and maybe more.

Here are four ways to approach the question of interests. Keep pencil and paper handy; you may want to make some notes as you go along.

Introspection

This is a matter of looking inside yourself and discovering, of all the things you've been exposed to, which you actually prefer.

Take school. If you're like most teen-agers, you've probably spent more waking hours in class than anywhere else. You've studied English, math, science, gym, music, art, history, languages, and who knows what else. How did you react? What were your favorite subjects? In social studies, were the portraits of Napoleon and Josephine more absorbing than the struggles for power? Or was it the other way around? In math, did you play around with numbers and equations, or were you sidetracked into wondering why anybody wanted six bushels of oranges, anyway? Try to separate the subject-matter from the teacher, the school and your friends in class. Was there any area you enjoyed more than the others? Trigonometry or textile design? Social science or printing shop? Don't think too hard about it; just jot down your responses as they come to mind.

Then there are the movies and television shows you enjoy most. Are you partial to adventure stories? Situation comedy? Documentaries? How about animal pictures, science shorts, political debates? Is it sports you watch most often, and if so, what kind? Once you identify the shows you prefer, it's worthwhile to pinpoint what holds your interest. Is it action? Scenery? Clothing? Or the emotions on people's faces? Questions like these will identify what matters most to you, the surroundings you prefer, the types of people you enjoy, the questions you find most challenging.

The same point of view applies to reading. Newspapers and magazines, books and cereal boxes, all offer something to read. Which hold your interests; which make you turn away? Some people are fascinated by long, complicated accounts of battle actions or trips over rugged terrain; others skip them to get on with the story. For another group, both plot and description are secondary to the characters and what makes them tick. Where do you fit in; what do you look for when you read? Are you partial to love stories, mysteries, biographies? Can you sustain interest in a long, involved novel, or do you prefer something you can finish at one sitting? Remember, there are no right or wrong answers here; it's your own reactions that are important. In answering questions like these, you're discovering what really interests you.

The Objective Approach

Here we turn to how you actually spend your spare time. What a person does with his free time may tell more about his interests than anything he says. It reveals, not only what he prefers to do, but how much initiative and energy he devotes to it. Mary feels she's interested in sports. Of her twenty free hours a week, she spends six listening to records, five reading, five with friends, two watching television, and only one each biking and playing tennis. Mary may admire the outdoor type, she may wish she were athletic, but she clearly prefers the sedentary life.

Check on yourself. For two weeks, keep a running account of how you spend your time. Don't change your habits, go on doing what you usually do; just make a note of it. Like Mary, you may find there's a gap between what you think you're interested in, and how you actually use your time. If so, try to analyze it. Are your interests too expensive? Are they unavailable in your community—and how hard have you looked? Could they be too strenuous? Maybe you enjoy reading about gardening, but you draw the line at getting your hands dirty. Or you may love to dismantle an automobile engine, but get bored and restless when it comes to learning the theory. If you find that some of your interests are more imaginary than real, don't take it too hard. At the same time you'll be discovering your true preferences, which will be much more to the point.

The Outsider's Point of View

Often, your friends know you better than you think. They notice when you really throw yourself into something, and when your attention wavers. They can compare your reactions to those of other people—even to their own. When you go to a concert, do you listen or tend to doze off? At a football game, are you alert every minute, or is your real pleasure in kidding around with the people next to you? There's nothing wrong either way, but in the first case football spells out sports, while in the second it means sociability and school spirit. Your friends can put you straight.

So can your teachers. Over the years, teachers get to know hundreds of young people. As a result, they're in a unique position to identify your strengths and weaknesses. You may think your paper on Zen Buddhism hits a new high, but your teacher can evaluate it in light of every other paper he's ever read on this and related themes. He can compare your energy, conviction and dedication with that of all the other students who've passed through his classes. If you're on good terms with any of your teachers, feel free to draw upon their insight and perspective. Make an appointment and talk it over.

Sometimes your parents can also tell you a few things worth knowing about yourself. If you're comfortable discussing such issues with them, it's a very good idea. But if, in your household, it would lead to civil war, better go elsewhere first.

Interest Tests and Inventories

Various check lists and inventories have been developed, comparing your interests with those thought to relate to different vocational fields. Generally, the tests list hundreds of items, in assorted categories. You choose the items that appeal to you. In some tests you choose one out of three, while in others you're allowed to check as many as you like. The responses on these tests needs analysis and interpretation; they're nothing you can take by yourself. They are usually available through such agencies as state employment offices, Youth Opportunity Centers, local mental health offices, and guidance services offered by organizations like the YMCA, the Jewish Federation, and so on. Your own school counsellor may be in a position to administer the tests. And of course, many private psychologists offer testing and vocational guidance, but their services are not cheap.

In any case, the tests won't provide ready answers to your questions. They are useful primarily as one more tool to help you get acquainted with yourself. Nonetheless, if you don't expect too much of them, they may be useful and interesting. Usually, such tests are organized around various categories. For example, one widely used test concentrates on the following areas of interest:

Scientific—an interest in knowing the why and how of things.

Social Welfare—an interest in people for their own sake.

Literary—interest in use of words and the manipulation of verbal symbols.

Systematic—keeping records, organizing information, computing.

Contact—meeting or dealing with people, in connection with one's business or profession.

Aesthetic expression—creating music, art, etc.

Aesthetic appreciation—seeing or experiencing works of art.

Another test gives rise to a second set of categories. As you can see, they overlap the earlier ones to a marked degree.

Mechanical	Literary
Computational	Musical.
Scientific	Social Service
Persuasive	Clerical
Artistic	

Of course, most people have interests in a variety of categories. Statisticians have gone to work on all these variations, and have come up with some highly technical results. For this and other reasons, it takes a skilled professional to interpret the responses on such tests. Nonetheless, the lists may help you sort out your own interests. Or they may help in a negative way, by enabling you to eliminate those areas which emphatically do not apply to you. Remember, in getting to know yourself, no single detail will tell you everything you need to know; it's only when you put them all together that a coherent picture begins to emerge.

ABILITIES

Knowing your interests tells something about your abilities, but less than you might think. Though there is some connection between what you enjoy and what you do well, the relation is tricky. You're not going to become a concert pianist unless you love music, but loving music by itself won't get you there. A person interested in antique furniture may have no ability at all as a cabinetmaker, and very little as an interior decorator. Or he may be a competent amateur, without even approaching the professional class. So interests, while important, are only a start; the next step is finding out what abilities and aptitudes you actually possess. You can get this information from at least a half-dozen different sources.

Achievement Tests

These are of two kinds. There are the ordinary tests your teachers are always giving you in school, to determine what you've learned. They measure how much arithmetic you know, how much spelling, history, geography, grammar, science. Very often they have a lot to do with your final grade.

Then there are standardized printed tests, given to large groups of students in the entire district, state, or even country. They compare your achievements with those of students in your grade elsewhere. Most schools use standardized tests somewhere around the third grade, and again at the eighth or ninth. Many will share the results with you and your parents—in some communities they are required by law to do so, upon request—or at least point out your general strengths and weaknesses.

Aptitude Tests

The relation between aptitude and achievement is controversial, and it's hard to be sure which comes first. Certainly, there's overlap in both directions, and the amount of experience you've had at a particular task shows up in tests as increased aptitude. Nonetheless, aptitude tests are designed to measure, not merely what you already know about a subject or skill, but also your individual capacity for mastering it. Special tests are available to measure specific aptitudes considered important in various fields of work. The most widely accepted of these is the General Aptitude Test Battery (G.A.T.B.), developed by the U.S. Department of Labor and administered to millions of people over the past 25 years. The G.A.T.B. has been given not only to the job applicant, but to people actually working successfully at hundreds of different occupations. On the basis of their responses, aptitude profiles have been prepared for just about every kind of work you can think of. The test itself sets up nine categories of aptitude:

General Learning Ability   Clerical Perception
Verbal Aptitude   Motor Coordination
Numerical Aptitude   Finger Dexterity
Spatial Perception   Manual Dexterity
Form Perception

Other tests are available to measure such specifics as mechanical comprehension, abstract reasoning, clerical aptitude and mechanical aptitude.

At best, these tests provide statistical information about your chances for success at different kinds of work. They direct you to various occupations which, in terms of your own aptitudes, you should be able to handle. For a given set of aptitudes, they may suggest dozens of compatible occupations—with no guarantee that you would enjoy any of them! Above all, they cannot direct you to a specific job which is the one perfect job for you; as a rule, there is no such job. Perhaps their most useful purpose is to warn you away from fields for which you are totally unsuited—and that's important, too!

Counselors know the strengths and weaknesses of these tests. They know that a person whose numerical aptitude is poor is unlikely to become a computer programmer, no matter how much time and effort he invests. Similarly, a person with little spatial perception would do well to stay away from architecture. On the other hand, through determination and practice, some skills can be strengthened. For example, Robert had an overwhelming interest in electronics, but his finger dexterity—an important aptitude for this work—was only fair. With suitable exercises recommended by his counselor, he improved to a point where he got a job and did well. This suggests why test results must be studied in the light of the individual's other qualities, and why they should be administered and interpreted by professionals who are trained in their use.

Where can you get such tests? Your school counselor can either administer them himself, or tell you where to go. The General Aptitude Test Battery is offered only through your state employment office, and is often given to high school seniors at school. The vocational services mentioned earlier may also provide batteries of aptitude tests.

School Grades

Admittedly, school grades depend on all sorts of things: the standards of the school, competition from others in the class, the teacher's grading practices (some teachers never give an "A"), how you and the teacher get along, and a host of additional factors. Nonetheless, over the years they reveal a good deal about your abilities and aptitudes. If you've always dashed off your English compositions an hour before class, and still pulled down 90's and 95's, you don't need an aptitude test to know you have verbal skills. By the same token, if you limped through all of algebra and geometry without a single test grade over 75, an aptitude test in math won't tell you anything new, either. If, term after term, with one teacher after another, your grades in history, or science, or French, remain within a certain range, the chances are that those grades are a good indicator of what you can do.

Evaluation of Physical Qualities

Maybe you never counted physical qualities among your resources, but they certainly make a difference in what you do. Are you physically strong enough to lift heavy objects? Are you particularly tall or short—and how might this limit your choice of occupation? Are you color blind? It doesn't matter for a waitress or plumber, but it can eliminate you from certain electronics fields where color-coded wire is used every day. People with allergies should be wary of such environments as florist shops, dry cleaners and woodworking or metalworking operations. Those with a tendency toward bronchitis do well to avoid fume-laden areas like garages and chemical plants.

Some jobs have uncommonly high demands with reference to personal appearance. An airline stewardess must meet specific requirements for physical proportions, and have even teeth and a good skin. Models are required to have precise body measurements so they can wear standard sizes of clothes. Radio announcing demands good speech and a clear, effective voice. Some of these personal requirements can be achieved through long, usually arduous effort; others are simply a matter of natural endowment. Examine yourself realistically. If you're determined to get into radio, are you willing to undergo the speech training required to become an announcer? Or might you find radio production as rewarding, and a lot more feasible? If airlines fascinate you, are you really prepared for a constant regimen of diet and grooming, or would you be just as happy in some behind-the-scenes job like being a telephone reservation clerk?

Hobbies

Your hobbies tell not only what you really choose to do, but how you go about it. Interests indicate a general direction; your actual aptitudes determine how you proceed and how far you go. If your hobby is photography, do you keep reshooting until the light is exactly right; do you patiently redo a portrait until the expression is just what you want? If so, then for you photography has a lot to do with art. Perhaps your primary interest is in technical data—the effects of different lens openings, papers, chemicals, and so on. In this case your hobby may be more of a science. Or is your greatest pleasure in the elaborate new darkroom equipment that enables you to use your mechanical skills? All of these are reasonable, legitimate approaches to photography, yet each draws on a different aptitude. If your interest is sewing, what do you enjoy most: designing, choosing patterns and fabrics, trying all the fascinating attachments on your sewing machine, or putting in the beautiful hand details that make your clothes different from anyone else's? For that matter, how are you at following the complicated diagrams and instructions that come with the patterns? This is still another type of skill, and one which is essential in certain types of technical work. To identify your hobby as photography, sewing, model-building or chess, is only a first step. Look a little further, and see in what direction you branch out.

Special Skills

There's a whole area of specific, usable skills that are often taken for granted. For example, Tom's been playing the piano for nine years. He'll never be what he calls "good"—where "good"means of concert calibre—but he's certainly good enough to accompany a beginning dance class, a choir rehearsal, or a roomful of kindergartners. Similarly, Helen's always spoken Polish at home. She's completely at ease in the language; she can speak it, read it and write it. Helen never thought anything of this skill; yet the command of a second language can open many doors. Other assets, often overlooked, include a talent for cooking or sewing, an agreeable telephone voice, a driver's license, and the ability to operate a tractor, switchboard, fork lift or power gardening equipment. Typing may be valuable when combined with other skills, even if your speed isn't impressive. So search out your special abilities; they may add up when you're deciding what to do.

Perhaps this is also the place to say a word about finances. It hardly qualifies as an "ability," but like piano-playing or a pleasant voice, it's one of those fixed, external realities that must be taken into account. What you do depends a lot on what you can afford to do. Options like travel and volunteer work are feasible only if you have outside financial resources. The Peace Corps provides you with room, board and pocket money, but it's no solution if you must also contribute to your household. The trade-off between present salary and future prospects depends on how badly the money is needed at this time. In general, young people looking for work are advised to put opportunity and type of work ahead of starting salary, but not everyone can afford to follow this advice. Only you know your financial situation. It's a fact of life; accept it as part of the total picture.

In discussing abilities, we've been emphasizing specific skills that can be evaluated in a very objective way. If you're looking for a job, these are what make the difference—not prospects or promises, but proof that you can handle the basic requirements of the job, right now. Maybe you already know of some weak spot that could keep you from getting the kind of work you want. It might be spelling, if you want to be a secretary, or arithmetic, if you're interested in retailing. Plenty of people have improved in areas like these. Sometimes, with the prospect of a good job ahead, a little private tutoring or a brush-up course in an adult evening school is all that's needed. But get the tutoring or the brush-up *first;* then go after the job. You may do beautifully, and everything will fall into place. On the other hand, you may have been right the first time; arithmetic, or spelling, or whatver it is, will never be for you.

TEMPERAMENT

By the time you've completed high school, you've developed some pretty well-defined responses to the situations you meet in life. These responses are related in turn to all the particular, distinctive qualities that give you your own individuality. What name should we give to these qualities? Sometimes the word personality is used, but too often personality suggests mere surface impressions. So we'll use another word: temperament. When we speak of temperament, we have in mind the deep-seated emotional and rational patterns which characterize the particular individual.

Even as people get older, this basic quality of temperament is unlikely to change very much. Of course, experience modifies it; you learn, in due course, to ignore or circumvent some of your feelings, and you may uncover capacities you weren't aware of before. But the framework remains essentially the same.

When we talk of temperament, we're talking about something very important in planning a course of action. Each of us has an ideal image of how we would like to be. We have another image of how we would like to *appear.* And we have still another—one we're not always ready to face up to—of how we actually are. In making decisions, and particularly decisions about careers, we often begin by trying to realize the ideal self. Only gradually do we modify this approach in terms of what we can actually do.

An oversimplified example may help here. John is an easy-going young man who has lots of friends and leads a happy social life. His school work is only fair; he'd rather enjoy himself than study. But on some level John is worried. In his fantasy, he'd rather be seen as more of a leader, someone who directs the activities of others and to whom others turn for direction. In choosing a career, John must deal with both aspects of himself, and try to reconcile them.

As with aptitudes, there are various ways to categorize temperament. One of the simplest is a three-way breakdown: are you oriented to people, to ideas, or to things? Of course, all of us have some interest in all three, so the question becomes one of emphasis. Let's see how it might work in practice.

John, when he sees a few classmates on the way to school, will call out to them, run to catch up, walk them to their classrooms for the sake of company. He really likes people, and would probably do well as a salesman or businessman. Andy has his mind on a science problem, and will avoid being interrupted by anyone, even a good friend. He is "idea"-oriented; he needs to do highly skilled work which will absorb all his energies. Joe spends his free time tinkering with his car or anyone else's. He enjoys company—as long as his friends work along with him and share his enthusiasm. Of course, not all cases are this clear-cut. For example, Dave will drop anything to get into a deep rap session—he doesn't care with whom. But it's not the people that interest Dave. To him, they're primarily a channel for sharing ideas; it's the ideas that have priority.

Needless to say, the three-way classification according to interest in people, ideas, or things, is among the simplest approaches to temperament. A somewhat deeper interpretation uses the categories described below. In general, each person falls somewhere along the scale from "not at all" to "very much." You may use the scales on the right to assess yourself. Keep in mind that a high number on the scale (6 or 7) means that the category really describes you, while a low number (1 or 2) means that it doesn't apply.

	Not at all						Very much
Autonomous—self-reliant; strong sense of personal freedom.	1	2	3	4	5	6	7
Curious—searches for new solutions; restless; interested in problem-solving.	1	2	3	4	5	6	7
Satisfied—easy-going; accepts things as they are.	1	2	3	4	5	6	7
Attention-seeking—wants to stand out; concerned with status; exhibitionistic.	1	2	3	4	5	6	7
Nurturing—takes care of others, helping, giving of oneself.	1	2	3	4	5	6	7
Idealistic—concerned with how the world ought to be.	1	2	3	4	5	6	7
Power-seeking—eager to control and dominate; seeks responsibility.	1	2	3	4	5	6	7
Realistic—concerned with making the best possible use of the world as it is.	1	2	3	4	5	6	7
Tolerant—accepts frustration, different viewpoints, variability.	1	2	3	4	5	6	7
Precise—enjoys accuracy, orderliness, organization.	1	2	3	4	5	6	7

Acquiescent—enjoys being given detailed instructions; dislikes responsibility and decisions.	1 2 3 4 5 6 7
Dependent—seeks assistance, follows leadership.	1 2 3 4 5 6 7
Conforming—prefers to follow an accepted pattern.	1 2 3 4 5 6 7

Where did you come out? If you scored four on most categories, ask whether you're really thinking through exactly where you belong. Most people fall to the right or left of middle; on some categories it may be far over in one direction, on others, just a little. Working this out will give you a "handle" on yourself, a new way to understand your own qualities and the kind of person you are. Meanwhile, let's see how some other people score.

We've all known people who want to run the show from the start. They gladly take responsibility for school projects, committees, meetings, and parties. They enjoy managing; even mix-ups turn into challenges for them. These people will score 6 or 7 on autonomy and power-seeking. They may also score strongly on curiosity and attention-seeking. In acquiescene and conformity they score only 1's and 2's. And when it comes to idealism, tolerance or precision, they could be anywhere on the scale.

Then there are those who do their own job to perfection and take pride in their work, but who would be irritated and miserable supervising the work of others. People like this often do so well that they get promoted to a managerial level—whereupon they go to pieces. A typical profile of this type may show 7 on precision, 6 or 7 on autonomy, but 1 or 2 on such categories as tolerance and power-seeking.

In general, no one temperament is "better" or "worse" than any other; the world needs all kinds of people to do all kinds of work. What is important is to recognize one's temperament and adapt to it, whatever it may be.

Take Bill. Bill is interested in sales management, and he feels he can learn fastest by being where the decisions are made. His temperament scores show him to be curious, realistic, and markedly attention-seeking. On conformity, he scores 1.

Bill surprises everyone by taking a crash course in typing and steno, and going to work as secretary to a department store executive. (His clerical skills leave something to be desired, but the boss likes his attitude!) His job will give him a ringside seat at the day-to-day operation of the store. It bothers him not one bit that every other secretary in the organization is female; in fact, he rather enjoys it. Situated as he is, he can't help being noticed; with any luck at all, his chances for promotion should be excellent.

John is also interested in management, and he can also type. (He learned how years ago, so he could help in his father's one-man wholesaling business.) But John's a quiet young man, who scored 6 in conformity. For him,

Bill's spot in the limelight would be a disaster. Instead, he goes to work for an import-export firm, where clerical jobs are commonly filled by men. His prospects are as good as Bill's because he's also chosen well—in terms of his own temperament.

In contrast to both of them is Tom. He is also interested in business management, but with a quite different attitude. Tom scores close to the top in two important areas: autonomy and curiosity. What this means in practice, unfortunately, is that he can't stand working for anyone else. He has to make his own decisions, for better or for worse. Tom's solution is to look for some small business of his own—a vending or rack route is what he has in mind—and learn while doing. To make this decision, he must be low in conformity; not many people his age would venture out on their own like this. However, he's aware of the risks, and is going ahead anyway. If he's also realistic enough to deal with concrete situations as they arise, chances of success should be excellent.

VALUES

In making decisions, different people attach importance to one factor or another. Claire makes good money as a waitress, but her friend Jo Ann turns down a similar job for the lower salary of a receptionist with a well-known insurance company. Fred rejects the comfort and cleanliness of office work in favor of the mobility of a taxi driver. Paul has a good eye for furniture design, but doesn't want to become an interior decorator. Let's examine these choices more closely.

Jo Ann, the receptionist, and Claire, the waitress, share many of the same traits. Each of them feels she's providing an essential service. Both use considerable manual dexterity, Jo Ann to handle a busy switchboard and Claire to manipulate her platters and trays. Both jobs require fastidious grooming. Why will Jo Ann work for less than what Claire earns?

The answer is that Jo Ann and Claire have different values; a different sense of what's important. When people actually buckle down and make their decisions, it's usually values that tip the scales.

Perhaps the key difference is that while Claire is concerned with earning money and feeling free, Jo Ann values status more highly. She feels good about herself, working with such a well-known firm. Somehow, the prestige and dignity of the company reflect on her, too. This is a very significant value; by comparison, the money is unimportant. Claire, on the other hand, enjoys the independence of being a waitress; she can get a job any day, anywhere in the country, and have money in her pocket that same evening. She likes the gamble of getting part of her income in tips; it lends excitement to her work. If the restaurant is doing well, she may earn more than her friends in other fields, and may be able to afford a spectacular vacation.

Fred, the cab driver, has a job in some ways similar to that of his cousin, a bank teller. Both deal with people all day, both handle money, and both are, in a way, confined to a limited space. But driving a cab makes Fred feel he's his own boss. He ranges all over the city, and nothing could convince him to work "cooped up indoors," which is how he sees his cousin's job. Then again, he works afternoons and evenings, enjoys seeing the nightlife of the city, and can sleep late in the morning.

Paul and Don are both interested in furniture design, but while Don prefers to study interior decorating, Paul has decided to be a carpenter. Don views design as solving a puzzle, fitting pieces together to create a whole; Paul prefers to create the separate pieces.

These are just a few cases where seemingly abstract values are translated into very specific actions. If values are this important, let's have a closer look at them.

Kinds of Values

One widely-used analysis of values identifies six basic groups. You can probably identify with one or, more likely, several of them. Notice that while the terms may be familiar, their meanings are somewhat different from what you might expect.

Economic—values concerned with practical, useful evaluation of alternatives, often in relation to income, working conditions, and so on.

Aesthetic—values concerned with form, harmony and beauty, usually in creative fields offering an opportunity to express one's own taste and judgment.

Theoretical—values related to concepts of truth, particularly with reference to scientific study and research.

Spiritual—values associated with religious feeling, often found along with aesthetic values.

Social—values built around interpersonal relations and love for people.

Political—values reflecting a drive towards dominance and power, although not necessarily in politics.

In some ways, these values resemble qualities of temperament. The basic difference is that while temperament appears to be innate, or nearly so, values are superimposed. They develop later in life, relate more to judgment in decision-making, and are more subject to change with maturity and experience. Until recently, young people tended to assume strong economic and political values that helped them shape aggressive business careers. As they grew older, these were replaced by social and spiritual values. Today, young adults seem to prefer social and aesthetic values from the start, but this, too, may change.

As with temperament, there is no need to rank or judge values. What is necessary is to recognize how powerfully they influence our choices. Some people value cleanliness so highly that they willingly take lower-paying jobs where their hands and clothes will not get dirty. Others forgo promotions and salary increases for the sake of remaining in a familiar community. For the person with strong social and political values, joining the police force could be ideal; if his values are aesthetic, the experience could be shattering.

When it comes to translating values into specific courses of action, people often go to extremes. On the one hand we have the pure idealist. He has defined his values, he intends to live by them, and he will not budge an inch. On the other, we have the confirmed cynic. As he sees it, the world provides no place for him and his ideals. He's quite prepared to deny his values during the eight-hour working day, and compensate by devoting himself to them completely on his own time. Most adults find themselves somewhere between these extremes. Their work and their lifestyle may not reflect all of their values to the maximum degree. They try to live by the most important ones.

The various resources and suggestions mentioned in this chapter are summarized in Exhibit 6–1 on page 61. Dealing with them is not easy. It's a long, demanding experience of looking inside yourself and trying to crystallize some ideas about the kind of person you are. You may find that the picture doesn't quite add up; there is a certain amount of confusion and contradiction. Don't let it worry you; no one in the world conforms completely to any single "type." The goal of this chapter is to help you to line up your interests and abilities, your major traits of temperament, and your values, so that you can see more concretely where to go from here.

Let's take Jo Ann the receptionist, as an example. Going through the classifications in this chapter, she comes out like this:

Interests: Aesthetic appreciation, systematic (collects stamps, maintains a recipe file).

     Contact (secretary of her club; takes minutes and sends out correspondence).

Abilities: Average student, no artistic skill.

     Better than average athlete; good coordination.

     Good at typing.

     Only fair at shorthand and bookkeeping.

     Seems to get along well with people.

EXHIBIT 6-1

A Guide to Knowing Yourself

A. Interests

    1. Introspection: school, movies and television, reading
    2. The objective approach: keeping track of your time
    3. The outsiders' point of view: friends, teachers, parents
    4. Interest test and inventories:

        Categories: a. scientific   systematic
                        social welfare   contact
                        literary   aesthetic expression
                                          aesthetic appreciation

                     b. mechanical   literary
                        computational   social
                        scientific   social service
                        persuasive   clerical
                        artistic

B. Abilities

    1. Achievement tests: classroom and standardized
    2. Aptitude tests:

        Categories: a. G.A.T.B.
                        general learning ability   clerical perception
                        verbal aptitude   motor coordination
                        numerical aptitude   finger dexterity
                        spatial perception   manual dexterity
                        form perception

                     b. Other: mechanical comprehension, abstract reasoning, clerical aptitude, mechanical aptitude, hand dexterity, etc.

    3. School grades
    4. Physical qualities
    5. Hobbies
    6. Special skills

C. Temperament

    Categories: a. people, ideas, things

                     b. autonomous   realistic
                        curious   tolerant
                        satisfied   precise
                        attention-seeking acquiescent
                        nurturing   dependent
                        idealistic   conforming
                        power-seeking

D. Values

    Categories: economic   spiritual
                        aesthetic   social
                        theoretical   political

Temperament: Highest in the following three categories:
                    Satisfied
                    Realistic
                    Attention-seeking
                    (There seems to be some conflict between "satisfied" and "attention-seeking," but Jo Ann tried to be as honest as she could. She does enjoy being noticed, and she is pleased with her appearance at all times; she always dresses very well.)

Values: Primarily social and economic. Has a strong sense of propriety and doesn't like disturbance. Likes to see things done right. Impressed by status.

Jo Ann's job as a receptionist is a good choice. Her work utilizes her greatest talent: the ability to get along with people. A shy person might be uncomfortable constantly dealing with strangers, but for Jo Ann, her highly visible position, combined with the prestige of the company, is altogether suitable. At the same time, operating the switchboard gives her a chance to use her dexterity and coordination.

Though this job serves Jo Ann so well, there are others that could be just as satisfying. She might enjoy working as a salesgirl in a good store; this would give less scope to her coordination, but more to her aesthetic sense. She could, with additional schooling, become a dental or medical assistant. Here she would have to decide whether the investment and study are worth it. There is also the danger that with all her feeling for people, she would draw back from seeing them in discomfort or pain. A job with an airline might suit her, although probably not as a stewardess; Jo Ann likes routine, while stewardesses must cope with the unexpected.

The important thing is that there is no *one alternative* for Jo Ann—or for anyone. Don't sit around waiting for the one perfect inspiration. There are many possibilities; as long as your choice conforms to the kind of person you are, you can grow and develop within it.

7

Work: What Is It?

Work is a very simple word to cover a very complex idea. In a down-to-earth sense, work is what a person does to earn a livelihood. But this is only the beginning. We all know that one person's work is another's play: the store manager spends his weekends gardening, the professional gardener boasts of his gourmet cooking, and the housewife volunteers one day a week to managing the Thrift Shop of her local hospital. So it appears that work is less a matter of what you do than of what it means to you, your community, and the people you work for.

WORK AND SOCIETY

Think of the incredibly complex and interdependent world of today. Every day we come in contact with a thousand things that had to be planned, designed, produced and sold by somebody. To these people, this is their work. Only through the combined efforts of every member can society be supplied with the innumerable goods and services on which each individual draws for his needs. To place a single telephone call may involve the contributions of a thousand people—operators, technicians, linemen, office clerks, even the people who print and distribute the directories. Your car represents the work of still other thousands—those who made the wires, screws, tires, gaskets and body sections; those who assembled these parts into the car you drive; the men who run the railroad or truck that delivered it to you. Everything in our world is created by somebody's work. Is it any wonder, then, that the relation to work is usually our strongest link with reality? When you think of work this way, you can understand what Ralph E. Denty, Jr., writing in the *Vocational Guidance Quarterly*, has in mind when he talks about "man's achieving a cooperative and unifying relationship with the universe through his vocation." Elsewhere, it has been suggested that "work, in its most universal aspect, represents man's attempt to impose human purpose on his environment."

WORK AND THE INDIVIDUAL

The person who thinks of work merely as a way to earn money finds the choice of work relatively simple. He chooses the job that promises the most money, either right away or in the long run. But when we stop to think about it, we see that work represents much more than that. Let's examine a few of the meanings we attach to our work.

Money

Our culture sets up the capacity to support oneself as a basic measure of adulthood. Money is needed to buy the basic necessities—food, clothing and shelter—which are required for survival. But often, we want more money than what's needed to survive. We want books, records, flowers, a prettier coat, a better meal—all the extras that add grace, comfort, or fun. According to our tastes, we want music, theatre, travel, works of art. Rightly or wrongly, society tends to accord a higher status to people who own more and "better" objects.

Money over and above one's needs also bestows considerable power on its owner. It enables him to buy the services of others, and gives him some authority over those who work for him. Again, we won't go into the question of whether money should make such a difference; the fact is that it does. So it's understandable that money is a very important meaning of work, and for some people, the only meaning.

Status

Whether or not they are aware of it, most people feel that certain kinds of work are in some ways on a higher level than others. These rankings are not necessarily related to earnings; a college professor is invariably ranked higher than a salesman, although his salary is likely to be much lower. One of the first questions people ask when they are introduced is, "What do you do?" The answer gives us an important clue to the person's earnings, his life style, where he fits in the hierarchy of the world's work. For some people, status is the one most important meaning of work; they will stay in jobs they don't particularly enjoy, year after year, in order to feel the pride of being a professor, an executive or a manager.

Participation

For many people, work is the medium through which they express their feelings about their fellowmen. They derive great satisfaction from knowing they are useful and they look for work through which they can express this. This is as true of auto mechanics, grocers and street cleaners as it is of doctors, teachers and social workers. Other people see their role differently; they seek power and authority, and find it in supervisory or managerial positions. Whatever our goals, most of us perceive them in terms of interactions with other people. Work provides an important arena for such interaction.

Personal Satisfaction

This is a wonderful feeling that we are competent, able people who fit well into the world we live in. In connection with work, this feeling is most likely to occur when we do something at which we are skillful, and know that our work is appreciated and valuable. It comes with recognizing that we, too, are involved with making the wheels go around; that we are part of the complex society around us.

Sociability

The people with whom we work usually see even more of us than our families. They share our on-the-job concerns, and understand our triumphs and frustrations. Often people will continue in jobs that are not otherwise rewarding because of their close feelings for their co-workers. Frequently, seasonal workers, temporarily laid off, will meet and socialize near their shops or offices, even though they are not working.

These are only a few of the implications of work. Now you see why, quite apart from the money, being unable to find work can be such a demoralizing experience, and why people who can easily afford to retire prefer to remain on the job.

WORK AND EMPLOYERS

Typically, employers are engaged in selling products or services. They employ others to help them do this profitably. Their primary objective in choosing and retaining employees is to use other people's talents, skills, and energy for the benefit of the company. To the extent that they pay fair wages and offer good working conditions, they are able to attract and retain a better staff. To the extent that the firm prospers and continues to offer stable employment, the employees benefit, too. Of course, this is an oversimplification, but it does make the point that employers are in business, not to provide an outlet for the employee's talents, but in order to make a profit for themselves or their shareholders.

For the past 40 years, the trend has been for employers to assume greater responsibility for the welfare of their workers. To this end, legislation has provided Social Security, unemployment insurance, workmen's compensation and minimum wages. Organized labor has succeeded in establishing the right to paid vacations, paid holidays, a shorter work week, health insurance, retirement plans and other benefits. The great majority of employers are decent, honest people who treat their employees fairly and often generously. But there is no way they can justify retaining an employee who, through erratic performance, undependable attendance, or personality difficulties, is causing the company to lose money.

Like every other person, employers have individual preferences and prejudices. Laws have limited their authority to exercise some of these. They may no longer refuse to hire anyone on the basis of race or creed, and are not supposed to discriminate because of age or sex. It is hoped that they will not turn down physically handicapped applicants whose disabilities do not interfere with their ability to do the job. The employer knows the value of a capable employee, and will often disregard personal preferences, in order to hire a skilled worker who will help the business. Just the same, the employee may have to adapt to the employer's way of doing things.

Just what does the employer expect from an entry-level applicant—someone who may offer some training, but not much in the way of experience? Basically, he is seeking someone who will become a well-functioning part of the firm, and help it advance. In practice, this might be translated into the following specific questions:

- Does the applicant have the necessary basic skills for the job—typing, electronics, bookkeeping, etc.?
- Does he have an idea of the goals and operation of the business? Does he express an interest in them?
- Is the applicant willing to learn? Very few young people are experts at anything. More important is a willing attitude that allows them to accept instruction and correction.
- Is he mature enough to meet the requirements of the job?
  - Appropriate dress. This doesn't have to mean high heels or a business suit. It means choosing clothing to meet the needs of the job. Blue jeans may be fine in a photographic processing plant. In an office or retail store, they may be out of place.
  - Tact in dealing with people. Some jobs take more tact than others, but there's no job where you'll always be able to suit yourself. Whether you're dealing with supervisors, co-workers, subordinates or customers, you must make the effort to get along with other people.
  - Responsibility. In general, this means you can be depended on to carry through your assignments. It could mean remembering appointments, writing out proper bills or receipts, answering mail; it might mean no more than arriving on time, every day, and putting in a fair day's work. The important thing is that you can be counted on to do your part of the job, reliably and promptly, without anyone checking up on you.

FOR WHOM IS WORK AN ALTERNATIVE?

So far, we've been theorizing about what work means to society, to the individual, and to the employer. Now let's turn to some more practical questions.

Depending on their particular goals, some young people are well advised to start job-hunting directly after high school. Whether you're one of them depends on how well you fit into one or more of the following categories.

You Want to Find Out What You'd Really Like to Do

Your teachers, your counselor, your parents' friends and your own buddies have been filling your head with advice, suggestions, and hot tips. You've been told to read up on jobs in the library, to study manpower projections for 1980, or to "do your own thing." Your head is swimming, your confusion is growing, and the prospect of becoming a hermit becomes more attractive by the day.

The answer is to dive in and discover the feeling of work; work in a store, for an advertising agency, on a farm, at an airport. At the airport, for example, you may only be loading food trays. But you'll be right there among the mechanics and pilots. You'll know the excitement of meeting a turn-around schedule—and the inevitability of weekend work. You'll find out exactly what kinds of jobs are available at airports, and what training is needed for each of them. You may decide that the pressure is too great; you wouldn't want it for all the glamour in the world. On the other hand, the thrill of being responsible for keeping the planes flying, even in a small way, may override every other consideration.

You Want the Money

If your family can't afford college tuition, or if it involves sacrifices you don't care to accept, you needn't be told about this. But the pressure to support oneself may be as much psychological as economic. Paying one's own way has always been a major sign of growing up. Many psychologists feel that the person who's still supported by his parents (and this describes most college students) hasn't quite made it. In fact, many college students are caught in a bind; on the one hand, they want to assert their competence and maturity, but on the other, they're held back by their dependency. If any of them privately wonders whether he even belongs in college, the whole thing can get pretty uncomfortable. Financially and psychologically, starting right in to work may be a much better choice.

Of course, if you're at the point in your life where you want to get out on your own, get married, or save up to travel, there's no question about your next move. Work is the one sensible answer.

You Feel You're Grown Up

Some people mature earlier than their contemporaries. They can't wait to get past the preliminaries and into the real, adult world. That's where energy, enthusiasm, and ideas are put to the test—not on some make-believe school project, but out there, where they're playing for keeps. The adventure of living your own life beckons irresistibly, and it begins with your entry into the working world.

There are many fields open to the high school graduate in this position. The telephone company and other utilities have elaborate training programs and are constantly looking for qualified young men and women. The same is true of many major companies, among them automobile and aircraft plants, banks, insurance companies and retail chains. Promotion opportunities are wide open in these fields. If you apply yourself seriously for four years, you may find that by the time you're 22, you're well into a career, instead of just starting to look for a job.

You Learn More Easily "Hands On"

This may be particularly true in mechanical areas. You read your science book over and over, and still miss the point about levers. But in the lab, you know exactly what will happen when you add more weight, or shift the balance point. Working with concrete things, you can understand relationships which escape you in the abstract. Vocational school may be one solution. Apprenticeship may be another. Getting a job could be the best alternative of all.

You Know Exactly What You Want to Do, and Further Schooling Isn't Necessary

Ralph fits into this category. He's been working part-time as a stock man in the local variety store for nearly a year now, and feels he has a real flair for merchandising. He's alert to what sells, and will probably be working on the sales floor soon. As an added advantage, he enjoys setting up merchandise displays. Ralph knows this is the field for him. He could go on to study merchandising in college, but he prefers to work full-time in the store. In the same four years, he will have tried a dozen different retailing specialties, and become close to expert at some of them.

What about the high school graduates who have wanted to become policemen or firemen since the age of five, and still want it? Often, they can't be hired under the age of 21. However, they may be able to qualify as trainees. Police Technician Trainees often learn important tasks which help qualify them when they reach the legal age. Alternatively, they may attend a community college which offers training in police or firefighting science.

Then there's the serious artist, dancer, musician or movie-maker, determined to work in his specialized field. First, it isn't easy. It's important to have outside corroboration of one's talent and creativity—but talent and creativity are only the beginning. Add to these the determination to seek out every opportunity and capitalize on it. If this describes you, you may be ready to go to work—provided there is any. Meanwhile, you could take temporary or part-time work (as discussed in Chapters 10 and 15); such an arrangement leaves you free to accept an offer in your own field, and allows time for practice or auditions.

You're Looking for Maturity

If you're like many high school graduates, your inexperience and limited contact have left you with a feeling of inadequacy when it comes to work. You're not sure you're mature enough to handle it; you're afraid of appearing awkward in the adult world. Actually, nothing will so quickly smooth out those rough edges as working. The employer who hires a beginner doesn't expect a professional. The job will usually be well defined, and within your ability to handle. You'll have supervision and ample opportunities to ask questions and learn the ropes. You'll discover that the adults working alongside you are not very different from you, and may have been beginners themselves, not long ago. Six months on the job, and you won't recognize yourself. You'll find yourself doing the very things you were afraid to think about, and doing them smoothly and efficiently.

You Want to Meet New People

You're tired of the school crowd and all their fooling around. You want to meet more solid people, who can give you a new slant on things. Work is one place to meet them. You'll find people who have been out in the world more, but are still close to you in age; it won't be hard to get acquainted.

In this case, of course, you'll want to work where there are plenty of other employees. Even if you're actually working by yourself, as you might be in drafting or keypunching, you'll have others alongside you. Strong bonds of friendship can develop over lunch or coffee breaks. Many large firms have organized activities for their staff: sports, bridge, dramatics and choral groups are typical. Others have classes, often during working hours. On the right job, you can earn money and make friends at the same time.

LEARNING ABOUT WORK

It should be apparent by now that for many young people going to work is a practical, direct and satisfying way to achieve a number of objectives. But once a person decides to look for work, the problem arises, "What should I do?" This ties in with a much broader question: "What is there to do?" The variety of places to work, the variety of jobs to be done there, the variety of skills and combinations of skills required to do the work, is almost endless. No wonder the next question arises on the heels of the last one: "How can I possibly choose?"

The question is reasonable. Choosing one alternative means rejecting a hundred others—for the time being, anyway. At some moments, these alternate paths seem far too inviting to reject, so the paralysis of indecision sets in. Later the opposite may occur. The actual job openings available to the inexperienced applicant seem so trivial, so remote from the life career he's dreamed of, that he's tempted to reject them all. And through it all there's a very human undercurrent of fear. For many young people the first serious job-hunt is a major step on the road to mature responsibility for their own lives. The adult world, after all, is the working world, where people not only make their own decisions, but live with the consequences. It does take courage to move out into it.

Perhaps the root of the problem is that people don't know what different jobs are available and what they entail. Here are some ways to find out.

Ask People You Know

Your parents, your relatives, the parents of friends, the counterman who serves you your daily soda—all are sources of information. Ask them questions like these: How do you actually spend your time on the job? How many people work with you, and how does your work tie in with theirs? Who tells you what to do? What do you like best about your job? What don't you like? How long did it take to learn the work? How are the day-to-day working conditions—hot, elegant, dirty, comfortable?

Classified Ads

Newspaper advertisements provide a vast amount of information about work. It's a good idea to get a major Sunday paper and read *each* ad thoroughly. This can take quite a lot of time—as much as two or three hours. Oh, if you have absolutely no interest in nursing or engineering, it may be all right to skip these categories. But don't skip too hastily; in general, you'll be surprised at the range of jobs under each heading. For example, look under "Medical." You'll find "Transcriber," "Records Librarian," "Photographer," "Radiation Technician," "Inhalation Therapist," "Medical Assistant," "Receptionist," "Insurance Biller," "E.K.G. Technician." You'll learn what background these jobs require, what they pay, whether they're plentiful or scarce. Interested in photography? One day's listings may include "Graphic Photo Technician," "Door-to-door Solicitor," "Photofinisher," "Photogrammetry," "Photo Production Manager," "Engraver," "Black-and-White Lab Technician," "Amateur to Train for Portrait Work." Reading through the ads, you'll learn about related areas; the person involved with computers should also check "E.D.P." (Electronic Data Processing), "Programmer," "Operator," "Systems Analyst." Try looking under "Technician;" you'll find it runs the gamut from "Electronic Technicians" to "Technical Illustrators." You may be far from ready for some of these jobs, but you should be aware of the scope within a given field.

Even if you know the kind of work you want, you'll learn a lot from the ads. Do you think you'd like to be a receptionist? You'll find that many receptionists are hired through employment agencies. Ninety-five percent of the openings require typing, usually at 50 words a minute or better. All require attractive appearance, exceptional grooming, a good telephone voice. As for the salaries, they range from $75 to $150 a week, with beginners near the low end of the scale.

Admittedly, not all jobs turn up in the classified ads. For example, "Travel" is a heading that seldom appears. Lots of people want to work in travel agencies, but it's a hard field to break into. Most travel agents start as typists, bookkeepers, and the like, and slowly work their way up to the more interesting jobs. Similarly, there are few calls for singers, instrumentalists, actors, radio announcers, dancers or others in the performing arts. Such jobs are usually filled by word-of-mouth, by agencies, or by ads in trade papers like *Variety* and *Show Biz*. So the newspaper ads won't tell the whole story, but you'll still find many jobs you might never have thought of by yourself.

The Occupational Outlook Handbook

The Occupational Outlook Handbook is the place to learn the details of the jobs you see listed in the ads. Published every two years by the U.S. Department of Labor, it describes over 800 occupations, with emphasis on new or rapidly growing fields. Each entry covers two or three pages, and explains in non-technical language the nature of the work, the kinds of places of employment, the necessary qualifications and training, the employment outlook (including the number of people now in the occupation and a consideration of future prospects), earnings and working conditions, and finally, sources of additional information. A sample discussion from this book is reproduced on page 72–74.

The Occupational Outlook Handbook also has sections devoted to the major industries and the occupations associated with them. For example, the section headed, "Aircraft, missile, and spacecraft manufacturing" describes the scope of the industry, and discusses the varying specific occupations involved, from engineers and technicians through production planners, clerical workers, sheet-metal workers, machine tool operators, metal processing occupations, assemblers, and inspectors. If there's an aerospace plant in your area, you'll get a pretty accurate idea of the jobs they offer, and where you might fit in.

Most important of all, *The Handbook* is so readable, you'll find yourself browsing in it long after your specific questions have been answered. It's brisk, relevant and easy to use. You'll find it in your public library, your

RADIOLOGIC TECHNOLOGISTS

(D.O.T. 078.368)

Nature of the Work

Medical X-rays play a major role in the diagnostic and therapeutic fields of medicine. Radiologic technologists, also called medical X-ray technicians, operate X-ray equipment under the direction of physicians who are usually radiologists (specialists in the use of X-rays).

Most radiologic technologists perform diagnostic work, using X-ray equipment to take pictures of internal parts of the patient's body. They may prepare chemical mixtures, such as barium salts, which the patient swallows to make specific organs appear clearly in X-ray examinations. The technician utilizes proper radiation protection devices and techniques that safeguard against possible radiation hazards. After determining the correct voltage, current, and desired exposure time, the technician positions the patient and makes the required number of radiographs to be developed for interpretation by the physician. The technician may use mobile X-ray equipment at a patient's bedside and in surgery. The technician also is usually responsible for keeping treatment records.

Some radiologic technologists perform radiation therapeutic work. They assist physicians in treating diseases, such as certain cancers, by administering prescribed doses of X-ray or other forms of ionizing radiation to the affected areas of the patient's body. They also may assist the radiologist in measuring and handling radium and other radioactive materials.

Other technicians work in the relatively new field of nuclear medicine in which radioactive isotopes are used for diagnosing and treating diseases. Their duties in assisting the radiologist may include preparing and administering the prescribed radioisotope and operating special equipment for tracing and measuring radioactivity.

Places of Employment

An estimated 75,000 radiologic technologists were employed in 1968; about two-thirds were women.

Approximately one-third of all radiologic technologists were employed in hospitals; most of the remainder worked in medical laboratories, physicians' and dentists' offices or clinics, Federal and State health agencies, and public school systems. A few worked as members of mobile X-ray teams, engaged mainly in tuberculosis detection.

Training, Other Qualifications, and Advancement

Training programs in X-ray technology are conducted by hospitals or by medical schools affiliated with hospitals. A program in X-ray technology usually takes 24 months to complete. A few schools offer 3- or 4-year programs, and 11 schools award a bachelor's degree in X-ray technology. Also, some junior colleges coordinate academic training with work experience in hospitals in 3-year X-ray technician programs and offer an Associate of Arts degree. In 1968, more than 1,100 schools of X-ray technology were approved by the American Medical Association (AMA). In addition to training programs in approved schools, training also may be obtained in the military service. Some courses in X-ray technology are offered by vocational or technical schools.

All of the approved schools accept only high school graduates, and a few require 1 or 2 years of college or graduation from a nursing school. High school courses in mathematics, physics, chemistry, biology, and typing are desirable.

The program in X-ray technology usually includes courses in anatomy, physiology, nursing procedures, physics, radiation protection, darkroom chemistry, principles of radiographic exposure, X-ray therapy, radiographic positioning, medical ethics, department administration, and the operation and maintenance of equipment.

Registration with the American Registry of Radiologic Technologists is an asset in obtaining highly skilled and specialized positions. Registration requirements include graduation from an approved school of medical X-ray technology and the satisfactory completion of an examination. After registration, the title "Registered Technologist, R.T. (ARRT)" may be used. To become certified in radiation therapy or nuclear medicine, technicians must have completed an additional year of combined classroom study and work experience.

Some technicians employed in large X-ray departments may be advanced to the job of chief X-ray technician as openings occur, and may also qualify as instructors in X-ray techniques.

Good health and stamina are important qualifications for this field.

Employment Outlook

Employment opportunities for radiologic technologists are expected to be very good through the 1970's. Part-time opportunities also will be very favorable.

Very rapid growth is expected in the profession, primarily as a result of the anticipated expansion in the use of X-ray equipment in diagnosing and treating diseases; more workers also will be needed to help administer radiotherapy as new knowledge of the medical benefits of radioactive material becomes widespread. X-raying of large groups of people will be extended as part of disease prevention and control programs. For example, many employers now demand that chest X-rays be taken of all employees, and most insurance companies include a chest X-ray as part of the physical examination required for an insurance policy.

In addition to the radiologic technologists needed for new jobs, replacement demands are expected to be high because of the large number of women who leave their jobs each year for marriage or family responsibilities.

Earnings and Working Conditions

Salaries of radiologic technologists employed in hospitals ranged from about $105 to $130 a week in 1968, according to the limited information available.

New graduates of AMA-approved schools of X-ray technology employed by the Federal

Government received an annual salary of $5,145 in late 1968. About one-sixth of all radiologic technologists working for the Federal Government in 1968, were earning $7,000 or more a year.

Full-time technicians generally work 8 hours a day and 40 hours a week but may be "on call" for some night or emergency duty. Most are covered by the same vacation and sick leave provisions as other workers in the same organization.

Precautionary measures to protect radiologic technologists from the potential hazards of radiation exposure include the use of safety devices such as individual instruments that measure radiation, lead aprons, leaded gloves, and other shieldings.

Sources of Additional Information

The American Society of Radiologic Technologists, 645 North Michigan Ave., Chicago, Ill. 60611.

The American Registry of Radiologic Technologists, 2600 Wayzata Blvd., Minneapolis, Minn. 55405.

school counselor's office and probably in the school liberary as well. Or you can order your own copy from the Superintendent of Documents, U.S. Government Printing Office, Washington, D.C. 20402. It costs about seven dollars (less than a penny an occupation), at which price it has a place in every home with children or teen-agers.

Of course, the information provided in *The Occupational Outlook Handbook* is general, and does not necessarily apply to any one particular job. Conditions vary between a large firm and a small one, and among the various companies in a specific field. But *The Handbook* remains the best place to start learning about a given occupation.

Your Local Library

Dozens of books are available, on specific fields or occupations. Some are over-optimistic; duties appear just a little more exciting than they really are, people a little more sympathetic, advancement a little more certain. However, if you allow for some exaggeration, you'll also find a valuable picture of the atmosphere, pressures, and satisfactions associated with various fields.

Get Behind the Scenes

In most businesses, the day-to-day activity, bustle and tension are quite different from what the public is allowed to see. If you know anyone working in a restaurant, a hospital, a factory, a large retail store or even the post-office, try to get the insider's point of view. Visit the kitchen, delivery area, switchboard; find out how much effort and coordination are required simply to keep the business going.

Plant tours are sometimes offered by large manufacturers. Even if you're not concerned with that particular industry, you're sure to find them interesting. Such tours cannot fail to impress you with the complexity of producing even the simplest objects.

Unanswered Questions? Ask for Help

Get back to the professionals—your school guidance office or the counselors at your state employment service. They're trained to provide information about every kind of work, and what they don't know, they can find out. One source available to them is the *Dictionary of Occupational Titles,* published by the U.S. Department of Labor. This enormous volume describes in minute detail the work involved in each of 22,000 job titles and is used almost exclusively by professionals in the field of placement and vocational counseling. A portion of one entry is reproduced on page 76. The book is hardly recommended for casual reading. It's included simply to give you an idea of the vast amounts of time, energy, and research which have gone into studying and analyzing the thousands of jobs required in our society.

Your school guidance office may have commercially published kits which describe, in simple terms, jobs which are likely to interest high school graduates. There are various such materials available, ranging from sets of index cards to elaborately cross-referenced pamphlets filling several file cabinets. They can be useful and informative. The school may also receive information from trade associations, describing their specialized fields. Again, such material tends to paint a rosy picture; balance it with more objective resources.

223. Stock Clerks and Related Occupations

This group includes occupations concerned with receiving, storing, shipping, and issuing supplies, materials, and equipment in a stockroom or warehouse environment. Includes taking inventories, keeping records, and requisitioning stock.

223.138 AMMUNITION FOREMAN (ammunition; explosives)

ammunition storekeeper
ammunition supplyman
magazine foreman

LINEN-ROOM SUPERVISOR (laund.)
manager, industrial garment

PETROLEUM-INSPECTOR SUPERVISOR (bus. ser.)

RECEIVING-AND-SHIPPING FOREMAN (any ind.)
chief clerk
shipping-and-receiving foreman
Receiving Foreman (any ind.)
Shipping Foreman (any ind.)

STOCK-CONTROL SUPERVISOR (clerical)

STOCK SUPERVISOR (ret. tr.)
head of stock
stockroom supervisor

SUPERVISOR, ASSEMBLY STOCK (clerical)

SUPERVISOR, STOCK (clerical)
manager, stockroom
shipping-and-receiving foreman
stock foreman
storeroom supervisor
warehouse foreman
warehouseman, chief

TOOL-CRIB FOREMAN (clerical)
foreman, tool crib
tool-clerk foreman

VAULT CUSTODIAN (motion pic.)
vaultman

223.368 MANAGER, FLOOR (whole. tr.)

PROCUREMENT CLERK (clerical)
award clerk
bid clerk
buyer assistant
purchase request editor
purchasing-and-fiscal clerk
purchasing clerk
purchasing-contracting clerk

223.387 AUTOMOTIVE-PARTS MAN (aircraft mfg.)

BOOK SUPERVISOR (clerical)

CHECKER (water trans.)
cargo checker
freight checker

marine clerk

FILM-LIBRARY CLERK (clerical)
film-vault clerk

FOLLOW-UP CLERK (elec. equip.)

LIBRARIAN (motion. pic.)

LINEN-ROOM ATTENDANT (hotel & rest.; medical ser.)
linen checker
linen clerk
linen-exchange attendant
linen maid

MAGAZINE KEEPER (any ind.)
powder man
powder monkey
powder nipper
prill man

MATERIAL CLERK (clerical)
material checker
stock editor
stock-record clerk
stores-auditor clerk
supplies clerk

Warehouse-Record Clerk (clerical)

METAL CHECKER (ore dress., smelt., & refin.)

TRUCK CHECKER (const.)
load checker
tallyman

MATERIAL DISPOSITION ANALYST (aircraft mfg.)

PARTS-ORDER CLERK (motor trans.)
parts clerk

PETROLEUM INSPECTOR (bus. ser.)

RETURNED - TELEPHONE - EQUIPMENT APPRAISER (elec. equip.)

SAMPLE CLERK (glass mfg.)

STOCK CLERK (clerical)
counterman
material handler
material keeper
stock attendant
stock checker
stock counter
stock-house clerk
stockkeeper
stockman
stockroom attendant
stockroom clerk
stockroom man
stock-service clerk
stock tender

IS THE JOB RIGHT FOR YOU?

By now, you have:

Identified some of your own qualities relating to different job situations, your ability to handle them, and your interest.

Decided that work is a reasonable alternative for you.

Examined sources for learning about different kinds of jobs.

Your next step is to make your choice.

To begin, recognize the realities. If you can't, simply can't, leave town, there's no use dreaming about the marvellous jobs 200 miles away. Depending on your age, you may be barred by law from certain types of work: night work, work in cocktail lounges, work involving occupational hazards. These are the hard-core facts; learn to plan around them.

When you're actually confronted with the available openings, a kind of premature depression may set in. "Check-out Clerk," "Assistant on Delivery Route," "Bank Teller Trainee," "Helper in Day Camp," "Beginning Clerical"—the choices may seem so routine, so far removed from you and the role you mean to play in the world, that you're tempted to give up before you begin.

In that case, remember that work is very different from school. Your duties may seem simple and even unexciting. But you will be held to a much higher standard of quality at a job than in school. If you're a cashier making change, a drill press operator turning out machine parts, a waitress filling orders, 65 percent is very far from passing. An occasional mistake may be condoned, especially at the beginning, but if it happens too often, you'll be out of a job.

Standards are higher in other respects as well. You're expected to arrive on time, every day, suitably dressed and ready to start work. There may be time for coffee breaks or an occasional cigarette, but by and large, you can't "cut class" or doze off.

So think of work as something new. You're not here to whiz through a half-dozen subjects with a minimum passing grade. You'll be learning responsibility, thoroughness, some specific useful skills and a feeling for the needs of the job. Your progress may not be as dramatic as it was at school, but after a while, you'll begin to notice a change. So will your boss.

With this behind us, let's get back to the jobs. When you read or hear about a particular job, consider it in terms of your own outlook and temperament. Here are some typical reactions:

Commission Salesman: "Oh, I couldn't take the insecurity of working on commission."
> *or*
"Great! I'll get paid what I'm really worth!"

Air Conditioning Installation Trainee: "I'll be moving around instead of being tied to a bench indoors."
> *or*
"That sounds like seasonal work. I need something steadier."

Hospital Attendant: "It's work that needs doing."
> *or*
"I'd probably catch something the very first day.'

Every one of these reactions is completely appropriate—in terms of the individual. What makes a job "right" is that you've matched it to yourself. Here, too, you can get help from professionals like your school vocational guidance counselor and the state employment service. They have a wealth of detailed, technical knowledge concerning skills and temperament requirements for various jobs. They're also familiar with elaborate theories of job satisfaction, developed from the viewpoints of management and of the individual worker.

In this area, too, professionals have access to an outstanding work: Volume II of the Department of Labor's *Dictionary of Occupational Titles*. This book groups thousands of jobs in terms of the "worker traits" required to perform them. The classifications are based on:

- Training Time
- Aptitudes
- Interests
- Temperament
- Physical Demands

Not surprisingly, these headings will remind you of the topics discussed in Chapter 6.

One page of this volume, the discussion of Customer Service Work, is reproduced on page 79. It tells us something we've already observed: that for any specific combination of "Worker Traits," there's a considerable number of suitable jobs. For example, customer service work, which involves customer contact and a modest amount of record-keeping, includes, among others, grocery checker, car rental clerk, retail receiving clerk in a cleaning and dying establishment, and lunch-truck driver. Each of these jobs calls for the same profile of "worker traits." In terms of skills and abilities, the person who can handle one can handle any of the others. Yet in practice these jobs would be very different. Which you prefer depends on your own personal interests. Outsiders can advise, suggest and recommend, but in the last analysis, the choice is up to you.

But don't let choice upset you. Remember, your first decision can be changed or even reversed anywhere along the way. For any person, with his individual combination of talents, skills, physique and temperament, there are dozens of appropriate occupations. Actually, with the world changing so fast, economists are convinced that each of us will work through several different careers or occupations in his lifetime. So don't be intimidated by your first job. Two weeks' notice and a courteous "goodbye" can undo your worst mistake.

CUSTOMER SERVICE WORK, N.E.C.

.468; .478

Work Performed

Work activities in this group primarily involve providing the public with a ready response for services or information requested. Includes such activities as recording or receiving payments for merchandise and selling miscellaneous specialties and general articles.

Worker Requirements

An occupationally significant combination of: Willingness to work in a service capacity; ability to understand and comply with requests of customers; ability to make simple arithmetic calculations when quoting and computing prices on merchandise and services; clerical accuracy in keeping simple records; and patience and courteous manner when dealing with the public.

Clues for Relating Applicants and Requirements

Experience as hat and coat checker at high school dances.
Experience as part-time salesman of raffle tickets for church bazaar.
Preference for public-contact work.
Experience clerking in dry cleaning establishment after school.

Training and Methods of Entry

Short demonstrations and on-the-job training are the usual means by which a person becomes familiar with this kind of work. In most cases, employers prefer workers with a high school education including some arithmetical and clerical training to keep simple records.

RELATED CLASSIFICATIONS

Inspecting and Stock Checking (.382; .384; .387; .484; .487) p. 271
Computing and Related Recording (.388; .488) p. 280
Cashiering (Drug Stores, Theaters, Restaurants, and Related Establishments) (.468) p. 269
Miscellaneous Customer Service Work (.863; .864; .865; .867; .873; .874; .877) p. 503
Miscellaneous Personal Service Work (Food Serving, Portering, Valeting, and Related Activities) (.868; .878) p. 507

QUALIFICATIONS PROFILE

GED: 3 2
SVP: 3 2

Apt:	GVN	SPQ	KFM	EC
	3 3 3	4 4 4	4 4 4	5 4
	4 4	5 3 3		5
				3

Int: 2 3
Temp: 5 2 3 Y
Phys. Dem: L 4 5

Moreover, whatever job you decide to accept offers a multitude of possibilities. For example, Jerry finds work with a resident buying firm; he keeps track of houseware merchandising trends across the country. Depending on his own particular skills and temperament, he may in time find himself interviewing salesmen or making the rounds of the trade shows. Ultimately, he could become a buyer. Or he may become interested in the moneymaking potential of a well-run housewares store, and try his hand at it. With a few accounting courses, he could move into the financial end of the operation. Only by actually entering the working world and functioning within it do the possibilities become apparent.

We've covered a lot of ground in this chapter. We've talked about the significance of work in general, what it consists of, and what it can do for you. The more important ideas are outlined in Exhibit 7–1 on page 80.

At this point, you're ready to start job-hunting. Approach it in a state of relaxed anticipation. The job you find may be better than you expected, or it may be worse; but it won't be a trap. Starting work isn't the end of your career; it's only the beginning.

EXHIBIT 7-1

Work: What Is It?

I. The General Significance of Work

  A. Work and Society
  B. Work and the Individual
    1. Money
    2. Status
    3. Participation
    4. Satisfaction
    5. Sociability
  C. Work and the Employer
    1. Employees as a source of profit
    2. Employer expectations:
      a. Necessary skills
      b. Interest in firm
      c. Willingness to learn
      d. Maturity to meet the requirements of the job
        (i) Appropriate appearance
        (ii) Tact in dealing with others
        (iii) Responsibility

II. For Whom is Work an Alternative?

Consider work as an alternative if:

    1. You want to find out what you'd really like to do
    2. You want the money
    3. You feel you're grown up
    4. You learn more easily "hands on"
    5. You know exactly what you want to do, and further schooling isn't necessary
    6. You're looking for maturity
    7. You want to meet new people

III. Learning About Work

  A. People you know
  B. Classified ads
  C. *The Occupational Outlook Handbook*
  D. Your local library
  E. Get behind the scenes
  F. Ask for help

IV. Choosing a Job

  A. Recognize the realities
  B. Expect your progress to be gradual
  C. Work in terms of your own outlook and temperament
  D. Ask for help if necessary
  E. Don't be intimidated by your first job

8

Finding a Job

Work begins, not when you're put on the payroll, but the day you decide to look for a job. The U.S. Manpower Administration claims that most people who have trouble finding work go about it in a half-hearted, disorganized way. Job hunting isn't something to fit in around watching television, catching up on your sleep, or visiting your old school. It's a job in itself, and one which may take more energy, imagination, and determination than the work you finally get.

Job-hunting can be organized into several steps:

- Laying the groundwork
- Finding the job opening
- The routine of job-hunting
- The interview
- Miscellaneous pointers

LAYING THE GROUNDWORK

As was mentioned in the last chapter, the first and most important step in looking for a job is deciding what kind of job you're looking for. Don't ask for a job doing "anything;" there's no such job. Every job has its specific responsibilities; the person who will do "anything" is showing both his ignorance of job duties and his lack of interest in finding out. There's quite a difference between applying for a job doing "anything" and applying for a job "where I can learn as much as possible about retail store operation." Better yet is understanding that if the store is big enough, there are a hundred different kinds of jobs within it. There are jobs in the receiving department, where merchandise comes in and is unpacked; there are jobs in the stock room, where employees keep inventory of how much merchandise, and of what kinds, is on hand at all times. There are jobs for

81

salespeople; some help the customer choose merchandise, while others simply direct him to the proper table. and look after the stock. There are cashiers and wrappers. There are buyers, section managers, merchandise managers and creditmen. There may be a delivery department, a customer service department, and a fleet of trucks. The person who asks for "anything" simply doesn't understand the operation.

You may find yourself undecided between two equally attractive, equally specific lines of work. In that case you can follow up on both. You're looking for "gardener" *or* "nursery salesman"—but you're still not looking for "anything."

Next, put yourself in a suitable frame of mind. You're embarking on a very important project. When people ask you what you're doing, don't answer, "Nothing." Tell them you're job-hunting—and continue by asking whether they know of anything. On the other hand, don't expect results the first week, or even the first month, particularly if you're looking for something off the beaten track. The early stages of job-hunting are like planting seeds; it takes a while before you see the fruit.

Finally, there are certain specific things you'll need for your very first interview. Line them up in advance; you may need them on short notice.

Have at least one clean, comfortable, reasonably conservative outfit for job hunting.

If you don't already have a Social Security number, get the necessary forms at your post office and mail them at once. There's virtually no steady job you can get without it. Once you have your Social Security number, memorize it; you'll be using it the rest of your life.

Have several names available, to offer as references. Teachers, previous employers, family friends, clergymen and responsible adults who know you well, are appropriate. Relatives are less acceptable, since they're presumed to be biased. You *always* ask the person if you may use him as a reference, no matter how confident you are. Usually, he'll be glad to agree. However, if he suggests that he really doesn't know you well enough, take the hint and find someone else.

Depending on your age and the kind of work you plan to do, you may need working papers. This varies from one community to the next; check with your school guidance office or the local branch of the state employment service.

Obtain a student copy of your high school transcript. Here and there, an employer may want to see it. Don't insist on presenting it, but have it ready in case it's asked for.

If the job you're after is covered by a union contract, get in touch with the appropriate union. Sometimes the union itself does the hiring, in which case you may not even be considered unless all the present members are employed. Or you may locate the job yourself, with the understanding that you'll join the union within a specified time period. Occasionally, union membership is optional. Procedures vary widely, so learn the ones that apply to you.

Lay in a supply of stamps and plain white business stationery. There's a lot of letter-writing connected with finding a job, particularly on weekends when businesses are closed.

Finally, prepare a resumé, and keep a few copies on hand.

A resumé is a simple, coherent outline of your background, education, and other qualifications for the job you want. A sample is given below, but other forms are also in use. The important thing is that it tell the interviewer, in a minimum of time, why you should be considered for his job opening. If you're listing work experience, it's not necessary to put down every baby-sitting or lawn-mowing assignment you ever had. However, you should include all relevant experience. If your resumé shows any great time gap—an interval unaccounted for, either by work or school—you may be asked what you were doing during that period. Be prepared to provide a reasonable answer.

Sample Resume:

```
Walter Stevens                    (Date of Resume)
234 Fifth Street
Piedmont, New York 14850
607-123-4567


Position Sought
     Photography equipment sales or stock work.

     Have good knowledge of standard American and
     imported cameras and equipment.


Background
     Sales: K-Mart Variety Store, October, 1972 to
     June, 1974. Sold all standard makes of cameras,
     lens attachments, tripods and related equip-
     ment. Also sold film, flash attachments and
     bulbs. Maintained stock on selling floor.

     Free-lance photography: Photography hobby for
     four years. Photography editor, Piedmont High
     School yearbook. Photographed special events
     and club groups for yearbook and school news-
     paper. Some darkroom experience. Good knowledge
     of black-and-white and color photography.
```

Other Interests
>   Member, Piedmont High School hockey team
>   Red Cross Senior Lifesaver

Personal
>   Date of birth: May 30, 1955   Height: 5'10"
>   Weight: 175 lbs.

>   Education: Graduate, Piedmont High School,
>   June 1974.
>   Business major: courses include
>   Business English, Business Law,
>   Bookkeeping, Merchandising.
>   Shop courses: Photography, Printing,
>   Metal Shop.

>   Honors: Winner, second prize, 1973 Piedmont
>   High School Photography Contest.
>   Letter in hockey.

References
>   Ms. Leila Howard, Faculty Advisor, Piedmont
>   High School Yearbook, Piedmont, New York 14850

>   Mr. Henry Allanson, Manager, K-Mart Variety
>   Store, 123 Main Street, Piedmont, New York
>   14850

People often ask whether one resumé can serve for all purposes, or whether it should be rewritten, with appropriate additions or deletions, for each particular job. The answer is somewhere between the two. You have no choice but to start with your own basic resumé, if only because personnel managers and employment agencies may ask you to leave a copy. However, if you're answering a specific ad, or have "inside" information about the firm you're applying to, it may be worthwhile to rewrite your resumé for the occasion. For example, Harold didn't think his Scouting experience worth mentioning on a resumé. However, when he applied for a job with a bank headed by the troop's principal supporter, he rewrote the resumé, working in his background in Scouting. Similarly, Mary didn't mention her modest talent at arts and crafts until she answered an ad from a private kindergarten; at that point it assumed new importance.

Should your resumé be printed? Probably not. Unless you're planning to send out your own mailing (and we'll have more to say about that later in this chapter), one clean, typewritten original should do the job; you can make machine copies as needed. With a printed resumé, you're less likely to make changes, even when you know they would improve your prospects.

Of course, if you're trying simultaneously for two different types of jobs, you'd do best to prepare two distinct resumés—one for each set of qualifications.

The several steps just discussed are summarized below. They shouldn't take more than a few days, and they'll make things a lot easier when you begin job-hunting.

A. Decide what kind of job you're looking for.
B. Put yourself in the proper frame of mind.
C. Line up the following necessities:
    1. A suitable outfit of clothes
    2. A Social Security card
    3. References
    4. Working papers (if needed)
    5. High school transcript
    6. Union materials (if needed)
    7. Stationery and stamps
    8. Resumés

FINDING THE JOB OPENING

Once the job-hunting preliminaries are taken care of, where do you go from there? How do you go about actually finding a job? There are at least eight possibilities:

- Through people who know you
- Through classified newspaper advertisements
- Through public employment services
- Through private employment agencies
- Through personal canvassing
- Through mailings
- Through placing your own advertisement
- Through civil service

People Who Know You

Friends, relatives, teachers, friends of parents and parents of friends— the people who know you personally—are in an excellent position to recommend you to a prospective employer. If you let everyone know you're looking for a particular kind of job, they'll automatically think of you when they hear of something suitable.

Some young people feel there's something cowardly about seeking help from such sources. Such hesitancy is usually due to inexperience and a lack of sophistication. Actually, the best jobs are apt to be filled in this way. If an opening occurs in your cousin's firm, *and if he knows you're qualified for the position,* he's helping both you and his employer by suggesting you. The employer avoids the advertising, interviewing, and reference-checking that would otherwise be necessary. If you're recommended by a person he knows and trusts, he's saving time and money by giving you the chance. So don't be shy about telling people what you're looking for, and why you think you're qualified.

Newspaper Advertisements

We've already discussed newspaper ads from a purely informative point of view; we assume you've put some time into reading them. Now your interest is more personal; you're out to get a job.

Of course, you've checked the categories you're interested in and all related categories. But have you discovered the interesting catch-all sections alphabetized under such words as "Airlines," "Gal/Guy Friday," "Part-Time," "Nights," "Student," "Beginner," "Temporary," "Trainee"? Somewhere among these listings, you may find exactly what you want.

At the same time, keep in mind the jobs you won't find at all in the papers. To begin, there won't be much for performers of any kind. There may only occasionally be ads for artists, writers, interior decorators, designers, and the like. If you've done anything along these lines, your samples will speak for themselves. And—although this may not be your problem right now—high-level openings are rarely listed in the ads. Again, they're handled by word-of-mouth, direct recommendation, or ads in professional and trade publications. But don't let these exceptions worry you; there should still be plenty of interest in the Sunday paper.

Some advertisements ask you to call a phone number and make an appointment. Others give only the address; they want to see the applicant in person, and don't care to be bothered with calls. Occasionally an ad will give only a box number. Whatever the form of your answer, the best you can hope for is an interview. The interview is your chance to convince the employer of your suitability for the job.

When you call the phone number listed in an ad (and the line may be busy, so keep trying!), you'll say something like this: "I'm calling in answer to your ad in today's *Times* for a 'Store Manager Trainee.' I graduated from high school last June, and since then I've been working at Grant's. May I have an appointment for an interview?" If they want any more information, they'll ask you. Basically, you want to be brief and to the point, giving enough details to indicate you're a suitable applicant for the job. You'll get to tell the rest at the interview. Don't say anything negative at this time, even if it must be said sooner or later; you might be prematurely spoiling your chances.

If there's a box number, you'll need to write a brief letter and enclose a resumé. A sample letter is shown on page 88. Since the resumé gives all the basic information, the letter itself can be short. However, it does provide the opportunity to mention specific details not included in your resumé—hobbies, volunteer work, special experience—which, in your opinion, particularly qualify you for this job. Notice also that the letter should mention the job for which you're applying; the employer may have advertised more than one opening that day. Finally, keep a copy of every letter you send out; otherwise, you'll become confused trying to remember just what you said and to whom. Address your letter as follows:
If the telephone directory lists several addresses, or is otherwise not clear, call up the paper and get the information first-hand.

If you're asked to report in person, put on that outfit you have ready, take along the papers you've prepared, and be on your way. *Plan to get there early.* Many firms will come to a decision after interviewing the first dozen applicants; the rest are told simply that the job is filled. If this strikes you as unfair, remember that employers are businessmen, not judges. They're not dispensing justice; they're just trying to get a job filled.

Public Employment Services

There are probably a number of free employment services in your locality. The largest and most accessible of these is usually the service offered by your own state. It should be listed in the phone directory; look first under the name of the state, and then under such headings as "Employment Service," "Human Resources Department," or "Labor, Department of." If you have trouble finding the listing, check with your school guidance office or the local Chamber of Commerce.

The state service is available at no cost, either to employer or job-seeker. It lists jobs in all categories, from casual day worker through executive administrator. Your local office may also offer special services to young people; typical are counselling and contact with employers looking for beginners. Usually, it also has listings of local civil service examinations and apprenticeship opportunities. To get the full benefit from this invaluable service, it's a good idea to report several times a week, since new job listings come in daily.

However, the state agency may not be the only free employment service in your area. Look into the following:

Box No. 0000
<u>Local</u> <u>Town</u> <u>Daily</u> <u>News</u>
Address of newspaper
  (find address in the telephone directory)
City, State, Zip Code.

Sample Reply to a Newspaper Advertisement:

234 Fifth Street
Piedmont, New York 14850
June 15, 1974

Box 123
The Piedmont News
Piedmont, New York 14850

Dear Sir,

I am writing in answer to your advertisement for a photographic sales clerk in the June 14th <u>Piedmont News.</u>

The enclosed resume will give you the details of my background and experience. However, I would like to add that many of the people who know me consider me well-informed about photography. They often come to me with their questions and rely on my advice. I think this would be an asset to your firm.

I would appreciate a chance to meet with you and discuss my qualifications. My phone number is 123-4567.

Sincerely yours,

Walter Stevens

Walter Stevens

Local Youth Employment Service: Some localities offer special services operated by volunteers. Your school guidance department will know if there is one in your area.

Schools: Most high schools and colleges offer placement services.

YMCA, YWCA, YMHA, YWHA: Organizations like these sometimes maintain free employment services.

Churches: Your church group may have an employment service; check with your minister.

Unions: Some unions offer a placement service for jobs they cannot fill from their ranks. On the other hand, some unions strongly discourage outsiders.

Fraternal organizations: Fraternal organizations sometimes have placement services for members or children of members.

Like the state agencies, the above-mentioned services are free. They may offer fewer special resources than the state agency, but their service may be friendlier and more personal.

When you call on any of these agencies, prepare as carefully as you would for a job interview; dress neatly and take along the papers you may need. An appointment may be necessary, so it's a good idea to phone in advance.

Private Employment Agencies

These exist in all areas. They are privately operated, and charge fees which may be paid by the job applicant or by the employer. As a rule, they are regulated and licensed by the state, and are usually responsible, reputable firms providing excellent service to both employer and applicant.

The private employment agency depends for its livelihood on satisfying the needs of employers quickly and appropriately. To this end, it often maintains close and continuing contact with a large number of firms. Employers use such agencies to do their pre-screening. They expect the agency to be highly selective, sending them only the very best-qualified applicants, whether trainees or experienced personnel. Often, they will pay the agency fee, making the job free to the applicant. Such jobs are described as "fee paid."

Some employment agencies handle only "fee paid" jobs. Others handle both kinds. When you're referred to a job by a private agency, you should be perfectly clear about who is expected to pay the fee, and how much it will be. Details are usually stated on the application you sign. In many states, the maximum fee is limited by law to one month's salary, but it is often much less. (The maximum fee for temporary work is ten percent of the earnings.) In any case, when the applicant pays the fee, most reputable agencies do not expect to be paid until he is actually hired. Some permit the fee to be paid over several weeks or even months. Agencies specializing in factory jobs or other high-turnover work may require some token payment in advance, to be applied against the fee if you obtain a job. Avoid any agency asking more than a few dollars just to register you; this isn't necessary for beginning jobs. Most often there is no registration fee at all.

There are some very real advantages to working through an agency. Since the agency earns nothing unless you're hired, the placement counsellor may try to develop a job for you. If you were referred but not hired, the counsellor may be able to tell you the reason; this is very valuable information the next time you go out on an interview. Finally, the agency may save you a great deal of time in finding a job; the extra salary you earn may more than cover the fees.

In larger cities, private employment agencies often specialize in a particular field: engineering, factory work, office work, restaurants, hotels, or the like. Some cover specific industries such as publishing, advertising, or social service. This specialization is very useful, not only for the experienced person, but also for someone with general skills who wants to get started in a particular field.

For example, consider the case of Jerry. Jerry studied business subjects in high school, and had hoped to go on to junior college, but family circumstances ruled this out. Now he wants to break into the insurance field —not in sales, but possibly as an adjuster. Jerry is well-groomed and offers good grades in English, bookkeeping, and math. He's not sure how he would fit into an insurance firm, or what kind of job to apply for. But he has heard that the insurance industry is eager to train and upgrade capable employees, and he thinks he has a good future in this gigantic industry.

The insurance industry does hire high school graduates for various positions, and Jerry can apply directly to the firms in his area. At the same time, he could register with a private employment agency specializing in insurance placements. Here the staff may be in touch with companies which are always interested in promising beginners. If Jerry impresses them favorably, they could provide him with a valuable referral. Jerry might be hired immediately on referral. Suppose his starting salary were $85 a week, and the fee he paid the agency were $110. This sounds like a large amount. But if he were able to start work even two weeks earlier, he would be ahead financially. If he were placed in exactly the kind of growth-directed spot he had in mind, it would be doubly worth it. And of course, if nothing comes of the effort, it costs him nothing.

Personal Canvassing

Canvassing is a matter of going to the place where you'd like to work, introducing yourself, and asking for the work you want. It's particularly successful for work in clothing stores, art supply stores, record shops, or any area in which your hobbies, interests, or background give you a particular claim. For certain rather uncommon jobs, particularly with small firms, it may be the best way for an outsider to get started. For example, Francine, who loves flowers and flower arranging, resorted to canvassing when she found that there was no professional florist training available in her community. She went through the classified directory, making a list of all the florists in town, grouped by location. She planned to approach each of them in mid-morning, when he was most likely to have time for her—but she was careful to avoid busy weekends. Several were uninterested, one or two simply didn't need her, but after a half-dozen tries she found a job which, while low-paying, offered exactly the opportunities she was looking for.

In canvassing, should you phone first to make an appointment? In general, no; it's too easy for someone to turn you down on the phone. When you walk in and explain your enthusiasm for the work and your willingness to accept a modest salary, the prospective employer may develop an unexpected interest. If he appears busy or disinclined to discuss your inquiry, you may suggest, "Would you like to think about it? I can phone Thursday for your decision." If you're interested in working for a pet shop, a gift boutique or a bicycle shop, this direct, walk-in-the-door approach may get the best results.

However, if you're going to canvass, there are a few things to keep in mind. Recognize that most businesses are seasonal to some extent. For example, sporting goods, photography and boating are at their height during the late spring and summer; clothing stores go through a lull during the summer and pick up again in the fall. If possible, begin your search just before the start of the busy season, certainly not when business is at its lowest ebb.

Also, bear in mind as you canvass that some small businesses can't afford extra help, even if they want it. Don't take refusals personally; keep trying. If you become discouraged after the tenth "No," you'll never get to the twelfth place on your list, which might be waiting for someone like you to come along.

Mailings

Mailings—sending out your resumé, along with a covering letter, to the companies you'd like to work for—can be a real door-opener, or they can be a total loss. To appreciate the difference let's look at your mailing from the employer's point of view.

Here he is, getting a letter from someone he never heard of. He doesn't know if you're skilled, intelligent or reliable; he doesn't even know if you're honest. Moreover, your letter has probably arrived at a time when he wasn't considering hiring anyone. If you're to break down his resistance, you must usually qualify in one of two ways.

(1) Your background or experience is *outstanding*. He sells skating equipment; you've been skating since you were five, you're Junior Skate Champion, and you know you'd be valuable to a firm like his.

(2) Your letter is so compelling that he can't resist meeting the author.

On the other hand, you may have your own reasons for using a mailing. If you want a job in another community, a mailing may enable you to line up a few prospects before you actually make the move. Also, if you're trying to get into some exotic field like taxidermy or musical instrument repair—a field in which there are few, if any, regular training channels— you might write to potential employers, wherever they may be, and see whether they're willing to hire and train you. Your interest in their special field might get you an interview; the rest is up to you.

How do you know where to write? Your best tool is the classified telephone directory of the city you're interested in. If you need out-of-town directories, check the local library; if they can't help, contact your Chamber of Commerce or telephone company. If you're concerned with the type of business rather than the location, you'll need a listing of business firms. The best-known of these is *Thomas' Register,* but your librarian may be able to suggest others that will serve as well. Incidentally, if you can address your letter to a specific individual—the personnel manager or appropriate official—so much the better. In the case of local firms, the easiest way to get this information is to phone the company and ask. The operator who answers your call will probably give you the name of the person involved, and may even check around a little on your behalf.

Two more details. If you're planning a mailing, you may save some money by having your resumés printed. Find out what it costs. Finally, don't expect much more from your campaign than a few interviews. Even if you're dealing with out-of-town firms, it is very, very unusual for a company to hire anyone without meeting him face to face.

Placing Your Own Advertisements

Placing your own ad in a newspaper or trade journal is a convenient, inexpensive way to let people know you're in the job market. Questions have been raised about the effectiveness of such ads, but all you need is one job; if your ad leads to the job you want, then the ad has been 100 percent effective for you.

As with mailings, ads work best when you can offer specialized, distinctive qualifications. The following examples demonstrate the point.

Young man, H.S. grad, good grades, seeks any interesting work; salary open. Phone ———.

Nothing here will make a prospective employer rush to the phone! Compare it to either of the following:

Young man, 19, H.S. grad, seeks employment—sporting goods manufacturer, distributor, sales. Thorough knowledge equipment for backpacking, tennis, scuba diving. Strong, willing. Phone ——— 3–6 p.m. or write Box ———.

or

Young man, electronics hobbyist, knows wiring, testing; hi-fi, stereo, tapes, intercoms. Wants to work and learn. Salary $85. Phone ——— between 8–10 a.m. or write Box ———.

In placing such an ad, give your phone number (including area code) and a time to call; otherwise you'll get panicky about missing your responses. Also, give a box number, in case the prospective employer prefers to write.

Where you place your ad depends on whether you're primarily concerned with location or type of work. In the first case, stick to the leading newspaper in the community of your choice; the papers are listed in the classified directory. But if it's the type of work that interests you, and you're prepared to move to the job, consider an ad in the appropriate trade journal. There are thousands of such journals, circulating throughout the United States. They're indexed in a huge volume called the *Ayer Directory*; your librarian can help you with it. For unusual types of work, an ad in such a journal can be a reasonable and inexpensive technique for introducing yourself. It has the added advantage of being cheaper than a mailing.

Civil Service

Civil Service refers to public employment where jobs are filled through competitive examination. The system is designed to give everyone fair access to jobs with the federal, state, county and municipal government. Many local school districts also fill jobs through competitive examinations.

Generally, civil service jobs are classified according to the skills and responsibilities required; appropriate tests are designed, and applicants rated and ranked. Lists of eligible candidates are drawn up, and whenever a particular job opening occurs, the next candidate on the list (or sometimes the next two or three) are called in for interviews. Don't let the idea of a test discourage you. Of course, those who score highest are at the top of the list, and will be appointed first. But usually a list is used for a year or more, so even candidates with passing grades in the 70's may be called, sooner or later.

Civil service jobs range from Laborer or Clerk-typist all the way to Systems Analyst. They occur at all management levels, and involve all degrees of responsibility. They even include such unlikely job titles as Display Artist, Typewriter Repair Man, or Carpenter. However, new tests are given only as the old lists are used up, so if you're interested in a particular job, you may have to wait awhile before you can take that particular test. Your state employment service can provide information on test schedules. Moreover, federal civil service jobs are often publicized in the post office, and local ones in your community newspaper.

Civil service jobs offer some interesting advantages. Salaries are usually comparable to those in private industry, although sometimes lower. Benefits are often generous, including paid vacations and holidays, medical coverage, insurance, sick leave and opportunities for transfer. In addition, most civil service positions offer some form of tenure after a probationary period. This means that once you've attained permanent status (which may take from six months to three years), you can be fired only for demonstrated cause; if cut-backs in work necessitate that you be laid off, you can expect to be placed in another department of the same government agency as soon as possible.

Promotion in civil service is usually by examination, and a straightforward promotional ladder is available to all employees who wish to compete. If you're good at taking tests, and willing to study for them, this type of advancement is very appealing. Salaries usually include definite raises at specified periods, so that the competent employee is assured of making more money without having to ask for a raise. Retirement benefits are also excellent.

For the beginner, civil service has an added charm: it provides a channel for working outside your own community. A state civil service appointment may take you anywhere within the state; a federal appointment may, at your request, take you across the country. Of course, you're not required to accept such appointments, but for many young people, they're a distinct attraction.

One immediate disadvantage of civil service is that getting a job can take a long time. You may have to wait a half-year for the test you want, another three months before the list appears, and a year beyond that before your appointment comes through. If you're interested in breaking into civil service, it's best to take your tests as they become available (many people take more than one) and put them out of your mind. If a job materializes, that's time enough to think about it.

Civil service has been criticized on the grounds that duties, promotions and salary are very explicitly defined; there is little scope for variation or creativity. In these circumstances, the extremely dynamic, competitive individual isn't likely to find an outlet for his ambition. On the other hand, the conscientious, steady worker may feel very much at home here.

Incidentally, you may have heard that civil service jobs are less demanding than their private counterparts. Don't believe it. Salaries of government employees come out of taxpayers' money, and the employees are expected to earn their pay. Though the benefits are excellent, the workload may be heavy, the supervision close, and the working environment rather shabby compared to private industry.

We've given a lot of space to sources of job information. Don't choose one or two of them, and let it go at that. Pursue three, four, five, even all eight at the same time, if they apply to you. Work them in together; word-of-mouth *plus* newspaper ads, *plus* a little canvassing, *plus* an ad of your own and a civil service test, if they seem appropriate. You could find yourself with a half-dozen jobs to choose from!

The material in this section is summarized in Exhibit 8–1 on page 95.

EXHIBIT 8-1

How to Locate a Job

A. People Who Know You
   Parents, family friends, relatives, teachers, friends, parents of friends
B. Newspaper Ads
   1. Classifications
      a. Type of work (for example, "programmer")
      b. General category (for example, "trainee," "recent grad")
   2. Type of response: phone, letter, personal visit
C. Public Employment Agencies
   1. State Employment Service
   2. Other: Youth Employment Service, schools, YMCA, YMHA, etc., churches, unions, fraternal organizations
D. Private Employment Agencies
   1. Fee paid by:
      a. Employer
      b. Applicant
   2. Type of work offered:
      a. Specific jobs (e.g., clerical, data processing)
      b. Specific industries (e.g., hotels, insurance)
      c. General
E. Personal Canvassing
   1. Suitable for:
      a. Small businesses
      b. Unusual skills or occupations
   2. Things to avoid:
      a. Busy time of day or week
      b. Slack season
F. Placing Your Own Ad
   1. Newspapers (local or out-of-town)
   2. Trade journals
G. Civil Service
   1. Types: Federal, state, municipal, school board
   2. Advantages:
      a. Generous benefits
      b. Stability of employment
      c. Channels for advancement and promotion
      d. Opportunity to work out of town
   3. Disadvantages:
      a. Long delay before appointment
      b. Little scope for variation, creativity
      c. Heavy work load

THE ROUTINE OF JOB-HUNTING

Looking for a job *is* a job: full-time, five days a week. That's what you'd be giving the boss; why should you do any less for yourself?

Arrange a daily schedule. Start by checking the newspaper ads each morning, early enough so you can phone or get to an interview before noon. If there's nothing new in the ads, try an employment agency that day. Or you might visit the personnel office of a large company or store; such offices are usually open nine to five, and often no appointment is needed. Try to set up at least three meetings each day. Avoid the end-of-the-week slump; Thursdays and Fridays may be the best time to be interviewed for jobs starting the following Monday. And again, even if you don't have a definite appointment, be sure to get an early start.

One reason for job-hunting so aggressively is that finding a job is governed by the laws of probability. If twenty people apply for one job, 19 of them will *not* get that job. If it's a job requiring little skill or experience, as many as 50 people may apply; *49 of them will not get it.* This doesn't mean that these 49 will never get a job; it means only that none of them was the right person at the right moment. Now, if you go to one interview a week, these odds are pretty discouraging. If you go to one a day, the chances are a lot better. And if you build it up to three a day, then the prospects are good that before long, *you'll* be the one person in 20 who lands the job. One of the most important elements in job-hunting is exposure; the more interviews you arrange, the sooner you're likely to start working.

There's another way you can benefit from lots of interviews. Handling an interview is a special skill; it takes practice. At your first interview, you may have stage fright, stammer and wonder afterward how you could be so stupid. By your fourth or fifth, you're conducting yourself like an old pro. You know what questions will be asked, and you've developed suitable answers. You've learned to side-step questions you'd rather not answer head on. You've found a more effective way to describe your skills. If the employer gives tests, you'll discover that they resemble each other (sometimes they're identical!); you're more relaxed and your performance improves each time. You develop a feeling for the unstated requirements of the job and for the interpretation of an ad. After answering three ads headed "Manager Trainees" and finding they're all door-to-door sales jobs, you get to recognize the pitch. A month of daily job hunting will teach you more about the labor market than a year of reading statistical reports.

At the end of an interview, the prospective employer will probably say something like, "We're still interviewing; we'll call you back." *Do not stop your job-hunting and wait for his call.* This is the most common mistake of the inexperienced job-hunter. The employer is very encouraging—but he has just one more interview before he decides. Or he wants to check with the vice-president, who'll be back the day after tomorrow. Or the person who was leaving is staying another week. There are many valid reasons for employers to postpone their decisions. That's their problem, not yours. It's certainly no excuse for you to drop your own job-hunting activity. Above all, do not stay home waiting by the phone. If you're worried about missing the call, point out to the prospective employer that while you're very much interested in his job, you're out of the house most of the day; ask when *you* may call *him*. (This makes sense for another reason; very few employers will bother to contact you if you have *not* been hired.) Meanwhile, get right back on the job-hunt. Your very next interview may offer a much better opportunity, and they may be willing to hire you on the spot. The worst thing that can happen is that you'll get that other call after all, and have two jobs to choose from. There's nothing wrong with that, either. Just as an employer is free to choose from several applicants, so you can consider several jobs, and select the one that seems most promising. Just thank the other employers and explain that something else came along.

THE INTERVIEW

Every source, every job-hunting technique, every connection, can do only one thing for you: get you in for the interview. In most cases, the fact that you're there at all is a point in your favor; you're being interviewed because the employer thinks you may be able to do the job. Keep that in mind. The company is open to hire, and thinks you're a prospect, or they wouldn't even be talking to you. Remind yourself of this when the butterflies hit your stomach.

Things will go more smoothly if you make some preparations in advance.

First, return to Chapter 7 and remind yourself of what work means to the employer. Remember, no matter how bright, amusing and creative you may be, the primary concern of the employer is what you can do for the firm. Try to see yourself in this light.

Second, find out what you can about the company; how large it is, how long it's been in business, what it makes or does. Not only will the employer be flattered at your interest, but the interview itself is bound to proceed more smoothly.

Third, dress appropriately. Even if the interviewer himself is tolerant about clothes, he must consider the impression you'll make on customers and other employees. Don't expect people to know you have better clothes at home; dress as you would for the job itself.

Fourth, be sure to bring along your Social Security card, resumés, and all the other documents mentioned earlier. Organize them neatly in a folder or envelope; don't have them all over the place.

Finally, come on time. Better yet, come early. Every employer stresses punctuality—for others, if not for himself.

A job interview is essentially a talk session. What you say—and even more important, what you don't say—can decide whether or not the job is yours. Here are a few dos and don'ts.

- *Do* play up your strong points. Make it quite clear that you have the skills for the job; be prepared to demonstrate your typing, shorthand, machine operation, or whatever may be required.
- *Do* listen carefully. Give the interviewer a chance to spell out the nature of the job. Above all, don't interrupt!
- *Do* stick to your point. The interviewer needs to learn quite a bit about you in a rather short time, so go easy on jokes, anecdotes or other irrelevancies.
- *Do* prepare to leave when the interviewer indicates that he's done. Thank him, shake hands, and be on your way. Detaining him with a few last questions will only leave a bad impression.

Now for the things to avoid!

- *Don't* talk about poor health or accidents. Give the impression that you're as vigorous as the next one. The very fact that you're applying for the job should mean you can handle it physically.
- *Don't* downgrade anybody—not the teacher who was unfair, the previous employer who gave you a raw deal, the political maneuvering that kept you from being promoted. You may be absolutely right—but nobody wants to hear about it.
- *Don't* highlight your shortcomings. If you're terrible in math, you shouldn't be applying for a job where math is important. And if it's not important, why talk about it? The same goes for your academic record, work history, extra-curricular activities, and so on. Unless they do you credit, don't mention them; if they're important to the employer, let him take the initiative. As far as you're concerned, concentrate on the positive qualities that relate to the job.
- *Don't* dwell on mutual acquaintances. If you and the employer do have mutual friends, a mention of the name is enough. The subject of the interview is *you*.
- *Don't* try to give the impression that you know everything; you don't. Far more important are your capacity and willingness to learn.
- *Don't* over-emphasize the issue of advancement. Of course you hope to advance; no one expects you to stay at a beginner's job forever. But the employer would like to feel that you'll remain there long enough to render some service.

At some point in the interview, you'll probably be asked what salary you expect. This always poses a dilemma. You don't want to quote so high a figure that you eliminate yourself entirely; but you would like every dollar of what the employer was prepared to pay. How can you find out the prevailing wage for this kind of work?

You can get an idea from your local employment service, from newspaper ads, from private employment agencies and possibly from the people you know. The problem is that usually there's a range of salaries; low, medium, high. For example, the pay for a trainee bank teller may range from 80 to 95 dollars a week. Where do you fit in?

The higher salary will probably go to the person who has had some business experience, some public contact, or an outstanding academic record. The lower amount may be offered to someone just out of school, with no experience of any kind. Newspaper ads often hope to attract applicants by quoting a top figure, intended for the most highly qualified applicant. Actually, the employer may accept someone with fewer qualifications at a lower rate. Private employment agencies also offer salaries at the high end of the scale; this is because the employer expects them to pre-screen and refer only the most qualified applicants.

If you're asked what salary you expect, use your judgment; try to gauge where in the range you fit in. You're not likely to be off by more than a few dollars, and it shouldn't worry you too much. If there's real opportunity with the firm and you do your job well, you'll be earning more before long.

If the interviewer doesn't bring up the question of salary, don't be afraid to ask about it yourself. Make sure it conforms to federal and local regulations governing minimum wages. These regulations vary for different types of work; some are not covered at all. Your state employment service can answer your questions about minimum wages.

What about benefits? Vacations, medical benefits and paid holidays are offered by many firms. If they're not mentioned during the interview, it's perfectly reasonable for you to ask. But don't attach too much importance to such factors; at this early stage of your career, they're secondary to the type of work and the opportunities it offers. The same applies to hours, overtime requirements, lunch breaks, and the like. Ask about them if you wish, but wait until the end of the interview, and don't give them top priority.

Whatever your daydreams, it's not likely that the interview will end with your being hired. As we already pointed out, employers, however encouraging they may be, often have a host of reasons for postponing their decisions. So thank everyone, be sure to leave your phone number—and continue to your next appointment. Practice does it; each new interview will be a little smoother than the one before it, until finally you leave the ranks of job-hunters and join those of the newly employed. (For a review of this section see Exhibit 8–2 on page 100.)

MISCELLANEOUS POINTERS

When Things Go Wrong

No job-hunt carries with it the guarantee of being hired, and people have been known to keep trying, week after week, and still not land anything. What are the possible reasons?

1. You may really lack the qualifications for the job you're after. Maybe you majored in art, your fabric designs were tops, your poster won the gold medal, and your

EXHIBIT 8-2

The Interview

A. Advance Preparations
 1. Review what work means to the employer (page 65)
 2. Learn what you can about the company
 3. Dress appropriately
 4. Bring necessary documents
 5. Come on time
B. At the Interview:
 1. Do:
   a. Play up your strong points
   b. Listen; don't interrupt
   c. Stick to the point
   d. End interview when indicated
 2. Don't:
   a. Talk about poor health or accidents
   b. Downgrade anybody
   c. Highlight your shortcomings
   d. Dwell on mutual acquaintances
   e. Pretend to know everything
   f. Over-emphasize advancement and promotion
 3. Salary and Benefits
   a. Learn salary range from newspapers, agencies
   b. Place yourself within the range
   c. Don't worry about it
   d. If the interviewer doesn't mention benefits:
     (i) feel free to ask
     (ii) don't give them top priority

lettering is meticulous. You still won't be hired as the art director for the local retail store. Consider instead a spot as trainee in advertising production or display.

2. All industries have their busy and slack seasons; it may be the wrong time of year for the kind of work you want. Try a temporary job doing something else until more opportunities open up in the field of your choice.

3. You're pricing yourself out of the market. You may want $100 a week because that's what it takes to pay off the car you plan to buy. But your particular skills and experience may not be worth that salary. Lower your sights, and buy the car next year.

4. You don't act the part. This may sound silly, but the employer wants to see you as part of the company. If your dress, hair style, or slouchy way of lounging in your chair create a negative impression, you'll need a heavy load of qualifications to counterbalance it. Some personnel counsellors say that no qualifications will outweigh the employer's sense that you won't manage to work within the organization and become a harmonious part of it.

5. You may just be having a run of bad breaks. Keep the probabilities in mind, and don't give up.

Getting a Job Out of Town

If you're planning to move to another city, you may want to line up a job before you get there. This isn't easy, but there are a few steps you can take.

- Get the Sunday classified section of the chief newspaper in the city you're moving to. Find out what kinds of jobs are open, and what the prevailing salaries appear to be. Keep in mind that a newcomer is less likely to be hired than a resident of the city. For one thing, his references are harder to check; for another, employers are apt to feel more secure with somebody who's been around awhile.
- Run your own ad in the paper (see page 92).
- If you know what kind of work you want, send a mailing to the appropriate firms (see page 91).
- Check with the local branches of banks, retail chains, utilities, and other companies large enough to have an office in your new community. Find out from them the procedure for getting a job there.
- Send for appropriate civil service announcements; don't overlook state and municipal civil service agencies.
- If your family, friends, or teachers know anyone in the town you're going to, obtain letters of introduction. When you arrive, they may open doors which would otherwise be locked.
- If possible, go out to your destination for a week or two of intensive job-hunting. Even if you don't land anything, you'll learn what to expect. (While you're there, scout around for a place to live. You'll need to know what accommodations are available and what they cost.)
- Check the possibilities for temporary and casual jobs. Such work may tide you over until you find what you really want.
- Take enough money to last at least a few months.

Changing Jobs

No one expects you to stay in a job that's not working out. If you can't stand the routine, if you're not getting the chances you want, if there's not a friendly face in the crowd, it may be time to quit. You could even come out ahead. It's often easier to get a promotion or raise by changing jobs than by waiting it out in the old one. The experts call this diagonal mobility. As you move over, you also move up; each new job takes you a little higher, professionally and financially, than the last one. So don't feel disloyal. It's your life; you're certainly entitled to improve it.

But it helps to understand just why you're leaving. Perhaps you haven't been on the job long enough to discover its rewards. The fun of retailing is in watching the merchandise come in, guessing what will sell and staying to check your hunches. Waiting tables is a lot pleasanter if you've been around long enough to develop steady customers. It all takes time.

Or perhaps you're confusing the problems of your particular job with those of work in general. Work takes a lot of getting used to. You're expected to arrive, depart, take your break and eat your lunch on schedule. To put in a productive eight hours. To dress in a certain way. To keep your opinions to yourself. No wonder your first job may come as a shock. So before you quit, compare notes with your friends. Are their jobs really any better than yours, or are you all suffering from that first-job syndrome?

There are other reasons for leaving jobs. Sometimes the hours don't work out. You can't get along with your supervisor. You spent months priming for that choice spot, and it went to the boss' nephew. Your friend's doing the identical work elsewhere, and earning fifteen dollars a week more. You're repeating the same tasks over and over, with no opportunities for anything better. Or you just hate the place—the work, the people, everything about it. All of these are sound reasons for leaving a job, but try to understand which apply to you; you don't want to make the same mistakes twice.

Should you look for a new job while still at the old one? It isn't always easy. You can answer newspaper ads, send out resumés, make phone calls on your coffee break. If you can schedule interviews during lunch or after working hours, go ahead. But don't, as a rule, take off from work for this purpose. Your prospective employer may feel that if you're cheating on your present boss, you're not likely to treat him much better.

Some jobs are so scarce that you can't quit work while you look for them; the risk is too great. The same is true of civil service; months may elapse between taking the test and getting appointed. And of course, a good deal depends on your financial situation. If you have some savings, perhaps you can afford to give up work awhile. Or you might find something part-time to tide you over while you concentrate on job-hunting. In general, it may be possible to do some preliminary exploration while still employed, but the actual legwork of job-hunting is best accomplished when you can give your energies to it full-time.

However you manage, keep in mind that your employer will have to replace you, reorganize the work, or make other changes. He may even want you to help select and train your successor. So give him notice. Two weeks are customary; if the requirements of the job are unusual, give him a little more. Once in a long while, your boss may react by firing you on the spot. If you belong to a union, call it to their attention. Otherwise, find whatever comfort you can from knowing that you're civilized, and he's the boor. On the next job, you still give notice. It's a basic human courtesy.

At the beginning of this chapter, you were merely getting your Social Security number; now you're switching to your second or third job. There are a lot of details in between; they're summarized in Exhibits 8–1 (page 95), 8–2 (page 100), and 8–3 (page 103). Look them over, but don't try to memorize them; they'll come to life for you when you're out there, looking for that job.

Good luck!

EXHIBIT 8-3

Miscellaneous Pointers

A. When You're Not Having Any Luck:
   1. Check your qualifications for the job you're after
   2. Avoid slack seasons
   3. Don't price yourself out of the market
   4. Act the part
   5. Remember, it might just be a run of bad luck

B. Getting a Job Out of Town
   1. Study classified ads from the city you're going to
   2. Place your own ad
   3. Send out a mailing in the new city
   4. Check local branches of large firms
   5. Look into civil service in the new community
   6. Ask for letters of introduction
   7. Visit the new city; try job-hunting
   8. Check temporary and casual jobs
   9. Take enough money

C. Changing Jobs
   1. Reasons
      a. Haven't been on job long enough to enjoy its advantages
      b. The first-job syndrome
      c. Unsuitable hours
      d. Friction with supervisor
      e. Lack of opportunity
      f. Inadequate salary
      g. General dislike of job or work environment
   2. Job-Hunting While Working
      a. Do what you can:
         (i) Answer ads
         (ii) Make phone calls
         (iii) Send out resumés
         (iv) Make appointments during free time
      b. Problems:
         (i) Unusual jobs hard to find
         (ii) Civil service: takes a long time
         (iii) Finances
      c. Give notice in advance

9

Occupational Education

A high school graduate interested in studying X-ray technology can attend any of 216 schools, in over 38 states and the District of Columbia. Eleven institutions prepare students for a career in aircraft engineering technology. Bartending is taught in three schools; at least one each offers glass etching, piano tuning, and saddle-making. Or, if making saddles isn't your thing, you can learn electronic technology in 520 schools, stenography in over a thousand, and cosmetology—the art of making people more beautiful—in a whopping 2,477.

Schools like these, concentrating on education for employment, are known as occupational education schools. They include:

Junior and Community Colleges. About 1000 such schools are serving over two million students. Apart from the usual liberal arts, these schools offer occupational studies ranging from accounting to veterinary science. Often such programs lead to an associate degree in arts or applied science.

Private Occupational Schools. These schools, also known as proprietary schools, are frankly in it for the money; to remain in business they must give value for money. Today, a million and a half students are enrolled in over 10,000 such schools.

Adult Education Schools. Schools like these may be sponsored by two- or four-year colleges, by the local Board of Education, or by YMCA and similar groups. Courses, usually given in the evenings, cover a multitude of occupational subjects.

Correspondence Schools. Correspondence schools are equipped to teach virtually every area of occupational education; one school alone offers 225 courses. They are ideal for the student who cannot leave home or study full-time.

Area Vocational Schools. Generally government-sponsored, these schools train or retrain young people and adults in job areas related to the needs of local industry. They may be restricted to state or local residents.

Hospital Schools. Such schools offer training in nursing and other health-related occupations. Many charge little or no tuition, and some provide living quarters as well.

Company Training Schools. Examples are the computer-operator schools maintained by IBM, training in floor covering installation at Armstrong Linoleum, and courses in telephone technology sponsored by the Bell Telephone Company. The student attends full-time for a period of several months and is usually paid while learning.

Manpower and Rehabilitation Programs. Most such programs are directed to the needs of the educationally, physically, or economically disadvantaged.

Today, close to five million high school graduates are enrolled in occupational schools. They attend full- or part-time, days or evenings, winter or summer, for a few months or a few years. These young—and some not–so–young—people are learning everything from diamond setting to marine technology. What they share is a common goal: they want the skill and know-how to get started on a career. Some choose occupational education because they question their endurance or ability to finish college. Others see schoolteachers scrounging for jobs while technicians and secretaries have their pick. And some share the viewpoint of Columbia University's Paul Rosenbloom, who writes:

> The current clichés regarding vocational and liberal education are rooted in a tradition dating back to Plato. . . . He designed a model system of liberal education for a society, like the Greek society he knew, in which most work was done by slaves. A free man was a man of leisure. . . . If he did anything so well that he could support himself at it, he lost caste. Any man who worked for a living was not much better than a slave.
> The public school movement and the land-grant colleges introduced a new concept of education for a free man. If a man can support himself, then he is to that extent his own master. So vocational education becomes the basic form of liberal education for United States society.

TYPES OF TRAINING

Over 500 courses are offered in today's occupational schools; a partial list appears in Exhibit 9–1 on pages 108–111. Many of the classifications shown barely existed a decade ago. In the health field, the proliferation of services has created a demand for therapists and technicians of every kind; for each doctor there are six to ten workers in related fields. The picture is similar in science and engineering, where the ratio of technicians to professionals is three to one. These technicians participate in research, development and design, they provide production guidelines, and in general bridge the gap between the theory of the engineer and the skills of the mechanic. Today, one-third of all technician jobs are unfilled; meanwhile, new openings appear daily in such fields as radar, laser technology, plastics and electronics. Skills like these can hardly be "picked up" in a few weeks on the job; special training is indispensible.

Surveys by the U.S. Office of Education suggest that the training pays off. One such survey of 606,872 graduates showed that of those available for placement, 80 percent were placed in the specific occupation for which they completed training or in a related occupation. By field, the percentages were:

agriculture	67%
home economics	76%
distributive	78%
trade and industry	80%
office	81%
technical	90%
health	92%

This impressive record reflects the foremost characteristic of occupational education: concentration in the area of study. Relevance is built in; every course is slanted toward the specific career goal of the student. Thus, the photography student spends most of his time on equipment, lighting, composition, and darkroom techniques. He'll learn some optics, chemistry and art. If he plans to go into business for himself, he may even pick up a little accounting, business psychology, or commercial law—but virtually all this material is introduced only as it applies to photography. Unlike his college counterpart, he'll never be called on to analyze Chaucer, consider the causes of the French Revolution, dissect grasshoppers, or do push-ups in the gym.

Not that occupational education is easy; on the contrary, it may draw on a wider range of abilities than does college. The would-be physical therapist, mechanic, tailor, automotive technician, is held to strict professional standards; there's no room for the half-trained amateur. Plumbers, electricians, health employees, and the like must meet rigorous state licensing requirements; in other fields, standards are set by the appropriate union. In some two-year technical schools, the level of work in engineering, math and science is so high that graduates have transferred to four-year engineering colleges and received full credit for all courses completed.

Nonetheless, the atmosphere of an occupational education classroom is relaxed and friendly. Teachers and students are apt to be on a first-name basis. Snacking and cross-conversations are the order of the day; students are encouraged to work together and compare notes. Classes are small

EXHIBIT 9-1

Occupational Education Schools: Partial List of Courses Offered

AGRICULTURE

Agri. banking and credit
  management
Agri. business man-
  agement
Agri. engineering &
  mechanics technology
Agri. power equipment
  technology
Brewing technology
Dairy technology
Feed and fertilizer
  technology
Fisheries
Floristry
Forestry technology
Horticulture
Irrigation technology
Landscape architecture
Livestock procurement
  & distribution
Nursery management
Veterinary technology
Wildlife management
Wood industry tech-
  nology

APPLIED AND VISUAL ART

Advertising art
Architecture
Architectural design
  technology
Architectural rendering
Book-binding
Cartography
Cartooning
Ceramics
Darkroom techniques
Drafting, mechanical
Fashion design
Furniture design
Gemology
Glass-blowing
Illustration:
  medical
  technical
Interior design
Layout
Photography, basic
  movie technology
Photography:
  still medical
Sculpture
Sign painting
Silkscreen printing
Weaving

BUSINESS & CLERICAL

Accountancy
Advertising
Apartment house
  management
Banking
Bookkeeping
Business administration
Business machine
  operation
Claims investigator
Clerical
Computer operation
Computer programming
Court reporting
Escrow and title
Estimating
Insurance adjusting
Keypunch operation
Management training
Manufacturing tech-
  nology
PBX receptionist
Purchasing agent
Receptionist
Secretary (legal,
  executive, medical,
  bilingual, etc.)
Stenography
Tax preparation
Typing

CONSTRUCTION

Air conditioning
  technology
Assessors
Building construction
  technology
Building inspection
Carpentry
Contracting
Drafting (industrial,
  piping, reinforced
  concrete)
Earth moving machinery
  operator
Electrical wiring tech-
  nology
Estimating
Floor covering
Glazing
Heating technology
Masonry
Painting, paperhanging
Plastering
Plumbing
Steamfitting
Tile setting
Urban renewal tech-
  nology
Zoning and subdivision
  technology

DISTRIBUTIVE EDUCATION

Auctioneering
Buying
Checker, cashiering
Credit and collection
Fashion merchandising
Food store management
Insurance sales
Market training
Merchandising (retail
  and wholesale)
Petroleum marketing
Real estate sales
Retail management
Securities clerk

ELECTRIC & ELECTRONIC

Aviation electronics

EXHIBIT 9-1 (Continued)

Computer technology
Cyclotron maintenance
Electrical power technology
Electronic drafting technology
Electronic engineering technology
Microwave technology
Power lineman
Radar technology
Radio, TV technology
Sound systems technology

HEALTH

Child care & guidance
Clerk, medical
Cytotechnology
Dental assistant
Dental lab technician
Dentistry, mechanical
Dietetics training
Electrocardiograph technology
Environmental health technology
Histological techniques
Hosp. admitting clerk
Infant care
Inhalation therapy
Instrumentation technology
Lab. assistant
Lab. technology
Medical assistant
Med. records librarian
Nurse's aide
Nurse, practical
Nurse, registered
Occupational therapy
Operating room technology
Optical dispensing
Optical lab. technology
Orderly
Orthopedic asst.
Physical therapy aide
X-ray technology

Radiation therapy

MECHANICAL

Aircraft:
Aircraft assembly
Aircraft sheet metal
Power plant mechanics

Automotive:
Auto air conditioning
Automotive technology
Body & fender repair
Brake specialist
Diesel technology
Engine tune-up
Front end & wheel alignment
Marine & small engine repair
Mechanic, Diesel
Motorcycle repair
Tractor mechanic
Transmission specialist

Other:
Air conditioning
Appliance servicing
Assemblers, mechanical
Business machine servicing
Camera repair
Electroplating
Instrument repair
Locksmith
Metal trades technology
Oil burner service
Radio, TV repair
Refrigeration
Sheet-metal work
Water treatment
Watchmaking & repair
Welding

MISCELLANEOUS

Cabinetry
Foreign service officer
Modelling
Specifications writing
Surveying
Technical writing

OTHER ENGINEERING TECHNOLOGIES

Architectural
Ceramics
Chemical
Civil engineering
Industrial engineering technology
Instrumentation
Irrigation engineering
Hydraulic
Marine
Metallurgical
Mechanical
Mineral
Oceanographic
Paper
Petroleum
Plastics
Quality control
Testing Technology
Textile
Vibration
Welding

PERFORMING & COMMUNICATIONS ARTS

Acting
Broadcasting
Costume
Creative writing
Communications, telephone
Dance
Disk jockey
Educational media technology
FCC license
Journalism
Pantomime
Playwriting and production
Radio announcing
Speech arts
TV production
Theatre production
Ventriloquism
Writing

EXHIBIT 9-1 (Continued)

PRINTING

Color separation
Engraving
Imposition and plate
  making
Lithographic technology
Linotype operator
Printing technology
Type setting
Webb offset technology
Zinc plate making

SERVICES

Baking
Bartending
Dealers, gambling
Dog grooming
Dog training
Dressmaking
Drycleaning
Electrolysis
Community organization
  aide
Fabric repair
Family assistance
  worker
Hotel and motel
  management

Interpreter
Laundering
Law enforcement
Locksmithing
Moving (local and
  long-distance)
Park and recreation
  worker
Polygraph technology
Restaurant practice
Sewing machine
  operator
Tailoring
Upholstery
Waiters, waitresses
Wigmaking

TRANSPORTATION

Air:
Aircraft field services
Airline communications,
  FAA
Airline reservations
Flight training
Helicopter training
Stewardess, air
Tower control

Freight:
Cargo supervisor
Dispatcher
Freight claims handler
Rate analyst

Highway:
Auto damage appraiser
Attendant, service
  station
Driver (bus, diesel,
  truck)

Sea:
Decompression chamber
  operator
Deep-sea diver
Deck officer (merchant
  marine)
Marine engineer
Navigation technology
Pilot (merchant marine)
Ship building

Other:
Aerospace engineering
  technology
Traffic management
Travel agent
Travel guide

and provision is made for extra practice and drill. The instructor may not hold a college degree but he's qualified through years of experience; he knows all the pitfalls in the field, and it's his job to steer the class past them. Typically, he deals with his students on a one-to-one basis, providing encouragement, supervision and advice as indicated; if the students fall behind, it is he who is accountable. The college tenure system, whereby teachers may become permanent fixtures regardless of their ability to teach, is unknown in most occupational schools; the instructor who can't deliver is out of a job.

The occupational school graduate can find work quickly, at a respectable salary, doing something he likes to do. As in any field, promotions occur, and as in any field, some people—the resourceful, the concerned, the uncommonly skilled or adaptable—are promoted more often than others. Advancement is usually within the field, in contrast, say, to teaching, where it may entail switching to administration. Financially, the graduate can approach or even outstrip his college counterpart, especially if he ends up in business for himself. A recent *Wall Street Journal* article quoted a high school graduate, first in his class, who decided to become an electrician. "A lot of my friends agree with me that college just isn't worth the hassle anymore," he says. "You can earn just as much in the trades as you can in a profession, and you don't have the expense of four years of college training."

Certainly the person who can do a job and do it well is his own man. If he happens to be the stuff of which company presidents are made, well and good. But if not, he can still attain a measure of self-satisfaction and self-respect which may be difficult for the ambitious junior executive. Should he ever want to resume his studies, he can sign up for college courses and perhaps work toward a degree; here, as everywhere, his maturity and practical experience will be an enormous plus.

SHOULD YOU ATTEND AN OCCUPATIONAL EDUCATION SCHOOL?

But let's come back to you. How can you decide whether occupational education is right for you? Start by asking the following questions; if you answer with more yesses than nos, then it may be a pretty good bet.

1. Are you a good student—but not when it comes to abstract learning?

Are you interested in electricity and chemistry but not in abstractions like life, matter and time? Do you enjoy music and books without caring to philosophize about them? If so, you may belong to a group of students who have real academic ability, but who prefer concrete, useful studies to broad abstract ones. They're the ones who get bogged down by the stream of reports, comparisons, analyses and papers expected in college. Yet these same preferences may give them an edge in business, aeronautics, health services and other occupational fields.

2. Are you absorbed in one subject—perhaps science, technology or any of the arts—to the exclusion of everything else?

If you cut all your history classes to work in the art studio, or if you whiz through physics and trigonometry while panicking at the thought of foreign languages, this may mean you. Here, too, we have the students whose passion is dressmaking, radio/TV or recording electronics, ceramics, nursing or tinkering with cars. In college, the freshman is expected to be an intellectual jack-of-all-trades; everyone has heard of the student so discouraged by required courses that he drops out even before starting on his own area of specialization. In adult life, however, your single-mindedness can be invaluable. If you have a long-standing interest in some marketable field, then occupational training may be exactly right for you.

3. Are you ready to choose a field and stick with it?

The great asset of occupational education is that you train in the precise field in which you plan to work. However, this asset can turn into a liability; if you change your mind, your training may not be worth very much anywhere else. For example, the applied optics taught to a student optician is useful in only a few related areas, in contrast to a beginning college physics course which lays the groundwork for a variety of later work. We noted that technical students who went on in engineering received two full years of college credit for their work; but had they switched to history or languages, they would have salvaged very little. So before you start occupational training, make sure you're pretty well committed to your field.

With one exception. Some training demands so little in time or money that it may be useful, if only as a stopgap measure. As we will see, typing and keypunching are examples; other possibilities include bookkeeping, dry cleaning, dental assisting, glazing and operating certain business machines.

4. Do you want to complete your studies in a relatively short time?

Young people with family or personal responsibilities know they can't count on year after year of study. Others have marriage on their minds; a few are deterred for reasons of health. The fact that most occupational education takes only a year or two (and some can be completed in a matter of months) may make it a natural choice.

But even without such pressing reasons, many students want to wind up their schooling and be done with it. Such students shy away from school, not for lack of ability, but because they can't take much more of the same old grind. For them, occupational training offers both a change of pace and a reasonably short program of study.

5. Are you anxious to earn your own way?

The question of financial pressures, both economic and psychological, was considered in Chapter 7. We saw there that if money is on your mind, finding a job can make a lot more sense than going on to school.

However, your own needs may dictate a solution somewhere between the two. Arnie, for example, was ready to start working, but he felt that, for him, any successful career would require a background in technology. He chose automotive repair. Lynn, in the same position, was alarmed at her lack of skills; she signed up for a short, intensive course in secretarial work. Carol made no bones about wanting to work where there were lots of men; with some artistic ability, she decided on a program in drafting. All these individuals wanted to start work, but felt they lacked the know-how. In such cases, an inexpensive, practical program of occupational education may be a good compromise.

6. Are you free to leave home if necessary?

In certain fields, training can probably be found within a few miles of wherever you live. In others, however, schools may be few and far between. Photography and drama schools concentrate in large cities; nursing schools are near major hospitals; schools of forestry or agriculture are usually found in rural areas. Sometimes local training, while available, is of lower calibre than that offered elsewhere. All this adds up to the fact that the occupation-oriented student, like the one who is college-bound, may end up out of town.

Most occupational schools don't maintain dormitories. As a rule, however, they do what they can to locate comfortable, convenient quarters for their students.

7. Are you reasonably mature for your age?

In college a professor may condone a sloppy piece of work for the sake of a few good ideas, but in occupational schools a sloppy job is simply unacceptable. Such schools, geared to the commercial market, must insist on a high standard of performance. In the resulting atmosphere, the student may find little room for temperament, self-expression, or letting off steam. No one expects him to be a paragon of maturity, but he should be fairly stable and in command of himself.

8. Are you confident of your ability to make your own way?

Some people have the confidence, talent, and sheer nerve to keep them moving in the right direction, come what may. These lucky individuals may not need the protective structure of college. They feel ready to take on the whole world; all they need is an entering wedge. Occupational education may be that wedge.

Of the above eight questions, some will be weighed more heavily than others, but each of them can help you make your plans.

INVESTIGATE THE FIELD

Occupational education begins with the question, "What kind of training do I want?" And this boils down to "What do I want to do?"

The choice of work was discussed in Chapter Seven; everything said there applies here, too. However, if you're interested in occupational education, you'll want to ask some additional questions.

First: I'll be putting a lot into this training. How much do I really know about the field? What special talents does it take? Have I ever tried it? Watched people working at it, or talked to them? What about salary? If this becomes my career, what sort of life can I look forward to?

Second: Who offers this type of training? Can I afford it? How long does it take? Is the school close enough to home? If I can't manage it, what are the prospects for study in related areas?

Third: I plan to earn a living in this field. What are the job prospects over the next five or ten years?

Fourth: I've chosen my field, and I have my pick of a half-dozen schools. How can I decide among them?

Researching Your Choice of Occupation

If you go directly to work, you'll discover new things about the job every day; what's more, you'll be paid while learning. But occupational training can absorb your time and money for months and even years before you put your choice to the test. It therefore makes sense to investigate the field in advance.

A good place to start is in the office of your school guidance counsellor. She has books, pamphlets, suggestions and tests that can steer you in the right direction from the outset. If you want to read on your own, start with *The Occupational Outlook Handbook*. This work, described in Chapter 7, discusses over 800 occupations; it's the best single place to start.

Your next stop might be the local library. Check here for an entire book or pamphlet devoted to your field. But remember that many such books paint too rosy a picture. To offset this trend, try some trade journals in the field; they're written for professionals and offer hard-core facts. As we noted, the thousands of American trade journals are indexed in the *Ayer Directory*; no matter how remote your interests, you'll probably find some sort of publication listed there. Once you locate a suitable journal, the publisher will most likely send you a back copy upon request. It may give you an altogether different picture of your field. For example, a boy who enjoys food preparation may plan to become a chef; only in the pages of a trade publication like *Nation's Restaurant News* will he discover how much of a chef's time is taken up with questions of portion control, leftovers, and whether to prepare 100 servings of corned beef and 65 of shrimp or the other way around.

But no amount of reading can convey the sounds and smells of a job, the physical strain, the interaction with other people. If at all possible, put yourself into the job, if only as the lowliest assistant. If you want to be an automobile mechanic, try hanging around a garage. Did you anticipate all the emergency work, nights and weekends? Can you cope with the cloud of customer suspicion? If you care about health work, invest some time in your local hospital—perhaps as a volunteer. Did you really get along with the patients? Or would you be happier behind the scenes, in an office or laboratory?

This is also a good time to investigate the special talents and abilities involved. Some are obvious: a radar technician needs an aptitude for physics and mathematics; a dental mechanic should have a touch of the artist along with his manual skills. But other requirements may not occur to you. Do you have to stand all day—and if so, can your feet take it? Would allergies or color blindness pose a problem? Some jobs, such as policeman, bartender, and pilot, usually require a minimum age of 21; will you be old enough?

Talk to the people on the job. Do they find it interesting, year after year? What about increased responsibility or job satisfactions? Are they exhausted at the end of the day, or have they energy for other interests? Speak to the boss, too; find out what he's gotten out of his career—and, incidentally, what qualities he expects in his employees. The views of a few people shouldn't change your outlook overnight, but they'll give you a better background on which to base your own judgments.

Look into salaries. *The Occupational Outlook Handbook* gives starting, average, and high salaries for most occupations, but the human reaction can mean a lot more than numbers. It's important to know whether employees live in relative comfort and are content with what they earn. If they depend on overtime, is it available regularly? Evaluate salaries, not by your present standards, but by those which will apply when you graduate. You'll want to support yourself, perhaps travel; you may want to get married.

If possible, visit a school in your field. Would you want to give it a year or two of your life? Are the advanced students still enthusiastic? Are graduates being placed in suitable jobs?

But most important of all is the day-to-day feeling of the job. Once you start working, you'll see more of your co-workers than of your own family; make sure they're the kind of people you get along with. Look closely at the job itself. Are you on your own, or under supervision? Can you use your own initiative? Can you take a break when you want to, or do you work in tandem with others? Will you be required to travel? Can you find a job anywhere, as in office work or automotive repair, or are you restricted to particular locations? How about emergency work—and don't think only of doctors; plumbers can also tell you a thing or two about emergency calls!

In short, try on the job for size. You can't anticipate every detail. Nor are you tying yourself down for life; if you do make a mistake, you'll be able to correct it. But start by checking things out ahead of time. The suggested steps are outlined in Exhibit 9–2 on page 116.

Researching Availability of Training

Once you've chosen a field, the next step is finding a school that offers it. Again, start with your guidance counselor; her know-how may save you weeks of chasing around. If you want to proceed on your own, look into

EXHIBIT 9-2

Steps to Help You Choose Your Field

A. Read:
   1. *Occupational Outlook Handbook*
   2. Specialized books and pamphlets
   3. Trade magazines

B. Visit:
   1. Library
   2. Scene of the job
   3. Appropriate occupational school (if possible)

C. Talk to:
   1. Guidance counsellors
   2. People employed in the field
   3. Employers

D. Write:
   1. Trade publications (if necessary)

E. Keep Asking:
   1. What is the job like?
   2. What are the opportunities for advancement?
   3. What is the salary range?
   4. Where are the jobs located?
   5. What is the expected demand?
   6. What is the feeling of the job?

the resources of your community. See the listings under "Schools" in your classified directory (all private schools, of whatever type, are listed there). Investigate the colleges near you; junior and community colleges offer high-quality occupational training at moderate cost, and the evening divisions of some four-year colleges may have training in selected areas. For information on state-sponsored programs write your State Board of Education (this, along with the capitol city and the state, are all the address you need). Your local Board of Education can tell you about evening and summer programs within the community. If your field is a popular one like cosmetology, the above steps will probably lead you to a good school within commuting distance.

However, if your passion is something like aeronautical design or animal husbandry, you'll want to consult one or more directories.

This is a good point at which to ask whether you prefer a private occupational school or a junior college. Private schools have several advantages. They are widely distributed, they admit students at frequent intervals, and they are less likely to be concerned about high school grades. Moreover, they are often very sensitive to the needs of a community or industry, and they may be far ahead in advanced areas like holography and laser technology—or fashionable ones like poodle grooming.

If you decide on a private occupational school, the following directories are excellent sources of information. All three include hospital schools, and the first two also list correspondence schools.

The Blue Book of Occupational Education. New York: Macmillan Information. Revised periodically. This reference work lists over 12,000 occupational schools, including junior colleges, arranged by state and cross-indexed under 586 courses of study. Information on tuition, length of program and housing are provided when available.

Lovejoy's Career and Vocational School Guide. New York: Simon and Schuster, 1973. *Lovejoy's* lists about 3500 schools offering 218 courses of study; it does not include junior colleges. Some information is provided on tuition, program length and housing. Available in paperback.

Vocational Training in New York City . . . Where to Find It. Kurtz, Marion, ed. New York: Vocational Foundations, 1973. Despite its title, this book covers the entire metropolitan New York area. It's an excellent source if you plan to study in this part of the country.

Lists of approved occupational schools are often furnished by professional and trade organizations. Leading organizations in a few fields include:

National Council of Trade and Technical Schools
2021 L St., NW
Washington, D.C. 20036

ANA-NLN Committee on Nursing Careers
American Nurses' Association
2420 Pershing Road
Kansas City, Mo. 64108

United Business Schools Association
1730 M St., NW
Washington, D.C. 20036

National Association of Schools of Art
1 Dupont Circle, NW
Washington, D.C. 20036

National Home Study Council
1601 18th St., NW
Washington, D.C. 20009
(covers correspondence schools in all fields)

Registry of Medical Technologists
P.O. Box 4872
Chicago, Ill. 60612

National Association of Cosmetology Schools
599 S. Livingston Ave.
Livingston, N.J. 07039

Department of Transportation
Federal Aviation Administration
Washington, D.C. 20590
(aviation industries)

Other such organizations are listed in *Lovejoy's Career and Vocational School Guide, The Blue Book of Occupational Education* and *The Occupational Outlook Handbook.* If these don't serve you, two directories, the *Directory of National Trade and Professional Associations of the United States* and the *Encyclopedia of Associations,* are sure to be useful; your librarian can help you with these.

On the other hand, you may decide on the occupational training offered in junior or community colleges. Fees are usually lower than in private schools. Training, while still career-oriented, may include some "liberal arts" courses in English, beginning mathematics or social science. Finally, if you decide to continue your studies, transfer from a two-year college to a four-year one is relatively simple. The following directories list two-year colleges both by state and by course offerings; additional information is included on tuition, residence facilities and entrance requirements. (Note: Many two-year colleges serve only the immediate area, and are not permitted to accept outsiders.)

American Junior Colleges. Edmund J. Gleaser, Jr., ed. Washington, D.C., American Council on Education, 1971.

Directory of the American Association of Junior Colleges. Washington, D.C.: American Association of Junior Colleges, 1970.

Barron's Guide to the Two-Year Colleges, by Graham R. William. Woodbury, N.Y.: Barron's Educational Service, 1972. Available in paperback.

Comparative Guide to Junior and Two-Year Community Colleges, by James Cass and Max Birnbaum. New York: Harper and Row, 1972.

1972 Junior College Directory. Washington, D.C.: American Association of Junior Colleges, 1972.

Let's see how this works. Lisa lives in Akron, Ohio. She intends to study cosmetology. No problem; her telephone directory lists three schools from which to choose. Barry, in Grand Rapids, Michigan, wants to study medical record technology. His own city doesn't offer anything, but *Lovejoy's* lists seven schools, two of them correspondence schools. Ann, in Los Angeles, wants to become a physical therapy aide. *The Blue Book* mentions five schools, two of them in California; moreover, *The Occupational Outlook Handbook* refers her to the American Physical Therapy Assocation for more information. Kenny, in Harrison, Pennsylvania, is anxious to learn real estate and insurance, preferably in a junior college; *Barron's Guide* cites five in his home state and a dozen more in nearby New York. Finally, Steve is interested in toy design, a field mentioned nowhere at all. (Someone suggested to him that there may not be enough demand for toy designers to justify special training, but Steve doesn't give up that easily.) The *Encyclopedia of Associations* directs him to the Toy Manufacturers of America (there are also separate organizations for manufactures of dolls and of stuffed toys); off goes a request for advice.

Financial Aid

By now you may be wondering how you'll pay for all this training. This need not be a hopeless problem. Today most schools, including private occupational schools, have financial aid programs based on need rather than grades; you can get help even if you're not near the top of your class. (This help may be in the form of part-time work or loans to be repaid upon graduation.) State and private agencies offer similar programs. Moreover, the U.S. Office of Education, recognizing the value of occupational training, offers at least five important plans: the National Direct Student Loan Program, the Guaranteed Loan Program, the Basic Educational Opportunity Grants, the Supplemental Educational Grants, and the Work-Study Program. All of these plans apply to approved occupational schools as well as to college, and all defer repayment, if any, until you leave school. The highlights of each plan are indicated below.

The National Direct Student Loan Program (NDSL)

This program is for students who are enrolled at least half-time in an approved vocational program, and who need a loan to meet their educational expenses. As a vocational student, you may borrow a total of $2,500. Repayment begins nine months after you graduate or leave for other reasons. You may be allowed up to ten years to pay back the loan; during the repayment period, you will be charged three percent interest on the unpaid balance. No payments are required for up to three years if you are serving in the Armed Forces, Peace Corps or VISTA.

Apply through the financial aid officer at your school. He can also tell you about loan cancellation provisions for borrowers who go into certain military occupations.

The Guaranteed Student Loan Program

This program enables you to borrow directly from a bank, credit union, savings and loan association, or other participating lender who is willing to make the educational loan to you. The loan is guaranteed by a state or private nonprofit agency or insured by the federal government.

You may apply for a loan if you are enrolled or have been accepted for enrollment at least half-time in an eligible vocational, technical, trade, business or home-study school, or a school of nursing. You do not need a high school diploma in order to borrow.

The maximum you may borrow is $2,500 a year (in some states it is less). Your interest may not be more than seven percent. The total amount you may borrow for vocational study is $7,500.

If your family income is low to moderate, you may qualify for Federal Interest Benefits. In this case, the federal government will pay the interest for you until you must begin repaying the principal. To apply for these benefits, you must submit to the lender a recommendation from your school as to the amount of money you'll need.

If you don't qualify for Federal Interest Benefits, you may still borrow, but you will have to pay your own interest from the time you take out the loan until it is paid off.

In any event, the loan must be repaid. Payments begin between nine and 12 months after you graduate or leave school, and you may take up to 10 years to pay it off. However, you must repay at least $360 a year.

You do not have to make payments for up to three years if you're serving in the Armed Forces, the Peace Corps or VISTA, or if you return to full-time study.

For further information and application forms, contact your school or lender.

Basic Educational Opportunity Grants

This program makes funds available to eligible students attending approved colleges, junior colleges, vocational schools, technical institutes, hospital schools of nursing, and other post-high school institutions.

To apply for a Basic Grant, you must complete a form called "Application for Determination of Expected Family Contribution." You can get a copy from your high school, post office, state employment office, the school you're planning to attend, or by writing to:

Box G
Iowa City, Iowa 52240

Within four weeks of returning the form, you will receive a "Family Contribution Analysis Report." Complete this form (it's really fairly simple), and submit it to the school you're planning to attend; they'll determine how much aid you're eligible to receive. (You may submit copies of the Report to more than one school.) The amount of your award will be based on expected family contribution, the cost of attendance at your school, and a payment schedule prepared by the U.S. Office of Education.

Basic Educational Opportunity Grants need not be repaid.

Supplemental Educational Opportunity Grants (SEOG)

These grants are for students of exceptional financial need who would otherwise be unable to continue their education. They need not be repaid.

You are eligible to apply if you are enrolled at least half-time as a vocational student in an educational institution participating in the program.

Under this program, the student receives between $200 and $1,500 a year. Normally, the grant may be received for up to four years, with a maximum of $4,000. If you are selected, your school must provide you with additional financial assistance at least equal to the amount of the grant. Apply through the financial aid officer of your school; he is responsible for determining who receives the grant, and the amount.

The College Work-Study Program

This program provides jobs for students who have great financial need and who must earn part of their educational expenses. You may apply if you are enrolled at least half-time in an approved undergraduate or vocational school.

The school arranges jobs on- or off-campus with a public or private nonprofit agency, such as a hospital. If you are eligible, you may work as many as 40 hours a week. In arranging the job and determining your work load, the financial aid officer of your school will take into account your financial need, your class schedule, your health, and your academic progress. The salary you receive is at least equal to the current minimum wage and may be considerably more.

Apply through the financial aid officer at your school. He is responsible for determining your eligibility and arranging the job.

Federal programs are apt to change frequently. For the most recent information on federal programs, write:

> Division of Student Financial Aid
> Bureau of Higher Education
> U.S. Office of Education
> Washington, D.C. 20202

If you're interested in other types of aid, try the financial aid officer of your prospective school. The following books may also help: they list programs sponsored by cities and states, fraternal groups, industries, and other sources you may have overlooked.

Barron's Handbook of Junior and Community College Financial Aid, by Nicholas Prioa and Vincent DiGaspari. Woodbury, N.Y.: Barron's Educational Series, 1971.

How and Where to Get Scholarships and Loans, by Juvenal Angel. New York: Regents Publishing Co., 1967.

Lovejoy's Scholarship Guide, by Clarence Lovejoy. New York: Simon and Schuster, 1964.

A National Catalog of Financial Aid for Students Entering College, by Oreon Kessler. Dubuque, Ia.: William C. Brown, 1971.

Scholarships, Fellowships and Grants. New York: Macmillan Information, 1969.

Scholarships, Fellowships, and Loans, by S. Norman Feingold. Arlington, Mass.: Bellman Publishing Co., 1972.

If you'll be living away from home, costs will be even higher. Some students solve the problem by moving in with relatives. Others take a room at the YMCA or similar organization, at least until they get their bearings. (Note: Don't count on this as a permanent arrangement; there may be a maximum length of stay.) Many schools maintain a housing service, but some regard housing as the student's concern. If so, an ad like the following often brings results:

Student, 19, male, entering XYZ Technical School, needs moderately-priced room near school. References exchanged.

The place you finally choose won't resemble your beloved room back home, but it will serve. You may even get to love it!

One problem remains. Suppose you discover, after all your researches, that the training you want is not feasible? Then it's time to look for a related area—where "related" refers to skills, purpose, social value, work environment or the like, depending on you. Thus, if you wanted rugged outdoor work, forestry is one answer, but surveying is another. If you dreamed of being a pilot and commanding huge planes, remember that air traffic control officers command them, too. Edward Morrison, Director of Vocational Research of the American Institute for Research, has divided general vocational capability into six major categories:

> Mechanical
> Electrical and Electronic
> Spatial (important in drafting and construction)
> Chemical-Biological
> Symbolic (verbal and numerical)
> People-Oriented

Morrison suggests that within each category, job requirements carry over from one occupation to the next; this may also be true of job satisfaction. So if you can't find training in diesel technology, try general automotive technology; if toy design courses are nonexistent, consider industrial design instead. Finally, Exhibit 9–1 on pages 108–110, groups related fields together; if one possibility can't be managed, move on to the next.

As you can see, locating the right type of school entails action on several fronts. The separate steps are outlined in Exhibit 9–3 on page 123.

Researching Job Prospects

You're interested in occupational training because you'll want a job. What are the prospects of getting it? What will be the demand in your field over the next decade?

Every year, government and private agencies spend millions of dollars trying to answer this question. Clearly, the answers can't be hard-and-fast. Projections for the future are based on certain assumptions: that the birth rate will remain constant, that standards of living will rise rather than fall, that military spending will continue as before, that future patterns of work, play, travel, education and medical care will resemble those of the past. Mistakes are inevitable. An unforeseen slowdown in birth rate affects the demand for teachers; a cut in government spending hits engineers; teenagers switch to blue jeans and the clothing industry nosedives. So projections of manpower needs should be interpreted as probabilities, not as promises.

The U.S. Bureau of Labor Statistics has projected manpower needs through 1980 in a variety of fields. Some of their results turn up under appropriate job headings in *The Occupational Outlook Handbook*. The

EXHIBIT 9-3

To Locate Schools in Your Field

A. Talk to:
1. Guidance counsellor
2. Librarian
3. Local Board of Education

B. Consult:
1. Local telephone directory
2. Directories of private occupational schools
3. Directories of junior colleges
4. Directories of trade and professional organizations (if necessary)
5. *Occupational Outlook Handbook*
6. School catalogs

C. Visit:
1. Suitable schools in your community and elsewhere

D. Write to:
1. Schools that interest you (for catalogs, etc.)
2. State Board of Education
3. Appropriate professional organizations

E. If You Need Financial Aid:
1. Contact financial aid officers of appropriate schools
2. Contact local lending institution
3. Write to U.S. Office of Education
4. Write to State Board of Education
5. Consult scholarship and loan directories

F. Keep Asking:
1. Where can I find this training?
2. How long does it take?
3. How much does it cost?
4. Must I leave home?
5. What are the related occupational areas?

material is also summarized in U.S. Department of Labor Bulletin #1701, *Occupational Manpower and Training Needs,* which can be ordered for seventy-five cents from the Superintendent of Documents, U.S. Government Printing Office, Washington, D.C. 20402. Your local library should have the *Handbook* and other manpower projection information available.

When looking at projections, keep in mind that they should all be considered with the following reservations:

First: The mere fact that a given field is in demand doesn't automatically make it right for you. Even though a projection says that 48,000 licensed practical nurses may be needed annually for the next ten years, unless you have the right personality, aptitudes and skills, you won't be one of them. Similarly, if you love working outdoors, you'll be miserable as a lab technician—even though the prospects look good on paper. Choose a field in terms of yourself; then, if the demand appears small, it's time enough to consider a related one.

Second: Don't be dazzled by percentages; they can be very misleading. Over the next ten years the number of dental assistants will increase by 100%, but the actual *number* required will be only 2400 a year. By contrast, the percentage increase for bookkeepers is only 18.9%, but the annual requirement is a substantial 78,000. Percentages may be impressive, but the head count may give a better picture.

Third: The projections are for the *entire* United States. If you plan to remain in your present community, local conditions may easily outweigh national ones. Thus, if you are interested in real estate, a building boom in your part of the country makes your prospects better than average, even though national demand is only moderate. A new hospital creates a local demand for medical personnel; a shopping center means more salespeople and cashiers; a local plant expansion causes a skyrocketing demand for technicians, draftsmen and machinists. For that matter, "local" may mean as close as your own family. If you want to be a hotel clerk and your uncle is in the business, national statistics needn't worry you.

Fourth: Published figures about the employment picture are usually a few years old. A lot can happen between the time they are compiled and the time you see them. We've already seen how an unexpected shift in birth rate affected the demand for teachers, and how military spending alters the prospects for physicists and engineers. Recent interest in fields like ecology, women's rights, pre-school education, and community health will cut down on some jobs and create others. You may not be as clever as the fellows who work for the Bureau of Labor Statistics, but you have the edge on them in one respect: you know what's going on right now. See how it may affect your choice of a career.

In any case, statisticians don't necessarily agree among themselves. For example, in his book, *Manpower Needs for National Goals,* Leonard A. Lecht of the National Planning Association stated that 995,000 cooks would be required by 1975, whereas the Department of Labor Statistics anticipated only 900,000 by 1980. The difference lies in Lecht's basic assumptions, one of which is a high level of government spending in many areas. This would mean increased employment and a period of prosperity for restaurants.

For reasons like this, statistical tables can confuse more than they clarify; you might prefer a different approach to the problem. Try talking things over with your guidance counselor or someone from your local employment agency; they have access to reports and bulletins you never heard of. Perhaps a social studies teacher in your own school takes a special interest in labor or economics. And people in your chosen field may have worthwhile views; they're at least as concerned as you are.

One last word about manpower needs: have faith in yourself. Whatever the national job market, all *you* need is one job. If you believe in your own talents and potential, give yourself a chance. No field is so over-crowded that it can't use a first-rate newcomer; you may be the one.

Choosing the Right School

Suppose you've chosen a type of training and located several schools, all equal in cost and convenience. How can you choose among them?

This question is particularly important in connection with private occu-pational schools. Most such schools are reasonably honest and reliable, but now and then a sharp operator appears on the scene. To protect the public, about twenty states require the licensing of private occupational schools.

Unfortunately, licensing requirements vary enormously from state to state. Almost all states have set standards of hygiene and safety, especially if the school is concerned with food, health or cosmetology. School build-ing and equipment may come under review, although most states phrase their requirements in such vague terms as "satisfactory" or "adequate." The background of director and faculty may be regulated; in such cases, emphasis is usually put upon practical experience. Some states consider the courses of study. Concern is often shown about the financial respon-sibility of the school; occasionally the institution is required to post bond. Finally, the school's advertising, sales methods and contracts may be regulated by law.

However, of the twenty states, very few have requirements in all of the above areas; in some, it's about as easy to start a licensed occupational school as to become a licensed peddler. Some states specify licensing for only a few types of school (barbering schools are a common example), while others specifically exempt some types. And states which require no licensing at all may nonetheless have excellent schools.

For reasons like these, state licensing practices rarely shed much light on the worth of any particular school. Your questions may be better answered by the local Chamber of Commerce or Better Business Bureau, especially if you're concerned about financial stability or other business matters.

In any event, the standards of a good school should go beyond business matters. Instruction should be competent and sympathetic. Classes must be of reasonable size; if special equipment is required, there should be enough of it. Instructors should keep abreast of recent developments in their fields. Entrance requirements should match the demands of the curriculum; a large number of under-qualified students may affect the level of teaching.

Supervision along these lines has become the responsibility of various accrediting organizations, each serving a specific type of school. To be accredited, the school must request an evaluation; it is then visited by an evaluating team including educators, professionals in the field, and others qualified to pass upon the school. Usually the organization charges a fee for the service.

Of the organizations listed on page 117 of this chapter, the National Home Study Council, the American Nurses' Association, the United Business Schools Associations, and the National Association of Schools of Art all serve as accrediting agencies. In the field of aviation, the Federal Aviation Administration exercises strict controls, although emphasis is on safety and legal requirements rather than on teaching. Other accrediting agencies include:

Engineers Council for Professional
  Development
345 E. 46th St.
New York, N.Y. 10017

Council on Medical Education
American Medical Association
535 N. Dearborn St.
Chicago, Ill. 60610
(in connection with other
professional agencies)

Cosmetology Accrediting Commission
25755 Southfield Rd.,   Suite 207
Detroit, Mich. 48075

Accrediting Commission for Business
  Schools
Suite 401
1730 M Street, NW
Washington, D.C. 20036

National Association of Trade
  and Technical Schools
2021 L Street, NW
Washington, D.C. 20036
(accredits courses of study
rather than schools; serves
a variety of fields)

Still other accrediting organizations are listed in *The Occupational Outlook Handbook*. Any of these organizations will provide a list of approved schools upon request. *The Blue Book of Occupational Education* also provides information. Keep in mind that new schools may not have had the chance to become accredited. Moreover, some first-rate established ones bypass the accrediting procedure altogether, depending instead on their own standards and reputation.

Junior and community colleges present an altogether different picture. Most public colleges are inundated with applicants, and have little reason to misrepresent their offerings. Furthermore, all colleges, public or private may request review by one of the six recognized accrediting associations listed below:

Middle States Association of Colleges and Secondary Schools
New England Association of Colleges and Secondary Schools, Inc.
North Central Association of Colleges and Secondary Schools
Northwest Association of Secondary and Higher Schools

Southern Association of Colleges and Schools
Western Association of Schools and Colleges

Among them, these six organizations cover all of the United States, as well as Puerto Rico, the Virgin Islands, the Canal Zone, and Mexico. Their evaluations are recognized throughout the academic world. The directories of two-year colleges listed on page 118 all include information on accrediting.

Whatever kind of school you're interested in, it's possible for you to do a little private accrediting of your own. Start with a thorough examination of the school catalog. Look for information on buildings, equipment, library, counseling and placement services. Check the entrance requirements. If you can't meet them, you're obviously in trouble; on the other hand, if you appear over-qualified, you may find the level of instruction too low. Watch for unsuspected charges and fees. The courses themselves should cover whatever you need to know in the field; if you can't evaluate them yourself, check with someone who can. Make sure there's a list of instructors—preferably with each one's qualifications.

If you can manage it, visit a couple of schools. Attend a few classes; then try talking with the students in the cafeteria or lounge. If they're still enthusiastic after a semester or two, the place must be doing something right. Equally important, you'll find out whether you're at home with the school and with the people there.

However, a school may be "good" in yet another sense. How is it regarded in the field? Is its diploma a mark of merit or just a formality? If the graduates of several schools apply for a job, which is likely to be hired?

Answers to such questions are limited by personal experience. One man has luck with School A, another with School B. Nonetheless, a few tactful inquiries may teach you a good deal.

As usual, start with your guidance counselor. Over the years, she's probably been gathering this kind of information. Moreover, she's paid to look after your interests, not those of some industry or school. Employers and experienced employees may have lots to tell. So will personnel managers in your field, if you're lucky enough to find any who will talk to you about it. Finally, check on the experiences of graduates once they start job-hunting. (But be careful; some private schools reward students with a cash bonus for each new recruit!)

In a few "glamour" fields you may have trouble finding any worthwhile schools, because in these fields the school contributes relatively little to success. A young man of average speech and personality may earn a diploma in disk-jockeying, but it won't rate him a job. A short, chunky girl will find her posture and grooming much improved by a charm course, but she won't find herself on the cover of *Vogue*. In areas like modelling, travel, photography, performing arts, and hotel management, the school should be checked as carefully as possible. The placement record is particularly important. Don't be taken in by promises of lifetime placement service; the "service" may be nothing more than putting your name on a list which is never used again.

Finally, every school has its strengths and its weaknesses. You'll never find the perfect school; there isn't any. Choose the one that comes closest to meeting your needs. The suggested steps are outlined below in Exhibit 9–4.

EXHIBIT 9-4

Steps to Take in Choosing a Specific School

A. Talk to:
  1. Guidance counselor
  2. Personnel managers
  3. Other employment agency personnel
  4. People working in your field
  5. Students training in your field
  6. Graduates in your field

B. Write to:
  1. State Boards of Education (for licensing information)
  2. Local Chambers of Commerce
  3. Local Better Business Bureaus
  4. Schools (for catalogs)
  5. Accrediting agencies (if necessary)

C. Read:
  1. School catalogs—with care!

D. Consult:
  1. *Blue Book of Occupational Education* (for information on accredited private schools)
  2. Directories of two-year colleges (for information on accredited colleges)
  3. *Occupational Outlook Handbook* (for accrediting agencies)

E. Keep Asking:
  1. Does the school meet health and safety standards?
  2. Is it financially responsible?
  3. Is their contract legal? What does it require of me?
  4. Are there any hidden costs?
  5. Are the facilities adequate and up-to-date?
  6. What are the qualifications of the instructors?
  7. What are the entrance requirements? Do they appear too high or too low?
  8. Is the school accredited? By whom?
  9. How is it regarded in the field?
  10. What is its placement record?

10

Learning to Type

In the last chapter, we had a lot to say about choosing a vocational school. Think it over carefully, try the work first, do a lot of investigating. Now we're retracting some of that advice, at least with reference to one specific area: learning to type.

We're not talking about shorthand, bookkeeping, or other office skills. If you're interested in the broad area of office work—and it's a substantial, rewarding field—then everything in Chapter 9 still applies. But learning to type is in a class by itself. The investment in time and money is so small, and the return so great, that it becomes an alternative for an altogether different kind of person: the one who simply doesn't know what to do with himself, but wants to make good use of his time while finding out. Call it a stop-gap if you like—but a stop-gap that will pay off for years to come. The ability to type 45 words a minute, smoothly and accurately, will get you a job almost anywhere. If you can type 55–60 words a minute, your choice of jobs is even better. We're addressing the boys now as well as the girls; in this day and age, there's no reason for girls to have a monopoly on the benefits of knowing how to type.

The demand for typists appears to be insatiable. According to the U.S. Bureau of Labor Statistics, 4,657,000 typists were employed in 1969, and the additional demand during the '70's promises to exceed a quarter-million a year. If this seems excessive, bear in mind that virtually every word in every newspaper, magazine, and book must be typed (often more than once!); that all business correspondence is typed; that every bit of information fed into a computer must be entered by way of a keyboard or a keypunch (which has a lot in common with a typewriter). Day after day millions of typewriters pour forth billions of words—and every last one of them calls for a typist.

Yet this eminently useful skill can be acquired at low cost in a couple of months. It's taught everywhere: in junior and community colleges, in the YMCA and similar organizations, in evening and summer schools, and in over a thousand private schools throughout the country. There are books and records from which you can teach yourself. In private schools, which offer a concentrated program and may provide practice time, you can get a basic course for a hundred fifty or two hundred dollars. Elsewhere, your tuition may be fifty dollars or less. That, and the willingness to apply yourself for a few months, will provide a skill you'll use for the rest of your life.

Typing jobs can be found almost anywhere, on any schedule, at any time. Claire wanted the experience of living in a big city; she took the bus, checked in at the local Y, and found a job within a couple of days. Linda is building up a free-lance typing business from her own home. Bill, who's serious about music, prefers to work only half-days; he's a typist for a small firm whose schedule dovetails with his own. Beginning typists start at eighty or ninety dollars a week, or they can earn as much as five dollars an hour in part-time work.

But for the high school graduate, the greatest advantage of typing is that it enables him to choose a field and learn it from within. A recent edition of *The New York Times* contained openings for typists with a medical office, a music publishing company, an advertising agency, an educational research project, an airline subsidiary, a non-profit social agency, a real estate firm, and a department store—to name only a few. For a person interested in one of these areas, what better way to discover the pressures and rewards than to work at it awhile? Susan thought she liked the health field; she became a typist in a hospital and discovered that, when all was said and done, the atmosphere made her uncomfortable. Meanwhile, John went to work for a brokerage house, got caught up in the world of stocks and bonds, and now plans further training in the field.

Often, that training takes place right on the job. Typing is famous as a stepping-stone to better things. The vice-president of a cosmetics firm, the dress buyer for a merchandising company, a copywriter whose ads have attracted national attention, a manager at a major computer corporation—all of these, and thousands like them, started as typists. The eager young person who wants to learn a business from the ground up is welcome anywhere. But he can't just learn from the sidelines; he must at the same time do some productive work. Typing provides the perfect solution.

What if you don't know what field you'd like to enter? Typing solves this problem via the temporary job. In the last decade, agencies specializing in temporary office help have sprung up all over the country. They offer jobs which may last for several days or for several months. The "office temporary" is expected to stay with the assignment as long as it lasts, but once it's over she's free until she requests the next one. Moira's first assignment, with a law firm, bored her to tears. Her second, with a plastics corporation, was no better. However, the third job brought her to an import-export agency, and something about it captured her imagination. She arranged to stay on; one of these days she'll be making her first trip to the Orient. Moira's luck is not uncommon; many typists turn temporary assignments into permanent jobs. Meanwhile, they're earning money, gaining experience, and meeting new people wherever they go.

But even if you never earn a dime typing, the investment is worthwhile. The average person can produce twelve to fifteen words of legible longhand a minute; even a beginning typist goes two or three times as fast. If you return to school, typing will save hours of cramped, tedious writing by hand (and some professors won't accept papers unless they're typed!). If you work in an office, the ability to type your own memos and rough drafts can be a real help. If you stay home with a family, you'll find yourself typing correspondence, tax returns, applications, and a hundred other documents. And if you're partial to volunteer or community work, your typing skills may be so much in demand that you'll decide to keep them a secret! Meanwhile, it's nice to know that if you should need some extra cash, the know-how is at your fingertips.

Suppose you're convinced. How do you choose a particular school? In Chapter 9 we outlined a number of steps, from investigating the school's finances to checking its placement record. However, when it comes to typing schools, you needn't bother. In the time required to compare a half-dozen schools, you can be typing twenty-five or thirty words a minute; a few more weeks and you'll have the knack. Of course, some teachers are better than others, but the big requirement is practice—and that's up to you. If you have a machine at home, you can learn at any reputable school. If not, you may give preference to a school which provides extra practice time. (But don't pay too much for the privilege; it may be wiser to attend a cheaper school and buy your own typewriter.) Either way, an hour a day for three months or so should do the trick. Typing, like bike riding, stays with you for the rest of your life, so the earlier you begin, the more good you'll get out of it.

11

Apprenticeships

The most ancient and respected of all vocational training systems is the apprenticeship. In primitive tribes the witch doctor trained his successor through apprenticeship. Leonardo da Vinci mastered his painting skills as an apprentice to another artist. In the Middle Ages, the apprentice was almost an indentured servant, starting as young as nine, living and working with his teacher until he could produce the "masterpiece" which would be accepted as signifying his mastery of his craft. Today, while the contract under which an apprentice works is still called an indenture, he is a well-paid, independent and respected member of the working community.

From earliest Greek days, conditions of apprenticeship have specified, in legally binding contracts, the duties and responsibilities of both master and apprentice. Today also, the conditions of apprenticeship are spelled out, including hours to be spent in classroom instruction, detailed enumeration of the tasks and skills to be learned on the job, and the exact salary to be paid for each six-month segment of the apprenticeship. The ultimate goal of the apprentice is to become a "journeyman"—a full-fledged, certified master of his craft.

Like a college education, completion of an apprenticeship program does not come easily. A graduate apprentice has earned what is equivalent to a degree in his craft. It has taken him between three and six years of classroom study, on-the-job training, and actual experience in every kind of work situation, every aspect of the field.

Apprenticeships are available in hundreds of different areas. Some of the most popular are listed in Exhibit 11–1 on page 134.

In examining apprenticeships in more detail we'll consider the following questions:

- What is an apprentice program?
- For whom are apprentice programs a reasonable alternative?
- What are the advantages of apprenticeships?

- Where can I get word of apprentice programs?
- What are the requirements?
- How do I apply?

WHAT IS AN APPRENTICE PROGRAM?

There are three kinds of apprentice programs:

- Registered programs planned by a Joint Apprentice Committee,
- Unregistered programs,
- U.S. Civil Service Programs.

Registered Programs Planned by a Joint Apprentice Committee

These are the most common types of apprenticeships. A program of this type is a schedule arrived at by the Committee, which includes representatives of management, labor, and education. The schedule designates

EXHIBIT 11-1

Leading Occupations Offering Apprenticeships

Aircraft Fabricator	Platemaker
Auto Mechanic	Pressman
Baker	Stripper
Barber	Leather Worker
Boilermaker	Machinist
Bookbinder	Meat Cutter
Brewer	Patternmaker
Bricklayer	Operating Engineer
Cabinetmaker	Painter, Decorator, Paperhanger
Candymaker	Photoengraver
Carpenter	Pipe Fitter
Carpet, Linoleum & Tile Layer	Plasterer
Cement Mason	Plumber
Compositor	Radio & TV Repairman
Cook	Refrigeration & Air Conditioning
Dental Technician	Mechanic
Electrician	Roofer
Electronics Technician	Sheet Metal Worker
Furrier	Stationary Engineer
Glazier	Steamfitter
Grading Equipment Operator	Stonemason
Ironworker, Structural	Tile Layer
Ironworker, Ornamental	Tool & Die Maker
Jeweler	Truck Mechanic
Lather	Upholsterer
Lithographic Photographer	Wood Carver

the precise activities required to master a trade, and the number of hours to be spent working at each of them over the duration of the apprenticeship. It specifies the salary to be paid for each six-month period, usually starting with one-half the journeyman wage and working gradually up to the full wage. It spells out exactly the conditions, benefits, responsibilities and duties of the employer and the apprentice. It specifies the time to be spent in related instruction, and where this instruction is to be received. The Committee sets up the standards for the particular craft or job, and may be national, statewide, or regional in scope. These programs are registered with the United States Bureau of Apprenticeship and Training, or with a state agency dealing with apprenticeship standards.

Unregistered Programs

These are programs set up by major employers who choose, for one reason or another, not to register them. It is important to keep in mind that such programs may be outstanding, measuring up to all government standards, even though they have not been officially registered.

U.S. Civil Service Programs

These are formal apprenticeship programs which can be entered only through civil service tests (see Chapter 8). They have all the benefits of civil service. Usually, these programs train in occupations required to meet special needs of the Armed Forces.

FOR WHOM ARE APPRENTICE PROGRAMS a REASONABLE ALTERNATIVE?

While there is an enormous amount of variation from one apprenticeship program to the next, they all require certain interests and aptitudes. Even more important, they call for a certain frame of mind. If you think you're interested, ask yourself the following questions.

1. Do I enjoy working with my hands—and am I good at it?
2. Am I patient enough to work with precision and persistence to turn out an excellent piece of work?
3. Do I know definitely that I want to learn a skilled craft?
4. Am I willing to invest the next two to five years learning in a stable, organized way, while working?
5. Is it important to me to earn a reasonable wage from the start?
6. How much do I value the security and regular salary increases that go with an apprenticeship?
7. Am I willing to settle down, make a choice now and stick with it?

Your own answers will help you decide whether apprenticeship is for you. An apprenticeship program is a long-term commitment, not to be undertaken lightly. Actually, many apprenticeship programs are more difficult to get into than Ivy League colleges, so those who are accepted value them highly. Still, the dropout rate is comparable to that for college —about 50 percent. The apprentice who drops out after two years may be in a better position than the college dropout, because while he has not completed his training, he has acquired some marketable skills along with work experience and references.

We've been referring to apprentices as "he" because in the past, opportunities were traditionally limited to young men. Today, however, the picture is changing. Women are or have been apprentice trainees in more than 60 of the 350 apprenticeable occupations in this country. For the most part, these women have been trained in cosmetology, bookbinding, cooking or printing. However, significant numbers are learning to be computer repairmen, dental technicians, electronic technicians, draftsmen, upholsterers and watchmakers. The Armed Forces have been particularly aware of their responsibilities in this area; they have accepted women apprentices in such fields as Combat Vehicle Mechanic, Electro-Plater, Gyro Repairer, Machinist and Sheetmetal Worker, among others. So the days are gone when women must regard apprenticeship as a closed field; opportunities exist, and new ones are opening every day.

WHAT ARE THE ADVANTAGES OF APPRENTICESHIPS?

One of the most interesting measures of how people feel about the work they do, is whether they would recommend others to follow in their footsteps. When a group of craftsmen who had come through apprenticeship programs in 20 different fields were asked this question, 95 percent said they would recommend that others get into an apprenticeship. This certainly indicates that the men who have gone through such programs think highly of the experience. But their response is not surprising, when we start listing the advantages of apprenticeships. Here are a few of them:

• Top quality training, combining practical on-the-job instruction by experienced craftsmen with enough classroom instruction to provide the necessary theoretical background for complete understanding of the field.

• Salary from the first day, with built-in, guaranteed salary increases as part of the contract.

• Regular union benefits from the start, with controlled working conditions, time off, holidays, health benefits, and the like.

- Better promotional opportunities. Management recognizes the thorough grounding the apprentice gets in all aspects of his craft, and the resulting superiority of apprentice-trained craftsmen. This makes the apprentice a most likely candidate for promotion. Harry Kursh, in his book, *Apprenticeship in America,* describes a study by Charles E. Koerble on promotion of apprentice-trained workers. He found that of 340 men who had completed apprentice training, 115 had moved up to management level positions in an average of under seven years. Nearly 35 percent had moved to management level positions during the first five years of their journeyman status.

- More interesting and creative work assignments. Because of their expert knowledge, journeyman are given the most demanding, self-directed assignments in the field.

- Opportunities for self-employment. Since graduate apprentices represent the brightest, most knowledgeable people in the trade, it should come as no surprise to find that within five years of completing training, 21.3 percent had advanced to contractors or employers in their industries.

- Better pay for comparable work. In the study mentioned above, 25 percent of completed apprentices were earning even *more* than the journeyman's scale five years after completion of training. Almost 62 percent of all brickmasons, 36 percent of machinists, and 35 percent of carpenters were earning above scale. As skilled craftsmen become scarcer, not only do journeyman scales keep rising, but so does the capacity of the experienced, well-trained craftsman to command rates even higher than these already impressive scales.

- College credit. Here and there, college credit is already being given for apprentice training, and the trend can be expected to continue.

WHERE CAN I FIND OUT ABOUT APPRENTICESHIP PROGRAMS?

With a journeyman electrician's wages running to about ten dollars an hour, and apprentices earning about five dollars to start, it's not hard to see why apprenticeship opportunities are very much in demand. The competition can be fierce, so getting in may take a carefully laid-out campaign over a couple of years. The first step, of course, is to learn about the programs as they are announced. Here's how to go about it.

1. While there are many broad, national apprentice programs, there are even more smaller localized ones. It's a good idea to get information as close to home as possible. A good place to start is your local State Employment Service Office. They can provide information about programs, both registered and unregistered, in your local area. There is sometimes more

than one program for the same skill; you'll probably want to apply to each of them. You may also inquire at the field office of the U.S. Bureau of Apprenticeships and Training, if there is one in your city. It will be listed in your telephone directory under "U.S. Government."

2. Apart from visiting your local agencies, try sending out a few letters. For general information about apprenticeships, write to:

U.S. Department of Apprenticeship and Training
Department of Labor
Washington, D.C. 20202

More specific information about opportunities in your area can be obtained from the nearest of the Bureau's eleven regional offices. These offices, along with the states they serve, are as follows:

Region I
(Conn., Maine, Mass., N.H., R.I., Vt.)
Room 1703-A
John Kennedy Federal Bldg.
Government Center
Boston, Mass. 02203

Region II
(N.Y., N.J., Puerto Rico, Virgin Islands)
Room 906, Parcel Post Bldg.
341 Ninth Ave.
New York, N.Y. 10001

Region III
(Del., Md., Pa., Va., W. Va.)
P.O. Box 8796
Philadelphia, Pa. 19101

Region IV
(Ala., Fla., Ga., Ky., Miss., N.C., S.C., Tenn.)
Room 729
1317 Peachtree St., N.W.
Atlanta, Georgia 30309

Region V
(Ill., Ind., Mich., Minn., Ohio, Wisc.)
219 S. Dearborn St.
Chicago, Ill. 60604

Region VI
(Ark., La., N. Mex., Okla., Tex.)
Room 312, Mayflower Bldg.
411 N. Akard St.
Dallas, Texas 75201

RegionVII
(Iowa, Kans., Mo., Neb.)
Room 2107, Federal Office Bldg.
911 Walnut St.
Kansas City, Mo. 64106

Region VIII
(Colo., Mont., N. Dak., S. Dak., Utah, Wyo.)
Room 314, New Custom House
19th and Stout Sts.
Denver, Colo. 80202

Region IX
(Ariz., Calif., Hawaii, Nev., Trust Territories)
Room 10451, Federal Bldg.
450 Golden Gate Ave.
San Francisco, Calif. 94102

Region X
(Alaska, Idaho, Wash., Ore.)
Room 1809, Smith Tower
506 Second Ave.
Seattle, Wash. 98104

A new office, serving the District of Columbia:
D.C. Manpower Administration
14th and E Sts., NW
Washington, D.C. 20004

Finally, 29 states maintain state apprenticeship agencies, as do the District of Columbia, Puerto Rico, and the Virgin Islands. These offices supervise apprenticeship training and standards within the state, and may also maintain an information guide to all programs registered in the state. Their addresses are given below.

Arizona
Arizona Apprenticeship Council
1623-B W. Adams
Phoenix, 85007

California
Div. of Apprenticeship Standards
Dept. of Industrial Relations
455 Golden Gate Ave.
P.O. Box 603
San Francisco, 94102

Colorado
Apprenticeship Council
Industrial Commission Offices
200 E. 9th Ave., Rm. 216
Denver, 80203

Connecticut
Apprenticeship Training Div.
Labor Dept.
200 Folly Brook Blvd.
Wethersfield, 06109

Delaware
State Apprenticeship and Training Council
Dept. of Labor and Industry
618 N. Union St.
Wilmington, 19805

District of Columbia
D.C. Apprenticeship Council
555 Pennsylvania Ave., NW, Rm. 307
Washington, D.C., 20212

Florida
Bureau of Apprenticeship
Div. of Labor
State of Florida Dept. of Commerce
Caldwell Bldg.
Tallahassee, 32304

Hawaii
Apprenticeship Div.
Dept. of Labor and Industrial Relations
825 Mililani St.
Honolulu, 96813

Kansas
Apprenticeship Training Div.
Dept. of Labor
401 Topeka Blvd.
Topeka, 66603

Kentucky
Kentucky State Apprenticeship Council
Dept. of Labor
Frankfort, 40601

Louisiana
Div. of Apprenticeship
Dept. of Labor
State Capital Annex
P.O. Box 44063
Baton Rouge, 70804

Maine
Maine Apprenticeship Council
Dept. of Labor and Industry
State Office Bldg.
Augusta, 04330

Maryland
Maryland Apprenticeship and Training Council
Dept. of Labor and Industry
203 E. Baltimore St.
Baltimore, 21202

Massachusetts
Div. of Apprentice Training
Dept. of Labor and Industry
State Office Bldg.
Government Center
100 Cambridge St.
Boston, 02202

Minnesota
Div. of Voluntary Apprenticeship
Dept. of Labor and Industry
110 State Office Bldg.
St. Paul, 55110

Montana
Montana State Apprenticeship Council
1331 Helena Ave.
Helena, 59601

Nevada
Nevada Apprenticeship Council
Dept. of Labor
Capitol Bldg.
Carson City, 89701

New Hampshire
New Hampshire Apprenticeship Council
Dept. of Labor
State House Annex
Concord, 03301

New Mexico
New Mexico Apprenticeship Council
Labor and Industrial Commission
1010 National Bldg.
505 Marquette, NW
Albuquerque, 87101

New York
Bureau of Apprentice Training
Dept. of Labor
The Campus, Building #12
Albany, 12226

North Carolina
Div. of Apprenticeship Training
Dept. of Labor
Raleigh, 27603

Ohio
Ohio State Apprenticeship Council
Dept. of Industrial Relations
220 Parsons Ave., Rm. 314
Columbus, 43215

Oregon
Apprenticeship and Training Div.
Oregon Bureau of Labor
Rm. 115, Labor and Industries Bldg.
Salem, 97310

Pennsylvania
Pennsylvania Apprenticeship and Training
  Council
Dept. of Labor and Industry
Rm. 1547, Labor and Industry Bldg.
Harrison, 17120

Puerto Rico
Apprenticeship Div.
Dept. of Labor
414 Barbosa Ave.
Hato Rey, 00917

Rhode Island
Rhode Island Apprenticeship Council
Dept. of Labor
235 Promenade St.
Providence, 02908

Utah
Utah State Apprenticeship Council
Industrial Commission
431 S. 6th St., Rm. 225
Salt Lake City, 84102

Vermont
Vermont Apprenticeship Council
Dept. of Industrial Relations
State Office Bldg.
Montpelier, 05602

Virginia
Div. of Apprenticeship Training
Dept. of Labor and Industry
P.O Box 1814
9th St. Office Bldg.
Richmond, 23214

Virgin Islands
Div. of Apprenticeship and Training
Dept. of Labor
Christiansted, St. Croix, 00820

Washington
Apprenticeship Div.
Dept. of Labor and Industries
314 E. 4th Ave.
Olympia, 98594

Wisconsin
Div. of Apprenticeship and Training
Dept. of Labor, Industry, and Human
  Relations
Box 2209
Madison, 53701

3. Get in touch with the local trade union in your field of interest. This organization may be actively involved in the Joint Apprenticeship Committee for your chosen craft. If applications are not now being accepted, ask them to send you an announcement.

4. Inquire at large companies in your area, employing this kind of workers. They may have an unregistered program for which you are, or can become, eligible. Find out what their requirements are, and how you should go about filing an application. If you're interested in a field which has no large employers, such as jewelry or dental technology, you may approach some local firms about the possibility of setting up an apprentice arrangement for you. If the employer thinks you show promise, then, with

the cooperation of the State Bureau of Apprenticeship Standards, he may be able to map out a program.

5. Ask journeymen in the field. They sometimes know of prospective openings ahead of time, or may be able to direct you to an interested employer.

6. Finally, consider the United States Civil Service Apprenticeships. Since these depend on examinations which are given only periodically, you should keep in touch with the nearest office of the U.S. Civil Service Commission. It wouldn't hurt to contact this office once a month, to get the latest information on application dates. Usually, two or more examinations are given at the same time, covering several different apprenticeship opportunities, and you indicate your preference. No experience is required, and as a rule the examination tests your aptitude to learn the trade, rather than your knowledge of it (see Chapter 6). Many public libraries have Civil Service Examination Study Workbooks on file; you can review these in advance, and possibly bone up on subjects that need improvement.

WHAT ARE THE REQUIREMENTS FOR APPRENTICESHIP PROGRAMS?

As you would expect, individual requirements vary from one program to the next. However, there are certain basic areas to check into.

Age Limitations

Most programs specify age limitations. Usually the lowest age is 18, and the highest between 26 and 30, with additional allowance for time served in the Armed Forces. A few programs do not specify an upper age limit, leaving the program open to people who have already spent part of their lives working.

Physical Requirements

Most programs require good physical health. Some specify visual requirements, and may exclude those who are color blind. In some industries, your capacity to lift and manipulate specified weights may be tested. If you know about these requirements beforehand, you can exercise to develop the strength and agility required—or find some less strenuous field.

Education

Many apprenticeship programs have no specified educational requirements at all. Others require high school graduation or the General Education Diploma (G.E.D.), a high school equivalency diploma. Some go into considerable detail about specific course requirements. For example, the

AN EQUAL OPPORTUNITY EMPLOYER

JOINT APPRENTICESHIP COMMITTEE
MOTION PICTURE EMPLOYERS AND
AFFILIATED PROPERTY CRAFTSMEN LOCAL NO. 44 - I.A.T.S.E. & M.P.M.O.
8480 BEVERLY BOULEVARD • HOLLYWOOD. CALIFORNIA 90048

NOTE: ONLY THE FIRST 35 COMPLETED
APPLICATIONS RECEIVED AND ACCOMPANIED
BY THE REQUIRED DOCUMENTATION WILL
BE CONSIDERED!

NOTICE OF APPRENTICESHIP OPPORTUNITY
Motion Picture Employers-Local #44 Affiliated
Property Craftsmen, I.A.T.S.E. & M.P.M.O.

Applications for the Propmakers Apprenticeship Program, jointly established
by Motion Picture Employers and Local #44 Affiliated Property Craftsmen,
will be distributed from ▮▮▮▮▮▮▮▮▮▮▮▮▮▮▮▮▮▮▮▮▮▮▮▮▮▮▮▮ APPLI-
CATIONS WILL NOT BE FURNISHED ON TELEPHONE REQUEST OR SENT OUT BY MAIL.

In order to obtain an Application, you must apply in person, during the above
stated period, only, to I.A.T.S.E. Affiliated Property Craftsmen Local #44,
at 7429 Sunset Boulevard, Hollywood, California. Hours: 10:00 a.m. to
12 Noon, and 2:00 p.m. to 4:00 p.m., Monday through Friday.

PLEASE NOTE THAT FILING AN APPLICATION DOES NOT CONSTITUTE A BONA FIDE OFFER OF
EMPLOYMENT. THE PURPOSE OF SOLICITING APPLICATIONS AT THIS TIME IS SOLELY FOR
THE PURPOSE OF ESTABLISHING A LIST OF ELIGIBLE SELECTEES FOR ASSIGNMENT AS THE
NEED ARISES.

BEFORE YOU REQUEST, OR RETURN, THE OFFICIAL APPLICATION FORM, IT IS IMPORTANT
THAT YOU MAKE A PERSONAL EVALUATION OF YOUR OWN QUALIFICATIONS IN ORDER TO
DETERMINE THAT YOU MEET THE BASIC MINIMUM REQUIREMENTS WHICH ARE AS FOLLOWS:

1) An applicant must have attained his 18th birthday and not yet have
attained his 26th birthday as of September 13, 1972. However, extra time
up to a period not exceeding four (4) years shall be allowed beyond
such 26th birthday to compensate for any time during which applicant
has been in active full-time duty in the regular Armed Forces of the
United States.

2) Successful completion of a minimum number of twelve (12) school
semesters in subjects as indicated below:

GROUP I	Woodworking Cabinet Making Carpentry	) 2 Semesters or more required) from this Group.)
GROUP II	Basic Math Basic Shop Math Algebra Geometry Physics	) 2 Semesters or more required) from this Group.)))
GROUP III	Crafts Plastics Leather Woodcarving Mechanical Drawing Machine Shop Auto Shop Electricity Shop Sheet Metal Welding Elec. Welding Acetylene Welding Heliarc Print Shop (Gr. Arts) Architectural Drawing	) The balance to complete 12) Semesters may come from this) Group.))))))))))))

OVER)

To become eligible for a personal interview with and final selection by the Joint Apprenticeship Committee, applicants must provide the following:

1) Completed, signed Application Form.

2) Authentic proof of age. (See attached "Instructions Concerning Proofs of Age").

3) High School Diploma or G.E.D. Equivalent.

4) Official transcript(s) of Junior High School, Senior High School and of any Post-High School Educational Records and Grades. "Student" copies of transcripts are not acceptable. Transcripts of credits obtained while in military service are not acceptable.

5) Copy of United States Military Service and Discharge (DD214), if any--required if requesting consideration for time spent in U.S. military service, if over age limit.

Applicants selected by the Joint Apprenticeship Committee will be required to pass a medical examination, including a Color Perception Test, arranged and provided by the Committee at no cost to applicant.

* * * * * * * * * * * * * *

HOURLY RATES OF PAY FOR APPRENTICES

7305 Apprentice Prop Maker

1st 1000 hours worked	$3.35
2nd 1000 hours worked	3.46
3rd 1000 hours worked	3.725
4th 1000 hours worked	3.995
5th 1000 hours worked	4.255
6th 1000 hours worked	4.465
7th 1000 hours worked	4.73
8th 1000 hours worked	5.00

* * * * * * * * * * * * * *

JOB DESCRIPTION

LOCAL #44 AFFILIATED PROPERTY CRAFTSMEN I.A.T.S.E.

The Propmaker fabricates, repairs, sets up, maintains, removes and stores props, miniatures and sets for motion pictures from wood, cardboard, plastic, rubber, cloth, metal, clay, and glass; uses hand tools and power tools; sets up and operates various machines such as saws, jointer, mortiser, molder, shaper shears, brake and drill press, soldering and arc or acetylene welding equipment. Does all types of rigging and construction using ropes, cables, chains and lines of all kinds. Installs and operates all such supplies of power as gasoline, diesel, air, water, electrical, manual and all accessories required on a rigging job.

Interested applicants should be strong and active to do strenuous lifting of various materials and equipment; should be able to work from high ladders and scaffolding and possess manual dexterity to be able to work with hand and power tools.

APPLICATIONS AVAILABLE FROM:

I.A.T.S.E. Local #44
7429 Sunset Boulevard
Hollywood, California 90046

(MUST APPLY IN PERSON)

HOURS: 10:00 a.m. to 12 Noon, and 2:00 p.m. to 4:00 p.m., Monday through Friday -- August 2, 1972 through September 13, 1972, only.

Property Craftsmen Apprentice Announcement (pages 142 and 143) in the motion picture industry specifies the following:

2 semesters or more chosen from: Woodworking, Cabinetmaking, Carpentry.

2 semesters or more chosen from: Basic Math, Basic Shop Math, Algebra, Geometry, Physics.

Balance, to complete 12 semesters, from: Crafts, Plastics, Leather, Woodcarving, Mechanical Drawing, Machine Shop, Auto Shop, Electricity Shop, Sheet Metal, Welding, Electric Welding, Acetylene Welding, Heliarc, Print Shop, Architectural Drawing.

If the list discourages you, bear in mind that this is one of the most difficult programs to enter, and their educational requirements are among the most demanding. Still, if this is what you want, you can complete your course work either at high school or at night school after graduation. And remember, many programs have no specific course requirements at all. Others may require only a shop course, an algebra course, or competence in arithmetic. If a high school diploma is required and you lack one, you can work on the General Education Diploma to become eligible.

Tests

Many programs administer a written test to help determine the applicant's aptitude for the field. Some use the General Aptitude Test Battery administered by the State Employment Service Office (see Chapter 6). Every program requires that those who pass the written test be given an oral evaluation or personal interview as part of the selection process. One program, for the ceramic tile setting industry, has no formal educational requirements, but gives a written General Assessment Test which counts for 60 percent of the score, and an oral interview rated as follows:

Attitude	10 points
Confidence	10 points
Oral response	10 points
Stability	10 points

Such an interview is even more meaningful than an interview applying for a particular job, since the apprentice will not only be working, but also learning. The Selection Committee wants assurance that the time and money it takes to train a man are not being wasted.

Previous Experience

In many programs, the applicant is credited in some way for previous experience. Sometimes he is not tested with new applicants, but is rated separately. Occasionally, work experience is credited against missing educational requirements. Or the experienced apprentice may be started at a higher salary than the novice. In practically every case, actual work experience is recognized and weighed.

Job Requirements

Some apprenticeship programs require that you actually have a job lined up, even before you begin. Finding the job has nothing to do with the union; it's strictly between the employer and yourself. If you're interested in a program of this type, start scouting around now. Look up some employers in the field (a letter of introduction will probably help), and convince one of them that you deserve to be hired.

HOW DO I APPLY?

If you've followed up on the suggestions given earlier, you already know about various apprenticeship tests and other opportunities. Nonetheless, applying to the program may be complicated by restrictions of various kinds. Most apprenticeship programs accept applications only during limited, specified times, even from those who have the basic qualifications. Some unions want to restrict apprenticeships, particularly when the industry is suffering economically, and there are not enough jobs for all the craftsmen already in the union. In 1972, the Property Craftsmen's Union mentioned above specified that applications would be distributed from August 2nd through September 13th. "In order to obtain an application you must apply in person during the above period at the specified address between 10 A.M. and 12 noon, and 2 P.M. to 4 P.M., Monday through Friday. Applications will not be furnished on telephone request or sent out by mail." As if that isn't enough to discourage applicants, there is a note to the effect that only the first 35 completed applications received and accompanied by the required documentation would be considered!

It's obvious that although applications are open from August 2nd to September 13th, the applicant who picks up his application on September 10th might as well not bother. In such a case, it would be best to have all the documentation ready before August 2, pick up the application at 10 A.M. August 2, fill it out immediately, and submit it the same afternoon. This would still be no guarantee of selection, but it would at least give you a chance. A properly submitted application would make you eligible for a personal interview with the Joint Apprenticeship Committee, which is in charge of final selection. Those selected by the Committee are required to pass a medical examination, including a color perception test.

This is the kind of apprenticeship program you've heard all the horror stories about. Most are more reasonable. For example, the Electrical Apprenticeship program in Los Angeles calls for high school graduation and one full year of algebra with a passing grade. Where there are specific course requirements, a school transcript or grade report is required. Applications are accepted continuously every Tuesday and Thursday at various locations but within limited hours. Applicants who qualify and pass the aptitude test (the notice does not specify when this is held, so the applicant would have to make sure where and when) must attend a "Scheduled Prep Meeting" to receive other necessary information. The Carpenters' Union in Los Angeles accepts applications continuously, tests are administered several times a week, and anybody who can find an employer to hire him can apply for membership and be tested that same week.

In entering apprenticeship programs, as in all situations where there are many applicants and few openings, it is helpful to know people whose recommendations will carry some weight. These may include journeymen who are already in the field, union officials, and employers. Sometimes even suppliers can help, by letting you know when applications will be accepted and where job openings may occur. As mentioned before, some programs require you to have the promise of a job before you will be accepted. In any case, work experience can give you the advantage of becoming acquainted with employers and journeymen who may help you be accepted into the program. Such work may also help you decide whether you want to spend the next few years mastering the job. So while you wait to be accepted into an apprenticeship program, your efforts could well be directed toward finding work in the field, or in a closely related one.

* * *

This chapter has provided a variety of details about apprenticeships. The information is summarized in Exhibit 11–2 on page 147. However, it would be unfair to leave the subject without mentioning the commonly voiced objection that in order to be accepted, you have to have a father in the trade. Many think that unless you have solid connections in the union or industry, you're wasting your efforts to apply at all. Despite government efforts to eliminate discrimination and nepotism, there is no doubt that a letter of recommendation or a personal "good word" can make a big difference—just as it would in banking, advertising, and just about any field you can name. This doesn't mean that if you're not closely related to someone in the field, it's useless to apply. It does mean that it helps to develop some relationship with people who can support your application. There may be some unfairness here, and various anti-discrimination agencies are trying to temper the situation. However, it's wise to be realistic. Explore the field of your choice so that you see the total picture. Don't be discouraged by generally pessimistic talk. But do sound out people in the field to learn just what your chances may be. And keep working at it; the rewards are substantial.

EXHIBIT 11-2

Apprenticeship Programs

A. What is an Apprentice Program?
  1. Registered programs planned by a Joint Apprentice Committee
  2. Unregistered programs
  3. U.S. Civil Service programs

B. For Whom are Apprentice Programs a Reasonable Alternative?
  Apprentice programs may be for you if you:
  1. Enjoy working with your hands and are good at it
  2. Have the patience to work with precision and persistence
  3. Know definitely you want to learn a skilled craft
  4. Are willing to invest two to five years in learning
  5. Want to earn a reasonable wage from the start
  6. Are willing to make a choice and stick with it

C. What are the Advantages of Apprenticeships?
  1. Top quality training
  2. Salary from the first day
  3. Regular union benefits from the start
  4. Better promotional opportunities
  5. More interesting and creative work assignments
  6. Opportunities for self-employment
  7. Better pay for comparable work
  8. Possible college credit

D. Where Can I Get Word of Apprenticeship Programs?
  1. Visit U.S. Employment Service office
  2. Visit State Employment Service
  3. Write U.S. Regional Office, Dept. of Apprenticeship and Training
  4. Write State Apprenticeship office
  5. Contact local trade unions
  6. Contact large companies in your area
  7. Contact journeymen in the field
  8. Look into U.S. Civil Service apprenticeships

E. What are the Requirements for Apprenticeship Programs?
  1. Age limitations
  2. Physical requirements
  3. Education
  4. Tests
  5. Previous experience

F. How Do I Apply?
  1. Restrictions on applications
  2. Personal contacts

12

Going Into Business
for Yourself

Every year about 400,000 new businesses get started. Every year, for whatever reason, nearly as many close. The typical new business lasts only two or three years.

Yet new businesses keep opening. Some of them prosper; a few make their owners very rich. For the rest, the businessman either muddles through, earning an unimpressive salary, or he gives up. Under these circumstances, why do people keep trying?

Louis L. Allen, president of the Chase Manhattan Capital Corporation, has one answer. In his book, *Starting and Succeeding in Your Own Small Business,* he suggests: "The reason why a man selects himself to head his own small business is because he *must* do it. The American dream is made up of such urges. The drives which force him to do this are as old as capitalism itself."

PROS AND CONS

Let's take a realistic look at small business and see what it entails.

First, it means coming up with your own ideas. That's fine if ideas are your strong point. But don't expect to succeed merely by copying what works for someone else; the way to attract customers is to provide added features the competition never thought of.

Second, it requires the muscle to carry out your ideas. If you want a bright, immaculate store, you personally may end up doing the scrubbing. If you think a telephone sales campaign is indicated, it's you who'll be manning the phone.

Third, it usually means an extended working day. Beginners in business can't afford much hired help. You may use your mornings in production, your afternoons in sales, and your evenings catching up on paper work. If self-employment interests you only because you think it's easier than a nine-to-five job, forget it!

Fourth, your income may be far below what you could earn on an ordinary job—at first, anyway. Even a sound business may take six months to a year before it starts showing a profit. Meanwhile, more often than not, the owner cuts down wherever he can, including his own salary.

Fifth, it ties up a lot of money. You'll be paying for advertising, printing, equipment, rent, before you take in your first dollar. There may be lawyers' and accountants' fees. Once the business is under way, it still takes time to collect your bills—while your suppliers are clamoring to be paid. Even in a modest service operation like sign painting or giving music lessons, your investment will amount to a tidy sum.

Sixth, it puts the problems and pressures squarely on your shoulders. Suppose you're running a lawn care service, and Mrs. Jones wants her lawn in top shape for a big Sunday party. Three days of rain have put you behind schedule—but she couldn't care less. Either you get her lawn mowed by Sunday afternoon, or you come up with a pretty convincing explanation. It's up to you.

Finally, you lose the benefits usually provided by an employer. These include health and disability insurance, sick leave, paid vacations, educational opportunities and the like—not to mention financial backing and a steady income.

On the other hand . . .

In your own business, it's you who reap the benefits. If your ideas are good, if you're willing to put in a fourteen-hour day, if you do everything from top-level conferences to sweeping the floor, you're the one who gets rich. You're free to back your hunches and live with the consequences. You can stop telling people your boss is an idiot. You *are* the boss; you stand or fall on your own merits.

WHO WILL SUCCEED?

Success in business doesn't require advanced education. A study of business firms showed that 19.4 percent of the owners had eight years or less of schooling, while another 33.3 percent had nine to eleven years. Nor does it call for exceptional intelligence. What it does require are certain values and qualities of temperament. Autonomy is essential; if you can't get yourself organized and functioning, there's no one to do it for you. Your values will probably emphasize money and status rather than, say, social service; even if your business is socially useful, you're not likely to start it for that reason. Louis Allen talks of a "willingness to 'pay the price' "—the ability to make the sacrifices and adjustments necessary to

keep your business alive. Above all, you'll need maturity. As a businessman, you're an adult, working among adults; don't expect them to make
allowances for your age.

More specifically, self-employment requires traits like the following:

- **Self-Discipline.** In any enterprise, there are always chores to be done—
inventory to be checked, bills to be sorted, delinquent payments to be
followed up, a new ad to be written. The businessman must handle
them without being prodded and without feeling sorry for himself. He
washes windows or dusts displays because he knows that a dingy store
keeps customers away and cuts down on his own profits. He delivers his
products or services as expected without fuss or excuses—it was raining
too hard, nobody could expect him to get through that downpour. It's
exactly the ability to get through the downpour that makes your customers deal with you rather than a competitor.

- **Responsibility.** To run any business successfully, you must be responsible to yourself, your customers, and your suppliers. If you miss a bill
or two, supplies may be cut off. If you promise more than you can deliver, you'll lose sales and recommendations. Particularly in a small business, dependability may be your strongest selling point.

- **Enthusiasm.** To be self-employed, you must believe in yourself and
your product. Enthusiasm is contagious; if you yourself glow with conviction, you'll generate interest wherever you go.

- **Sociability.** As a businessman, you're always on the lookout for new
customers. It helps to like people and get along with them. You may
also want to keep in the public eye through participation in community
or philanthropic groups.

- **Organization.** Businesses grow and develop best if they proceed according to plan. As a businessman, you'll need to set your goals, anticipate
difficulties, and keep moving in the direction you've mapped out for
yourself. Instinct, timing and "business sense" are important in any operation, but they're no substitute for careful, long-range planning.

- **Attention to Financial Detail.** A large part of business success depends
on figuring expenses and profits accurately. You must have an accurate
grasp of costs—not only for materials and labor, but for advertising, de-
liveries, overhead, waste. You should know how much of everything you
need, so that you neither over-buy nor run short. If you don't like record-keeping, or lack the patience for it, you may need a partner who can
handle this end of the business. Otherwise you could sell lots of merchandise and still go broke.

- **Stability.** Every business has its good and bad periods. Sometimes
there's nothing to do but ride it out and wait for times to improve. But

if you get too depressed, you may never muster the energy to steer the business back to normal. To work effectively at such times takes a stable, generally optimistic temperament.

- **Good Health.** Self-employment makes demands on your physical stamina. If you're prone to minor ailments like upset stomach or colds, if you're laid low by every virus that comes your way, or if you just run out of steam by mid-afternoon, then—even though none of it is your fault—you'd probably do best to avoid a strenuous business of your own.

In the booklet, *Checklist for Going Into Business,* the Small Business Administration tests these qualities with the following questions. Indicate whether you are "Above Average," "Average," or "Below Average" for each of the qualities below.

——Are you a self-starter?
——Do you get along with other people?
——Can you lead others?
——Can you take responsibility?
——How good an organizer are you?
——How good a worker are you?
——Can you make decisions?
——Can people trust what you say?
——Can you stick with an undertaking?
——How good is your health?

Allow two points for "Above Average," one for "Average," and none for "Below Average." If you scored 15 or better, you probably have the temperament to run a business. Between 10 and 15, you may need to develop these qualities—through application and effort, it *can* be done. Or look for a partner whose strengths dovetail with your weaknesses. Below 10, you'd do best to postpone self-employment a year or two, and then see where you stand.

TYPES OF BUSINESS OPERATION

If you're considering self-employment, chances are you already have some idea of what you would do. If you've been mowing and maintaining lawns for a half-dozen neighbors as a part-time job, you might be planning to buy a pick-up truck and a bigger power mower, and expand the operation. If you're really good at macramé, you could be wondering what's involved in producing enough bags and belts to supply retail outlets. If you've been clerking at the local sports shop, you may be weighing the possibility of starting something of this sort on your own. Basically, these three enterprises cover the three major types of business: service, production and merchandising.

Service

Here you are selling a service. Either you provide it yourself, or you coordinate the work of others. Service enterprises include such categories as child care, newspaper delivery, gardening, grounds maintenance (including cleaning pools or shoveling snow, depending on the season), window washing, poodle grooming, bookkeeping services, automobile repair, music or language instruction, tutoring—plus as many imaginative services as young people can dream up. Service is a natural for this age group. Since no inventory is required and the business can usually be operated from home, it requires a far smaller investment than other operations. What is necessary is some good advertising (the classified section of the local newspaper is often effective), circulars distributed among potential customers, a telephone-answering service or device, an acceptable level of performance, and a reputation for unfailing dependability. If service is all you're selling, you've got to deliver.

Service as a full-time business may be far more complicated than an occasional after-school job. A high-school student can look after a toddler or two on her own front porch, and no one will make a fuss; when she tries to develop a full-time child care service, she may find herself subject to all sorts of safety and health regulations. Assistants require bonding, insurance, and social security; your station-wagon may need commercial plates. And you'll have to look into the question of licenses and taxes. There's more to self-employment than finding twice as many customers.

A word of caution is also in order on pricing. For this type of enterprise to work out, you must set your prices carefully. A dollar an hour may be all right if all you want is some extra pocket money, but it's hardly a living wage. When self-employment is a full-time job, it's essential to charge enough so that once you're operating at capacity, you're earning a fair return. This must cover, not only your salary, but such expenses as telephone, advertising, car expenses, insurance, and a cash reserve for emergencies. You'll need time to get from one customer to another, and a break for lunch. You may want to provide yourself with health insurance. Figuring expenses is the critical factor in setting your prices at a workable level. If, after you take all these items into account, you can't arrive at a price people will pay, look for another type of work. Don't cut prices below the break-even point; you'll work yourself into bankruptcy.

Production

Helen's real passion is growing plants from cuttings; she started selling them when there was no room in the house for any more. She deals chiefly with supermarkets, who welcome them as a profitable, non-competitive line. Clem specializes in enamel-on-copper ashtrays, candy dishes, and the like. He started in a corner of the basement, but his designs proved so popular, he now rents loft space and has an assistant to help him. Donna began marketing her jewelry at sixteen, when she convinced buyers that only teen-agers could understand each other's tastes. Her instincts were right; the jewelry sold, and now she's well into a business of her own.

In these and other production enterprises, you're selling the *products* of your work. Often the business starts small; as demand increases, you expand the operation and hire others to take over the job of production. Clearly, in an operation like this, salesmanship is essential; no matter how superior your product, it won't do a thing for you until you line up some customers. If selling isn't your strong point, you might consider a partner to market your product while you concentrate on producing it better, faster, and more economically. Or persuade a salesman to add your items to the lines he already carries. The best choice is someone already dealing in related, but non-competitive goods.

Of course, we've been limiting ourselves to the very simplest of production enterprises. Other such fields include crafts, photography, small-scale printing, carpentry, light manufacturing, and home-made foods, clothing and novelties. These are the areas where risk and cash outlay are held to a minimum while you learn the ins and outs of the trade. For more serious production, the investment in rent, machinery, raw materials and inventory can run into hundreds of thousands of dollars. Let it wait until you're more of an entrepreneur.

Merchandising

Merchandising consists of buying products and reselling them at a profit. The sale may be made through door-to-door selling, vending machines, renting a shop, mail order or other channels. The cash investment can be considerable. In order to buy at a low price, you have to buy in quantity. This means you need a place to store the merchandise. It also involves laying out money which you won't get back until the merchandise is sold. There's a built-in gamble; you can never be sure how much you will sell, nor how long it will take. Merchandising calls for as much experience, investigation, calculation and planning as you can manage. It also requires all the advance information you can get; we'll have more to say about that later on.

DISTRIBUTORSHIP

One way to get into the merchandising business and minimize risk at the same time is *distributorship*. In an operation like this, you buy in bulk from a manufacturer or jobber, and resell to retail outlets. Sometimes your products go on the retailer's shelves. Sometimes they go into vending machines, which may belong, not to you, but to the company which placed them on location. Or they may go on racks in supermarkets, drug stores, or variety stores. You've probably seen racks like these and never given them a thought; they may hold toiletries, small housewares, stationery items, or inexpensive toys. But somebody has to keep those racks filled, find out which items sell best, test new items, and make sure the racks are varied and attractive enough to draw customers. That somebody is you—the distributor. The distributor may also track down more locations for additional racks, thereby increasing his outlets, volume, and profits. This kind of enterprise can start with little capital, and expand as far as your energy and imagination will take it. If you're interested, speak to your supermarket manager; he'll give you the names of some distributors working his store. And don't limit yourself to the items you've already seen on racks. Practically anything can be sold in this way, from sewing notions to imported giftware.

ROUTE SALES

A second way to get into merchandising is through *route sales*. Think of the ice cream truck coming down your street at the same time each day; the milkman, the bakery salesman. All of these are route salesmen. Some, like the milkman, aren't in business at all; they're simply employees of the company, working on salary and commission. But others are actually distributors. Of course, they use the company truck and trade-mark; but they buy the merchandise as independent merchants, resell it on the route and build up business in any way they can. In general, any product or service for which there is a recurrent daily or weekly need lends itself to this sales technique: pet foods, diaper service, laundry and dry cleaning, knives and scissors sharpening (both residential and industrial), snacks, dairy products, fresh fruits and vegetables. The catering truck bringing refreshments and lunch to industrial areas is another form of route sales. This kind of self-employment offers mobility, contact with people, and a great deal of freedom, both in developing your customers and in setting up your route. However, once you have it going, there's no freedom at all, because in route sales, dependability and regularity are the essence of the operation—being in the same place at the same time, day after day. In fact, some people make a business of acquiring a route, developing it, and then selling it, at a profit, to some less adventurous soul. If the field interests you, you can start as an employee and learn how it works and whether you can handle it. If all goes well, you can branch out for yourself.

FRANCHISES

Related to distributorship and route sales—although not limited to merchandising—are *franchises*. Basically, a franchise permits you to do business under the firm name of a large, well-known company. You get the benefit of the popular brand name, as well as guidance, promotional assistance, training, special recipes and formulas, and the advantages of bulk buying. Franchises have been particularly popular in snack bars and restaurants, rental services, cleaning stores, and clothing shops. Generally, a franchise requires a large outlay of capital. The chances are you won't be able to consider it unless you have financial backing and some kind of track record. Moreover, while franchises are basically an excellent business opportunity, there have been abuses. Before buying one, investigate it thoroughly through your bank or Better Business Bureau.

As we discussed the three types of business operation—service, production, and merchandising—it probably occurred to you that many enterprises straddle two of them, or even all three. For example, a restaurant serves, produces, *and* merchandises the food it sells. A newspaper route deals in both sales and service. Shoe repair is basically a service field, but the owner usually sells related supplies as well. So the three categories aren't meant to be hard-and-fast. Think of them primarily as a guide.

MANAGING YOUR BUSINESS

Common Reasons for Failure

So far, we've considered the qualities that make a businessman, and the types of business to choose from. Now we come to the most critical question of all: What makes a business succeed? Let's turn the question around a little. What makes a business fail?

Among experts in the field, there is almost unanimous agreement: the one overwhelming cause of business failure is poor management. Professor Frank Tucker of the Harvard Business School describes it as "the critical variable in small business success." Dun and Bradstreet, the well-known business firm, classified causes of business failure in 1965; the four leading causes were:

Cause	Percent
Incompetence	41.3%
Unbalanced Experience (not well rounded in sales, finance, purchasing and production)	21.4%
Lack of Managerial Experience	18.8%
Lack of Experience in the Line	9.9%

In short, these four causes—all of them related to management—accounted for over 90 percent of all failures.

Just what does a manager do? The job is so varied and far-reaching that a precise description is impossible. Speaking in more general terms, Louis L. Allen suggests: "The manager's job in a small business is first to create and then to direct a whole series of relationships between his company and its employees, suppliers, bankers, and customers."

This is a very tall order. It demands judgment, planning, versatility, resourcefulness, prudence and tact—just for a start! It requires sensitivity to employees, customers, social and economic changes. And all this is quite apart from the specific design, production and merchandising expertise needed for the business in question! The Dun and Bradstreet publication, *Patterns for Success in Managing a Business,* pinpoints 15 patterns of business success. These patterns are:

1. Gain Know-How
2. Start with Adequate Capital
3. Choose the Right Location
4. Have Skill at Buying
5. Control Working Capital
6. Have Sound Credit Management
7. Have the Right Draw (i.e., salary)
8. Have the Right Attitudes
9. Plan for Expansion
10. Recognize Limitations
11. Keep Adequate Records
12. Watch Balance Sheet—Not Just Profits
13. Desire to Learn
14. Be Willing to Take Advice
15. Stay Healthy

Yet even this impressive list mentions only the more objective requirements of a good manager. Louis Allen adds at least one more; a "feel" for the enterprise. "Every so often" he writes, "a situation comes along and one gets a reaction—a positive reaction—in his stomach. Trust these feelings; they are usually very reliable. An intuitive urge is an important ingredient in decision-making."

After poor management, the primary cause of business failure is insufficient capital. Capital is the technical name for the money you need to start and back up your business. Since it takes between four and six months for even the simplest business venture to start returning a modest income, you must have enough money to pay your expenses and sustain yourself for that length of time. And of course, it may take a good deal longer.

To appreciate the importance of capital, let's consider a very simple case: Jim, who wants to expand his lawn-mowing and grounds-maintenance activities to a full-time operation. Jim's first step is to calculate how much money he needs to give his venture a fighting chance. Since he'll be living at home, and his parents are willing to continue supporting him, his problems are smaller than most. Nonetheless, Jim would like to start paying his own way as soon as possible.

Jim begins by estimating his known monthly expenses as follows:

Salary	$400
Truck Payment	150
Insurance	40
Advertising	35
Telephone Service	25
Car Expenses	50
	$700
20% reserve	140
Monthly total	$840

This sounds like a formidable amount of money. It would be even larger, except that Jim already has the power mower, clippers, trimmers, and other equipment required for his work. Moreover, the only item he can really cut down is his salary. But even by cutting to the bone while living at home, he has irreducible expenses of over $400 a month—which, in a six-month period, comes to $2400.

How much is he earning during this time? He starts with ten customers who pay him $25 a month. At this rate he needs 34 customers to cover the monthly $840. (Of course, he could look for people who would order additional services and pay correspondingly more.) Jim is confident that he can build up his business at the rate of ten new customers a month. Meanwhile, however, he must make up the difference between his monthly expenses of $840 and his present income of $250. This difference amounts to $590 the first month, $340 the second (assuming he gets the ten customers as planned), and $90 the third—a total of $1020. But what about the possibility of some customers discontinuing the business—perhaps because they move, decide to do the work themselves, or find someone else to do it? Suppose only five customers make this decision in the entire three-month period. This cuts his income by, say $150. (The exact amount depends on when the customers leave.) So the capital needed to cover expenses goes up to $1170.

Now, this is a very simple case. There is no rent or inventory, equipment costs are minimal, and Jim continues to live at home. By contrast, the amount of capital required to start a modest fashion store is in the neighborhood of $45,000; a ski shop may call for as much as $50,000; even a boutique may need $20,000 or more. How to get this money will be considered a little later. Right now, the important idea is this: without financial backing, even a sound business venture doesn't stand a chance.

But even with adequate management and financing, businesses may fail. A small restaurant draws its trade from the factory across the street; the factory relocates, and the restaurant goes out of business. A very rainy season discourages shoppers; a sudden shift in fashion cuts the value of your merchandise in half; with a local water shortage, people give up extensive care of their lawns. Inflation, strikes, accidents, natural disasters—all have their effect on small business. You can't foresee everything; you simply anticipate what you can.

Increasing Your Chances of Success

Let's get back to the original question: What can you do to make your business succeed? You can proceed in at least three ways: gain experience, gather information and look into financing.

EXPERIENCE

The best way—perhaps the only way—to understand what makes a business tick is to become part of it. Even if you've been in the local snack shop or sportswear store a hundred times, you can't appreciate everything that's involved unless you've worked there. There are problems you never thought of: supplies, overstock, absenteeism, theft, bills to pay and bills to collect. Do you locate on a busy street at a high rent, or choose a cheaper spot a couple of blocks away? Do you hire that talkative boy with the bright ideas, or will he be too restless for routine production work? Do you pay the phone bill this month, or should you stall them and use the money to pick up some inventory at bargain prices? Do you allow teen-agers to have charge accounts because they're big spenders, or do you refuse because the teen-agers may never pay up? You think your new belt design is the best thing going; do you risk making up a few dozen in advance, or should you wait until the orders are in your pocket? The best way to answer questions like these is from experience—acquired, free of charge, while working for someone else.

If your goal is a business of your own, your first step is to get a job in the same type of business, or one as close to it as possible. But do more than just draw a paycheck. Actually immerse yourself in the place; familiarize yourself with all its problems. In Allen's words, get the "feel" of the business. Try every phase of the operation, no matter how menial; you may be doing them all when you're on your own. Watch your boss; with each decision he makes, ask yourself, "Why did he handle it this way? What was he thinking of? And how would I have done it?" Then see how things work out.

Get acquainted with suppliers, customers, co-workers. They can tell you what the competition is up to, and whether it's succeeding. If the firm subscribes to a trade journal, browse through it; you'll learn how other people are handling their problems. Let your employer know about your interest; for all you know, you may find yourself going into business with him. While there's no set rule, try for at least a year or two of experience before venturing into the field on your own.

INFORMATION

Self-employment touches upon so many areas, you can't possibly start off knowing them all. You'll need some background in law, accounting, psychology, merchandising, economics, design, financing, advertising, office work, personnel work, production and many more. Even if you can afford to hire experts, you'll need this information, if only to make sense of what they say. Where can you find it all?

The best place to start is the Small Business Administration, or SBA. This governmental agency exists for the express purpose of helping small business. The complete list of SBA offices, arranged by region, appears below. (For telephone numbers, check the directory; you'll find the Small Business Administration listed under "United States Government.")

SBA FIELD OFFICE ADDRESSES*

Boston	Massachusetts 02114, 150 Causeway St.
Holyoke	Massachusetts 01040, 326 Appleton St.
Augusta	Maine 04330, Federal Bldg., U.S. Post Office, 40 Western Ave.
Concord	New Hampshire 03301, 55 Pleasant St.
Hartford	Connecticut 06103, Federal Office Bldg., 450 Maine St.
Montpelier	Vermont 05601, Federal Bldg., 2nd Floor, 87 State St.
Providence	Rhode Island 02903, 702 Smith Bldg., 57 Eddy St.
New York	New York 10007, 26 Federal Plaza, Rm. 3930
Hato Rey	Puerto Rico 00919, 255 Ponce De Leon Ave.
Newark	New Jersey 07102, 970 Broad St., Rm. 1635
Syracuse	New York 13202, Hunter Plaza, Fayette & Salina Sts.
Buffalo	New York 14202, 111 W. Huron St.
Albany	New York 12207, 112 State St.
Rochester	New York 14604, 55 St. Paul St.
Philadelphia	Bala Cynwyd, Pennsylvania 19004, 1 Decker Sq.
Harrisburg	Pennsylvania 17108, 7–11 Market Sq.
Wilkes-Barre	Pennsylvania 18703, 34 S. Main St.
Baltimore	Towson, Maryland 21204, 7800 York Rd.
Wilmington	Delaware 19801, 6th and King Sts.
Clarksburg	West Virginia 26301, Lowndes Bank Bldg., 109 N. 3rd St.
Charleston	West Virginia 25301, Charleston National Bank, Suite 628
Pittsburgh	Pennsylvania 15222, Federal Bldg., 1000 Liberty Ave.
Richmond	Virginia 23240, Federal Bldg., 400 N. 8th St.
Washington	D.C. 20417, 1310 L. St., NW
Atlanta	Georgia 30309, 1401 Peachtree St., NE.
Birmingham	Alabama 35205, 908 S. 20th St.
Charlotte	North Carolina 28202, Addison Bldg., 222 S. Church St.
Columbia	South Carolina 29201, 1801 Assembly St.
Jackson	Mississippi 39205, Petroleum Bldg., Pascagoula and Amite Sts.
Gulfport	Mississippi 39501, 2500 14th St.
Jacksonville	Florida 32202, Federal Office Bldg., 400 Bay St.
Louisville	Kentucky 40202, Federal Office Bldg., 600 Federal Pl.
Miami	Florida 33130 Federal Bldg., 51 SW. 1st Ave.
Tampa	Florida 33602, Federal Bldg., 500 Zack St.

Nashville	Tennessee 37219, 500 Union St.
Knoxville	Tennessee 37902, 502 S. Gay St.
Memphis	Tennessee 38103, Federal Bldg., 167 N. Main St.

Chicago	Illinois 60604, Federal Office Bldg., 219 S. Dearborn St.
Springfield	Illinois 62701, 502 Monroe St.
Cleveland	Ohio 44199, 1240 E. 9th St.
Columbus	Ohio 43215, 34 N. High St.
Cincinnati	Ohio 45202, Federal Bldg., 550 Main St.
Detroit	Michigan 48226, 1249 Washington Blvd.
Marquette	Michigan 49855, 201 McClellan St.
Indianapolis	Indiana 46204, 36 S. Pennsylvania St.
Madison	Wisconson 53703, 122 W. Washington Ave.
Milwaukee	Wisconsin 53203, 735 W. Wisconsin Ave.
Eau Claire	Wisconsin 54701, 510 S. Barstow St.
Minneapolis	Minnesota 55402, 12 S. 6th St.

Dallas	Texas 75202, 1100 Commerce St.
Albuquerque	New Mexico 87101, 500 Gold Ave., SW.
Las Cruces	New Mexico 88001, 1015 El Paso Rd.
Houston	Texas 77002, 808 Travis St.
Little Rock	Arkansas 72201, 600 W. Capitol Ave.
Lubbock	Texas 79408, 1205 Texas Ave.
El Paso	Texas 79901, 109 N. Oregon St.
Lower Rio Grande Valley	Harlington, Texas 78550, 219 E. Jackson St.
Corpus Christi	Texas 78408, 3105 Leopard St.
Marshall	Texas 75670, 505 E. Travis St.
New Orleans	Louisiana 70113, 1001 Howard Ave.
Oklahoma City	Oklahoma 73102, 30 N. Hudson St.
San Antonio	Texas 78205, 301 Broadway

Kansas City	Missouri 64106, 911 Walnut St.
Des Moines	Iowa 50309, New Federal Bldg., 210 Walnut St.
Omaha	Nebraska 68102, Federal Bldg., 215 N. 17th St.
St. Louis	Missouri 63101, Federal Bldg., 210 N. 12th St.
Wichita	Kansas 67202, 120 S. Market St.

Denver	Colorado 80202, 721 19th St.
Casper	Wyoming 82601, 100 E. B St.
Fargo	North Dakota 58102, 653 2nd Ave., N.
Helena	Montana 59601, Power Block Bldg., Main & 6th Ave.
Salt Lake City	Utah 84111, Federal Bldg., 125 S. State St.
Sioux Falls	South Dakota 57102, National Bank Bldg., 8th and Main Ave.
Rapid City	South Dakota 57701, 627 St. Joe St.

San Francisco	California 94102, Federal Bldg., 450 Golden Gate Ave.
Fresno	California 93721, Federal Bldg., 1130 O St.
Honolulu	Hawaii 96813, 1149 Bethel St.
Agana	Guam 96910, Ada Plaza Center Bldg.
Los Angeles	California 90014, 849 S. Broadway
Las Vegas	Nevada 89101, 300 Las Vegas Blvd., S.
Phoenix	Arizona 85004, 122 N. Central Ave.
San Diego	California 92101, 110 W. C St.

| Seattle | Washington 98104, 710 2nd Ave. |
| Anchorage | Alaska 99501, 1016 W. 6th St. |

Fairbanks	Alaska 99701, 503 3rd Ave.
Boise	Idaho 83701, 216 N. 8th St.
Portland	Oregon 97205, 921 SW. Washington St.
Spokane	Washington 99210, Courthouse Bldg., Rm. 651

*Taken from SBA Publication 115-A

What can the SBA do for you? To begin, it offers over 150 free booklets on all aspects of small business operation. These booklets are brief, clear, and to the point. Typical titles include:

How Trade Associations Help Small Business
How to Analyze Your Own Business
The ABC's of Borrowing
Delegating Work and Responsibility
What is the Best Selling Price?
Checklist for Going Into Business
Finding and Hiring the Right Employees
Legal Services for Small Retail and Service Firms
Building Good Customer Relations
Six Methods for Success in a Small Store
Building Customer Confidence in Your Service Shop
Can You Afford Delivery Service?

In addition, there are bibliographies on several dozen types of business, including restaurants, handicraft stores, mail order, bookstores, job printing, hobby shops, apparel and accessory stores, pet shops and florists. To get the complete list of titles, send a postcard to your nearest field office asking for SBA 115-A, *Free Management Assistance Publications*. Once you have the list, all you need do is check off the titles you want, and mail it back.

The SBA also offers about 50 booklets for sale. These are more detailed and elaborate than the free ones. Typical titles are:

Human Relations in Small Business
Cost Accounting for Small Manufacturers
Handbook of Small Business Finance
Guides for Profit Planning
Selecting Advertising Media

Specialized booklets are offered in a number of areas, including service stations, bookkeeping service, restaurant, dry cleaning business, automatic vending machines, carwash, swap shop, shoe repair service, retail camera shop, pet shop, retail music shop and small, drive-in restaurant. Prices begin at thirty cents, and only four titles cost more than a dollar. Again, to get the complete list of booklets, write your local SBA field office; ask for SBA 115-B, *For-Sale Booklets*. When the list arrives, mark your choices as before, but this time mail the order, together with check or money order, not to the field office, but to the Superintendent of Documents, Government Printing Office, Washington, D.C. 20402. (Your payment should be made out to the Superintendent of Documents.) Allow a few weeks for delivery. With next to no trouble, and at minimum cost, you'll have an entire library of first-rate information on running your own business.

But the SBA does more than publish booklets. It holds regular workshops and film sessions on aspects of small business management. It makes loans, either on its own or in conjunction with your local bank. It provides consultants with whom you can talk over your ideas. The sole purpose of the SBA is to help people like you; take advantage of what it has to offer.

The SBA is hardly your only source of information. Many communities offer free or inexpensive courses in various aspects of business operation, including such subjects as bookkeeping, psychology, merchandising techniques and advertising. Typical are courses like "Law for the Small Businessman" or "Making Your Own Displays." Sign up for such courses if possible. You'll probably find the content so relevant to your own plans and goals, you'll be a better student than you ever were.

Of course, you'll also want to try your own library. There are dozens of books to help you; check the card catalogue under "Small Business" and "Management." While some of the books may be too technical, you'll find others that are just right. Talk over your needs with the librarian; she may have a file of clippings and pamphlets on the subject of self-employment. And while you're there, get the name of the appropriate trade organization; find out how they can help you.

Get acquainted with your local commercial bank. They can tell you what to expect in the way of competition, as well as whether the community can support a business like yours. For example, it takes a population of only 500 to support a small grocery store (assuming there are no supermarkets nearby), but 7,000 to support a florist, and 60,000 to support a photographic supply store. Visit your Chamber of Commerce; ask whether in your community, as in many others, local businessmen have formed a volunteer group to advise beginners. Talk to other people in your field, employees as well as businessmen. In time, you'll find you've built up an extensive background of information and know-how.

FINANCING

Capital was mentioned earlier in this chapter. It's needed to cover the expenses of starting a business, to maintain it until the business is self-supporting, to finance later expansion, or to compensate for a temporary drop in profits. Where can the money come from?

Savings

This is among the most common ways to finance a new business. You get a job, earn a salary, and put away what you can. There are several good reasons for building up your savings account. For one, as you're accumulating money, you're also accumulating experience; once you start the business, you'll have a much greater chance of success. For another, as the bank sees it, your savings demonstrate your own steadiness and motivation; if you put up part of the investment, they may be willing to lend you the rest. Finally, you may have no alternative; as a newcomer, anxious to start your own business, you may find loans pretty hard to come by.

Personal Loans

You could try to borrow the money from family or friends. However, this may put a severe strain on personal relations. You could find yourself in the awkward position of having accepted the savings of those closest to you, and reduced these savings to nothing. Before you solicit money from family and friends, make sure you really want the responsibility. In any case, these funds must still be repaid, often with interest, so your monthly expenses will be increased by the amount of repayment.

Bank Loans

Your local bank, especially one at which you have maintained an account, may be willing to lend you the money. You begin by approaching one of their staff with a plan worked out in detail. The plan should consider initial expenses, operating expenses and projected income. It should indicate how you expect to build up the business. It might also mention your own business qualifications. Finally, the plan should indicate when you expect to start repaying the loan, and how fast.

You'll also need character references, preferably from people who have had business or financial dealings with you. These could include school faculty who can vouch for your reliability, current customers (if any), former employers, and firms from whom you made major purchases, such as a car or stereo. Don't short-cut this part of your application; for many bankers, the character of the borrower is the one most important consideration.

The bank may decide to give you a loan, or it may not. It may request a co-signer—a responsible party who will guarantee repayment in case you default. Or it may be willing to participate in a loan with the Small Business Administration. This means that the SBA itself will guarantee the loan, if the bank is willing to make it.

Small Business Administration

While the SBA prefers to co-operate with local banks, it does, upon accasion, make loans of its own. There are many legal restrictions upon such loans, and they may be even harder to get than bank loans. However, if you're planning a business of your own, you should contact the SBA in any case. They can provide the statistics you need, the tax information, the

EXHIBIT 12-1

Factors in Starting Your Own Business

I. What Does a Small Business Entail?
   A. Responsibilities
      1. Having your own ideas
      2. Carrying out your ideas
      3. Extended working day
      4. Temporarily reduced income
      5. Ties up money
      6. "Headaches"
      7. Loss of fringe benefits
   B. Advantages
      1. You yourself benefit from your effort and ability
      2. Freedom to make decisions and carry them out

II. Traits of the Good Businessman
   A. General Qualities
      1. Autonomy
      2. Maturity
      3. Values emphasizing money and status
   B. Specific Traits
      1. Self-discipline
      2. Responsibility
      3. Enthusiasm
      4. Stability
      5. Sociability
      6. Organization
      7. Attention to financial detail
      8. Good health

III. Types of Business
   A. Service
   B. Production
   C. Merchandising
      1. Distributorships
      2. Route sales
      3. Franchises

IV. What Makes a Business Fail?
   A. Poor Management
      1. Incompetence
      2. Unbalanced experience
      3. Lack of managerial experience
      4. Lack of experience in the line
   B. Inadequate Financing
   C. Unavoidable External Events

V. What Makes a Business Succeed?
   A. Experience
   B. Information (from SBA, courses, books, Chamber of Commerce, bank, trade organizations, people in field)
   C. Financing (from savings, personal loans, bank loans, SBA loans)

simple bookkeeping formats for your particular kind of operation. The advice they offer may be the decisive factor in your success or failure. Think of the SBA as your basic resource for information and guidance; their money-lending authority is just an extra added attraction.

Starting a business involves a host of different considerations; some of them are listed in Exhibit 12–1 on page 165. They touch upon you, your background, your ideas, your community. The venture is neither simple nor easy; Louis Allen warns us that "starting and operating a small business is at once exhausting, exasperating, sometimes discouraging, always long hard work." But he goes on to say: "It is also the most unbelievably satisfying work a man can undertake. That is why there are so many small businesses in our country."

13

Volunteer Work

The first few times Ruth wheeled a patient to the auditorium, she was sure she'd lose control and the chair would go careening down the ramp. But now she never gives it a thought.

"I'm sorry I can't stay for the movie," she explains. "I have to be home for dinner. But I'll be back on Friday; you can tell me all about it."

Mrs. Draper nods. At 78, her hearing isn't what it used to be. But she knows she can count on Ruth; she settles back comfortably in her chair.

Carefully, David applies glue to the spine of the book he's rebinding. Fixing books for the museum is a far cry from his real interests—primitive art—but it does get him behind the scenes and into the museum's reference library. Already, he's looked into more art books than he knew existed. With luck, he'll get to meet the curator—and who knows what may open up next year?

Mrs. Martinez and the city social worker sit at opposite sides of the desk, but Evaline remains standing. It gives her a better grip on things.

"Look, mister," she says, "the upstairs tenant left his sink running, and this lady's mattress was soaked. Of course she threw it out; it was stinking up the whole house! You've got to get her a new one and you know it, so stop giving us a hard time!"

Mrs. Martinez looks up in amazement. Even if she doesn't understand all the words, there's no mistaking the tone of Evaline's voice. As part of a neighborhood youth group, Evaline's one concern is to protect the interests of the Spanish-speaking residents. Before she leaves, she'll have not only a voucher for a new mattress, but something extra to replace the blankets as well.

Ruth, David, Evaline—they're all working and working hard. They come early and stay late; they're deeply involved in what they do. But not one is getting paid. They're working as volunteers.

167

Florence Nightingale introduced non-sectarian volunteering more than a century ago, when she proposed that "there exists a certain proportion of gentlewomen" who might contribute their services as hospital nurses. Today volunteering is no longer limited to "gentlewomen" or to hospitals. An estimated forty million Americans perform some sort of volunteer work every year. They range from sub-teens, taking over from parents on Election Day, to retired businessmen, advising newcomers how to run businesses.

Volunteer opportunities can absorb as much time as you care to give them, from once a year to all day, every day, week after week. You can work at home or halfway around the world. You can utilize every skill you possess, from making phone calls to high-level management; if you're short on skills, you'll be trained. In one week, the Voluntary Action Center of New York City listed over 200 openings; a sample is given in Exhibit 13–1 on pages 169 and 170.

WHY PEOPLE VOLUNTEER

Why do millions of people contribute their time to working without pay? We can answer this question with another one: Why—apart from money —do people work in general? At least four factors have been mentioned: satisfaction, participation, sociability, and status.

Preeminently, volunteering provides the satisfaction of doing vital work that would not otherwise get done. When a group of pre-schoolers rocks with laughter at the story you're reading them; when an elderly, isolated man gratefully answers your regular morning call; when you run a foreign-language film so a class of pregnant women can learn to care for their babies and themselves—at such times you don't need a paycheck to demonstrate the importance of your work. Again and again, volunteers emphasize the immediate, intangible reward that comes of doing humane, necessary work.

But such satisfaction demands personal involvement. Eva Rainman and Ronald Lippett, authors of *The Volunteer Community,* suggest that participation is part of the democratic ideal. We grow up believing that improvement is possible, that the world can be bettered, and that such betterment can come about through the contributions of "ordinary" people, working together. Watching from the sidelines is not enough. Writing a check, however large, is not enough. What the volunteer offers is himself —his time, his warmth, his concern. These qualities cannot be mass-produced or computerized. They must be given freely, as a tribute to our common humanity.

As for the social aspects of volunteer work, they depend entirely on you and on the work you choose. If you're in a school, hospital or community

EXHIBIT 13-1

Typical Opportunities in Volunteer Work

Education:

Tutoring in: remedial reading; English as a second language; commercial subjects; black, Puerto Rican, and Chinese history; spelling; math; accounting; biology; chemistry; social studies.

Classroom assistant

Coordinator of above programs

(Note: These assignments are carried out in settlement houses, community centers, senior citizens' center, housing projects, schools, institutions, and hospitals.)

Arts:

Teaching: photography; photo oil coloring; dancing; arts and crafts; sewing; knitting; macramé; pattern cutting; crocheting.

Designing visual aids for police department training program

Developing arts projects for children and the aged

Developing an arts and crafts program for hospital patients

With Senior Citizens:

Providing information on reduced fare program

Helping with telephone calls to isolated elderly people

Assisting with: feeding elderly, letter-writing, shopping, recreation program in old people's home (bingo, trips, etc.)

Carrying meals from central kitchen to elderly people living alone

Being an advocate for the elderly—helping them receive full benefits from public and private resources

In Hospitals:

Assisting in: occupational therapy; pharmacy packaging area; gift shop; mail room; feeding patients; medical records department; x-ray department; central supply room; library.

Making and delivering surgical supplies

Being a "big brother" to child in outpatient psychiatric department

Operating book cart

Visiting sick, lonely people undergoing alcoholic detoxification

Conducting screenings for vision and hearing defects

Helping plan and carry out holiday programs

Tutoring sick patients

Supervising, entertaining children; preparing them for bed

With Physically Handicapped:

Being a driver or guide

Reading to blind students

Being a scorekeeper for blind bowlers

Training perceptual and motor skills

Escorting residents to job interviews

Job solicitation for residents, including follow-up

Helping retarded children with such skills as walking, talking

Working in sports

Physical therapy for severely handicapped children

Instruction and tutoring in all areas

EXHIBIT 13-1 (Continued)

Recreation:
    Teaching: grooming; carpentry; cooking; sewing, knitting, woodworking; dress design
    Coaching: volley ball; boxing; weight lifting; basketball; track; karate; tennis; badminton
    Counseling at day camp
    Guiding (for overseas visitors, museum exhibits, zoos)
    Training cheerleaders
    Helping teen-agers establish a social club

Ecology:
    Setting up recycling centers for glass, paper, metals
    Creating "vest pocket" parks in empty lots

Business Activities:
    Teaching money management
    Offering career orientation programs for students
    Developing a food co-operative
    Offering employment referral, job development, job solicitation
    Collecting and giving away scraps and excess unwanted material
    Advising and consulting with small minority businessmen
    Providing legal resources for senior citizens, consumer groups, immigrants

In Addiction Services:
    Acting as helper in group encounter sessions (recording sessions or doing follow-up work with individual problems)
    Compiling statistical data on rehabilitation patients
    Representing addicts who have been arrested
    Researching housing resources
    Assisting in storefront narcotics program
    Taking young addicts to parks and on excursions
    Assisting in planning and direction of youth programs

center, you'll make new friends you would never have met otherwise—people different in age, background, language, customs. At the same time, you'll be meeting other volunteers; many agencies sponsor meetings and get-togethers where volunteers can share experiences and voice common concerns. If, on the other hand, sociability plays only a small part in your reasons for volunteering, you're free to come in, do your job, and leave. It's up to you.

Status is more of an issue with older, seasoned volunteers than with newcomers. However, even teen-agers report that their volunteer work commands respect everywhere they go, and opens doors that would otherwise be quite firmly closed.

HIGH SCHOOL STUDENTS AS VOLUNTEERS

Moreover, if you're a high school student, you may have some special reasons for considering volunteer work:

- If you're interested in a field like social service, teaching, or library work, volunteering provides a taste of the work environment and its demands upon you. Lisa, for example, thought she wanted to teach, but in her daydreams teaching meant a respectful, adoring class, quiet and eager to learn. Volunteering as a second-grade teacher's aid soon taught her that nothing could be further from the truth. Her few months in the classroom saved years of preparation for a field which might never have worked out. On the other hand, had she chosen to remain in teaching, it would have been with a clear sense of what she could expect.

- If you haven't decided on what you want to do, volunteering offers a worthwhile use of your time while you continue the search. You may even find your work so absorbing, you'll adopt it as a career.

- If you're short on experience and marketable skills, volunteering can provide both. The days are gone when volunteering meant rolling bandages or crocheting booties. Volunteer work is first of all work, as demanding and practical as anything you could be doing for money. Jimmy gave two afternoons a week to the hospital gift shop, and learned a half-dozen skills, including gift-wrapping, dealing with customers, making change and taking inventory. Now his new-found abilities are paying off; not only has he been hired by one of the city's largest stores, but he's been earmarked for special managerial training. Laura ran a volunteer guitar class, worked out some effective teaching techniques, and now has a half-dozen private pupils—in addition to teaching the class. Denise, who was good with animals, gained experience as a volunteer at the local animal shelter; now she's setting up her own pet-sitting service.

- Volunteering may lead to paid work. Denise got her first pet-sitting customers through recommendations from other volunteers. Harold, who started as a library volunteer when he was fifteen, tried his hand at every aspect of the operation, from checking briefcases to helping order books. When funds became available for another paid assistant, Harold was the natural choice—not because he had "connections," but because he had shown what he could do. Many other volunteers have found that supervisors or colleagues provide them with job leads—again, not as a thank-you, but because they have proved their worth. A volunteer may be hired as a vacation replacement, or to help clear up a backlog of work. Sometimes the volunteer's contribution becomes so valuable that it's turned into a full-time, paid job, with the volunteer getting preference.

- If you want to see another part of the country or of the world, volunteering may provide the opportunity. Admittedly, the number of openings is small, and the volunteer is usually expected to provide his own transportation and pocket money. However, the possibility should not be ruled out.

On the other hand, let's face it: volunteer work means working without pay. Most of us can manage a couple of hours a week, but when we consider volunteering as an alternative to college, we're thinking of a more serious commitment: perhaps half-time or better. Not everyone can afford this. Moreover, while some parents are willing to go on supporting their unpaid sons and daughters, others dismiss volunteer work as a mere stalling operation (ignoring the fact that college may be more of the same, and at far greater cost!). Many authorities agree that for the undecided teen-ager, volunteer work may be more of an eye-opener than anything else he could be doing, paid or unpaid. But each household must deal with the question for itself. Exhibit 13-2 summarizes the qualities we've been talking about If you're interested in volunteer work, see how many apply to you.

EXHIBIT 13-2

Volunteer Work May Make Some Sense For You If:

- You can afford to contribute a substantial amount of your time without pay.
- You're not sure of what you want to do, but would like to use your time meanwhile in a significant and productive way.

or

- You know exacly what you want to do, and it calls for a specific volunteer commitment.
- You're interested in a field like teaching, social work, or health, and want a better understanding of what it's like.
- You need to acquire work skills, experience, and contacts.
- You want to meet new people, preferably outside your usual social circle.
- You're interested in living in a new community.

WHAT TO EXPECT

What can you, as a volunteer, expect of your assignment, and what in turn can be expected of you? You can get some idea by stopping at your public library and browsing through their material on volunteering. But the one most important fact to keep in mind is that volunteer work is a job like any other. As in paid work, you're expected to be suitably dressed, courteous and reasonably easy to get along with. You come to work regularly and on time. (This is especially critical if you work with the disadvantaged or ill; the eight-year-old who's been looking forward to your visit all week can't understand that since you don't get paid anyway, you decided to take the afternoon off.) As a volunteer, you'll probably report to a supervisor who will hold you accountable for the quality of your work; if you don't quite fill the bill, you may be offered a more suitable assignment.

On the other hand, the volunteer, like any employee, has the right to choose his job in terms of his own interests, temperament and skills. If you're terrified of insects, don't volunteer for farm work; if you honestly don't hit it off with kids, don't force yourself to become a tutor. Obviously, your own inclinations must be balanced against the areas of greatest need. However, the range of volunteer work is so great that whatever your interests, you can put them to use.

Once on the job, you should be taught about your organization: its history, methods and goals. Moreover, as your own experience and insight grow, you have the right to expect more responsible work. Douglas K. Kinsey, president of the National Center for Voluntary Action, has written: "Freedom of movement within the volunteer world is essential. Mobility from service to administrative positions is necessary because the first helps discover problems and the second helps solve them." And Judge Mary Kohler, director of the National Commission on Resources for Youth, notes: "These kids have imagination. They have insight. They have more ability to size up a situation and decide what to do about it than most adults seem to recognize." What this means to you as a volunteer is that you should feel free to voice your observations and suggestions. If your ideas seem to be discouraged (possibly by the professionals you work with), talk it over with someone in the organization. Maybe your proposals are too sweeping, too vague—or just too expensive. Maybe they've already been tried, without success. You have the right to find out.

As in paid work, give your volunteer assignment a fair trial; Winifred Brown of the New York City Voluntary Action Center suggests six months to a year. In any case, try to see your project through; only in this way will you fully appreciate its purpose and design. If, after all this, you feel your job is a dead end, look for something else. There's no reason to stagnate in volunteer work, just because you're contributing your time.

On some jobs, incidental expenses—travel, phone calls, lunches and the like—may add up to a sizable amount. Many agencies are prepared to reimburse their volunteers for such expenses. If it makes a difference to you, raise the question at your first interview.

FINDING THE RIGHT VOLUNTEER JOB

How can a new teen-age volunteer find a suitable job? While government programs like VISTA and the Peace Corps have received a great deal of publicity, the fact is that most opportunities occur in private agencies. So let's consider these first.

If you're already interested in a specific type of work—perhaps with a hospital, school or arts center—by all means go directly to the institution involved. Remember, you'll be going to a job interview like any other;

you'll want to dress appropriately, come on time, and observe all the courtesies that apply to job-hunting anywhere. (See Chapter 8.) If a volunteer program is already in operation, they'll probably be delighted to have you. If not, you might consider starting one; there's more on this subject later on.

However, if you're not sure of what you want, you have everything to gain by contacting an established volunteer agency. Unless you've made a career of volunteer work, you probably have only the barest glimmering of its scope and extent. The list given in Exhibit 13–1 (pages 169 and 170) could easily be expanded to ten times its length, and still not tell the whole story. Moreover, many volunteer opportunities are surprisingly specialized and sophisticated. The person who wants to be a lawyer can work in a law office; the would-be actress performs in street plays; the kid who's a nut for accoustics would be welcomed by Recording for the Blind. The likelihood that you could think of such possibilities on your own, much less find them, is remote. So it's not surprising that organizations have arisen to match volunteers and jobs. A good volunteer agency is like a good employment agency. A professional talks to you, pinpoints your interests, strengths and weaknesses, and usually comes up with something far more satisfying than anything you could have found for yourself.

Probably the leading volunteer agency today is the National Center for Voluntary Action. Based in Washington, D.C., it has over 175 Voluntary Action Centers throughout the country. These centers maintain files on hundreds of different volunteer programs, including the location, purpose, whom to contact, and a brief description of the program's operation and accomplishments. If you have any trouble locating the center nearest you —or, for that matter, if you have any other questions about volunteer work—you can write to the central office:

> The National Center for Voluntary Action
> 1735 I Street, NW
> Washington, D.C. 20006

Another national resource is the Department of Health, Education and Welfare; many of the programs administered by this agency are required by law to include community representation. Find the address of the nearest HEW office in your telephone directory (listed under "United States Government") or write to:

> Office of Youth and Student Affairs
> Department of Health, Education and Welfare
> Washington, D.C. 20001

Other organizations, while nationwide, direct themselves to more specific interests. A few are listed below.

Youth Organizations United, Inc. (YOU)
912 6th St., NW
Washington, D.C. 20001

(works primarily with ghetto and inner-city groups)

B'Nai B'Rith Youth Organization
Harvey Berk
1640 Rhode Island Ave., NW
Washington, D.C. 20036

(serves teen-age Jewish youth who want to work with other youth and community programs; emphasis on community service)

Youth Citizenship Fund (YCF)
2317 M St., NW
Washington, D.C. 20036

(supports functions pertaining to community affairs, including voter registration drives)

Southern Christian Leadership Conference
334 Auburn Ave.
Atlanta, Ga. 30303

(works with young people in the deep South, primarily young blacks, in matters of civil rights, community service, etc.)

National Information Center on Volunteerism, Inc.
717 Colorado Bldg.
Boulder, Colo. 80302

(concerned with volunteering related to court and other criminal justice procedures)

If these channels are not convenient, you can turn directly to the resources in your own town. These include such agencies as:

YM/YWCA, YM/YWHA
Churches (not necessarily your own; the need for volunteers may be greater elsewhere in the community)
Community Action Programs

Scout groups
Red Cross
Future Homemakers of America
Federation of Jewish Philanthropies

Some of these agencies may be more active in volunteering than others. Make inquiries where you live; it won't take you long to discover where the leadership lies.

Finally, there are the actual institutions that use the volunteers. These include:

Community centers
Hospitals
Schools (apply through the local school board or Board of Education)
Museums
Libraries
Police Department

Fire Department
Drug Abuse Prevention agencies
Anti-pollution organizations
Orphanages
Homes for the elderly
Centers for the handicapped

Of course, applying to one of these suggests that you've already pinpointed your type of work. This is fine if you've looked into the alternatives (or if you're so carried away by your choice that you don't care about anything else). In any case, a large, modern hospital or school may use volunteers in a dozen or more areas. Thus, a major rehabilitation center uses volunteers in all of the following:

Clerical Services	Art Department
Gift and Coffee Shop	Therapeutic Recreation
Admission Staff	Continued Therapy
Nursing Service	Social Service
Occupational Therapy	Vocational Rehabilitation
Physical Therapy	Placement

The volunteer office of such an institution can screen and direct you almost as effectively as a more broad-based agency—although whatever your assignment, it will, of course, be within the institution.

TRAVEL AND VOLUNTEER WORK

All of the above channels will direct you to volunteer work in your own community. What if you want to try another part of the country, or of the world? In that case opportunities may be far more limited, and standards higher. Often, such openings call for adults with specific skills. Expenses may also be a problem; even if room and board are provided, you are usually expected to pay your own fare. If academic credit is offered, there may be tuition charges as well. However, there are exceptions; by hunting around, you may find a particular, problem-free program that's exactly right for you. Begin by studying the booklet, *Invest Yourself*; you can order it for one dollar ($1.25 if you want it sent by first class mail) from:

> The Commission on Voluntary Service & Action
> 475 Riverside Dr., Rm. 665
> New York, N.Y. 10027

This publication lists some 26,000 specific openings in several hundred different projects all over the world. It fills you in on what the project does; how many volunteers are needed, and where; duration; costs; and how to get more information. Another, less extensive publication, the *International Directory for Youth Internships,* lists several hundred intern or volunteer positions related directly to work with the U.N. system here and abroad. You can get a free copy by writing to:

> International Directory for Youth Internships
> Marty Abraham
> c/o U.S. Committee for UNICEF
> 331 E. 38th St.
> New York, N.Y. 10016

Finally, information on overseas projects sponsored by UNESCO can be obtained from:

> The Coordinating Committee for International
>   Voluntary Service
> UNESCO—1 rue Miollis
> Paris 15e, France

STARTING YOUR OWN PROJECT

So far, we've assumed that you want to join in with some existing volunteer group. But what if you have your own ideas, and want to start a new service? In that case, you're in good company. A group of Philadelphia teen-agers decided that the health education in their schools was unresponsive to their needs; the result was a volunteer project using puppet shows and plays which has already reached over 5,000 schoolchildren. The Handicapables, a California organization for the physically handicapped, was founded single-handed by Nadine Calligiuri, herself a victim of cerebral palsy. Dr. Ivan Scheier was worried about the rehabilitation of juvenile offenders; out of his concern grew the National Information Center on Volunteerism, headquartered in Boulder, Colorado, and concerned specifically with volunteering in relation to courts and criminal justice. Your ideas may be just as valuable as these. To start carrying them out, you'll want to move in two directions.

First, try to interest others in your community. No matter how sound your proposals, you'll need all the help you can get in implementing them.

Meanwhile, benefit from others' experienced by contacting either—or both—of the following organizations.

> Clearinghouse, National Center for Voluntary Action
> 1735 I Street, NW
> Washington, D.C. 20006

Tell them what you have in mind, and ask for specific examples of similar programs involving young volunteers. You might also request their publication, *Volunteer Ideas for Youth,* which gives case histories of ongoing projects, publications lists, resource groups, etc., oriented to high school youth. Single copies are free.

> National Commission on Resources for Youth, Inc.
> 36 W. 44th St.
> New York, N.Y. 10036

This organization collects and distributes information on innovative programs in which youth assume rewarding and responsible social roles. It develops model youth participation programs and provides free how-to-do-it materials in print, on film, and on videotapes. It has on file descriptions of some 800 programs, and is gathering new ones every day. If you want information on a program or type of program, write to them; make your inquiry as specific as possible.

Either of these groups would be delighted to hear from you, and can provide valuable guidance and information. Until you hear from them, don't publicize your own idea too widely; you may want to modify it in

EXHIBIT 13-3
Channels for Finding Private Volunteer Work

I. Within the Community
  A. General National Organizations
    1. The National Center for Voluntary Action
    2. Voluntary Action Centers (175, throughout U.S.)
    3. Department of Health, Education and Welfare
  B. Specialized National Organizations: Youth Organizations United, B'nai B'rith, etc.
  C. Local Agencies: YMCA, YMHA, YWCA, YWHA, churches, community action programs, scout groups, Red Cross, etc.
  D. Specific institutions using volunteers: community centers, hospitals, museums, police and fire departments, schools, etc.

II. Outside the Community
  A. The Commission on Voluntary Service and Action (Order *Invest Yourself;* one dollar)
  B. *International Directory for Youth Internships* (Order the *International Directory for Youth Internships;* free)
  C. The Coordinating Committee for International Voluntary Service

III. Starting Your Own Program
  A. Find Support in Your Own Community
  B. Write to:
    1. Clearinghouse, National Center for Voluntary Action (Describe your own idea; ask for related material. Also, order *Volunteer Ideas for Youth;* free)
    2. National Commission on Resources for Youth, Inc. (Describe your own idea; ask for free material on related projects)
    3. Order the periodical, *Synergist;* free.

light of their recommendations. And keep them posted as you progress, so others can learn from what you do.

You may also be interested in the free periodical, *Synergist.* This publication, which appears three times a year, highlights student volunteer programs, announces related national events, offers free resources, and presents the thinking of knowledgeable persons in the field. You can get it from:

> National Student Volunteer Program, ACTION
> 806 Connecticut Ave., NW
> Washington, D.C. 20525

The suggestions discussed in this chapter are summarized in Exhibit 13–3 above.

FEDERAL VOLUNTEER PROGRAMS

If opportunities abound in private volunteer work, just the opposite is true of federally sponsored programs. The Peace Corps, which requires two years of service overseas, was once a haven for idealistic young people. Today it concentrates on teachers, engineers, technicians and certain other classes of professionals. Liberal arts graduates are considered, but they should have experience in such areas as agriculture, health, informal education or mechanics. Younger volunteers are not accepted at all.

Another government agency, Volunteers in Service to America (VISTA for short), places less emphasis on degrees. However, the younger applicant should still offer some college, along with experience in community-involved work. A teen-ager fresh out of high school might have a chance here—a very slim chance!—but he would have to be uncommonly mature or skilled, and present a strong background in community service. If all this applies to you, you'll probably be snapped up by a private agency with much less trouble.

A third federal program, the National Student Volunteer Program, is limited to college students.

All these programs are handled by a single government agency, ACTION. For more information, contact your regional ACTION director, *not* the Washington office. You can get his address and phone by calling this toll-free number: 800-424-8560.

This is the situation right now. It may very well change. Lately, there's been a growing interest in federally sponsored, teen-age public service programs. The report, *Youth: Transition to Adulthood* (previously discussed in Chapter 3) attaches great importance to such programs, and recommends that they be made available to anyone from 16 to 24. If you share this point of view, take some action yourself; write to your Congressman, and urge your friends to do the same.

Meanwhile, however, don't pass up the opportunities that exist today. With so much to choose from, you're sure to find what you want.

14

The Armed Forces

Somewhere near the back of the typical Army brochure, you'll probably find the following words: "Note: Information in this publication is subject to change. See your nearest Army Representative for the latest information." The same applies to the content of this chapter. It's given only as a suggestion and guide. In all branches of the Armed Forces, practices and procedures are subject to change without notice. Such changes are usually administrative and you aren't likely to know about them unless you find out on your own. Before you decide to enlist in the Armed Forces, talk to a representative; make sure the features which originally attracted you still apply.

If you're interested in the Armed Forces, begin by erasing from your mind all those funny television shows and movies you've ever seen. The Army is not a glorified summer camp with oversized kids playing tricks on their counsellors. It is not a continuous comedy of errors where recruits concentrate on outwitting their sergeants. The branches of the Armed Forces—Army, Navy, Air Force, Marines and Coast Guard—are very serious organizations. They aren't playing games. Their primary job is the military defense of the United States, and it's not a laughing matter. Today's members of the Armed Forces are well aware of this. As a group, they're well-trained, serious men and women with clearly defined objectives and goals. Some are using their enlistments to explore themselves and the world before deciding on long-range goals. Others are serving a single hitch during which they will learn a lifelong technical skill. Some are planning a career in the Armed Forces, leading to early, well-paying retirement. A few are using their service time to earn a college degree with no financial concern. And many are relishing the opportunity to live away from their families, in a new part of the world, among a greater variety of people than they ever thought possible. All are to some extent exchanging their personal liberty for the advantages of the service, and a good number think it's worth it.

Still, the fact remains that virtually the entire thrust of the Armed Forces is toward the military defense of the country. In the event of war, it mobilizes the most modern resources of every sort for the one purpose of fighting the enemy. Some of the most advanced research and development in science, medicine and technology is taking place in the military establishment, but there's a reason: the results are essential for national defense. To the young person who can accept this situation, both ideologically and practically, the Armed Forces offer unequalled advantages. Here are some of them.

ADVANTAGES

Excellent Pay

At present, starting pay for an enlisted man or woman is over $300 a month, plus free living quarters, meals, uniforms, medical and dental care, and athletic and social activities. This is easily worth $600 a month or more—a respectable salary for a beginner in any field! Moreover, the recruit receives all this without ever having to worry about such problems as locating a place to live, preparing meals, having utilities installed, and the like. Financially and practically, the mechanics of daily living are greatly simplified.

Excellent Training

The Armed Forces is known for the calibre of its training. In some mechanical and technical fields, this may take the form of on-the-job apprenticeships; elsewhere, it may involve highly developed programs using the most modern audio-visual and classroom techniques. Many of the training programs developed by the Armed Forces have been adopted by public and private vocational schools as the most effective way known to teach the material. What's more, this training has proven its value in civilian life. A study covering 85,400 men separated from the Air Force between 1968 and 1970 showed that 72% of those who were in high skill Air Force jobs found work in related civilian occupations.

As an added advantage, we have one of the newest and most attractive features of military service: training options. Each of the services has a list of available occupations which it will guarantee. When a recruit selects some field from this list, his choice is guaranteed; if it is not available to him on completion of basic training, he may choose to be released from the service. Of course, the list varies, depending on the branch of the service and its current needs. Moreover, the recruit is tested before being offered the options; he may select only those for which he is qualified. But even with these limitations, training options assure the newcomer that his assignment will dovetail with his interests and aptitudes.

Travel Opportunities

As a member of the Armed Forces, a young person can see more of the United States—and the rest of the world—than in any other way. Often he can choose the area in which he would like to be stationed. Options for foreign service vary from one branch of the Armed Forces to another, and will be described later in this chapter.

Vacations

Every enlistee in the Armed Forces is entitled to 30 days annually of paid vacation, from the first year. Such a benefit is virtually unheard of in private industry. Imagine being stationed in Europe and having 30 days to visit all the famous capitals and landmarks! Or being in Japan, with the time and money to explore the Far East!

Opportunities to Meet People

The circumstances of army life throw together people from all walks of life and all parts of the country. Shared activities, both good and bad, as well as off-duty social and sports events encourage intimacy and close friendships. Both for the shy person and the outgoing one, there is probably no environment so conducive to interacting with other people.

PX Privileges

Most military installations include a government store (called a Post Exchange, or PX for short) which is a combination supermarket and discount store. It sells anything you're likely to want to buy, from groceries to jewels. Prices are about 30 percent lower than those in typical civilian stores.

Education

The Armed Forces encourages recruits to continue their education, and there are extensive opportunities in all branches. Those who have not completed high school can work toward a General Education Diploma, the equivalent of a High School Diploma. A two-year community college plan allows the enlistee to combine military service with attendance in a regular college program. Fully qualified recruits may be paid while attending college for four years, so if finances are the chief obstacle to further education the Army may provide an excellent solution. Or, if you're less committed to further study, you can sign up for single courses, evening courses, correspondence courses, or a lighter schedule of college-level work. Wherever you start, academically, the Armed Forces will gladly enable you to continue along the road.

Family Benefits

Married military personnel often have family quarters available at low cost right on the post, or are paid additional living allowances for off-post quarters. All members of the family can avail themselves of full medical, dental, PX and social facilities.

Opportunities for Promotion

Qualified individuals are encouraged to seek promotion, and training for promotion is freely available. You can increase your skills at your present assignment, learn another field, or try out for non-commissioned officer training or officer training school. If you have the qualifications, you'll get the opportunity in the Armed Forces.

Special Options

Over the last few years, the Armed Forces has introduced certain options to make enlisting more attractive. The following are available in all branches of the service.

Buddy Option

This provides that if friends join up together, they are guaranteed basic training at the same center. Generally, they can also have their advanced training in the same area, if not the identical post.

Vocational School Option

Under this option, vocational school graduates, or high school graduates qualifying for selected vocational training, are offered special rapid promotion opportunities. The recruit, on completion of basic training, receives specialized vocational training leading to assignment at a higher rank. All branches of the service offer this plan in some form, although details may vary.

Medical Skills Option

This is similar to the Vocational School Option, but it applies to the enlistee with experience in medical or related work. It offers rapid promotion opportunities and special accelerated training for Medical Specialists in such fields as pharmacy, physical and occupational therapy, optometry, and the like.

Delayed Entry Option

This provides that after enlisting, a young person may wait up to six months before actually beginning his service. This gives him time to take a vacation, finish school, wind up his job, or in other ways prepare for the new responsibilities ahead. For seniority purposes, he gets credit for the earlier enlistment date, although he does not, of course, get active duty credit.

Other options are available in some, but not all, branches of the service and these are described later in this chapter.

Special Bonuses

Certain assignments (such as flight duty, combat duty, nuclear service, and hazardous duty) draw special cash bonuses. The amount ranges from $50 extra per month to the current $2,000 bonus for Combat Arms service. These bonuses may vary according to the branch of the service and its needs at any given time.

Veterans' Benefits

Some of the greatest benefits of military service come after it's completed. Most people have heard about these benefits, but don't know exactly what they cover. The honorably discharged veteran can receive educational benefits, either in a vocational school or in an institution of higher learning. The amount starts at over $200 per month, with increases if the veteran has any dependents; the exact duration of the benefits depends on the number of months of active service.

But educational benefits are only the beginning. Free testing, counseling, and placement services are available through the Veterans' Administration. Medical benefits can be obtained through Veterans' Administration hospitals. Guaranteed home purchase loans at interest rates lower than average make it easier for the veteran to purchase a home, provided he makes the purchase within ten years of his discharge. Low cost life insurance is also available to him. In most Civil Service employment, the veteran receives extra point credits, thereby placing higher on the list; in Federal Civil Service, veterans receive unqualified preference over nonvets. In any case, many employers prefer to hire veterans. Training received in the service makes the veteran a valuable employee. Moreover, some employers welcome the opportunity to help a veteran who has served his nation. The U.S. government also offers special financial inducements to employers who offer veterans on-the-job training.

Retirement

Any member of the Armed Forces may retire after twenty years of service at 50 percent of his final cash pay (excluding the value of meals, housing, and other benefits). This means that the young person who enlists at 18 can retire at 38 with a sizable income which continues for the rest of his life, even though he may be working at a second career.

Knowing Yourself

Perhaps even more important than all the objective benefits listed above is the opportunity for self-discovery. You'll be operating in situations demanding more maturity, responsibility, discipline and interpersonal dealings than you've ever faced before. You'll be testing your leadership qualities, your ability to get along with others, your self-control—not to mention your tolerance for frustration! Your physical endurance will be enlarged, as will your capacity to deal with emotional stress. Most enlistees find that the Armed Forces place unprecedented demands upon them—but these demands bring out resources they never knew they had.

Viewed in terms of its advantages, military service adds up to a tempting package, both for the person with definite plans and the one who's not quite sure where he's headed. But there are serious drawbacks to consider along with the benefits.

DISADVANTAGES

Physical Risk

You're in the military forces, and if the United States is at war, you'll be called upon to serve wherever you are needed. The demands of the situation determine where you will be and what you'll be doing; all options are waived during wartime. The likelihood is that you will serve in whatever capacity you've been trained, but even a cook runs a risk if he's cooking in a combat area. Of course, in times of crisis, civilians are called up, too. But any way you look at it, the Armed Forces can be very dangerous.

Regimentation

You'll be facing a lot of strict regulation. There's a time to get up, a time to eat, a time to stand formation and drill, a time to go to bed—none of them of your own choosing. In a month or two, all this may become routine and you may be too busy even to think about it; the truth is, *most* working people function according to a pretty set routine. But in the military you don't have the option to deviate from it.

Admittedly, over the last decade or two, military regulations have become more flexible than they ever were. Hair styles, mustaches, and the like are more a matter of individual discretion. Servicemen and women may dress as they please in their free time. Leaving the post is more routine. But while on duty, their clothing must be immaculately clean and pressed, shoes shined, beds made, quarters in perfect order. The sergeant is tougher than mother ever was.

Subordination to Authority

Each individual in the service has a clearly defined area of responsibility and is expected to accept the authority of those above him. As a member of the Armed Forces, you must carry out the orders of your superiors, even if you don't understand the reasons, or disagree with them. There are channels for suggestions, and even for examination of accepted procedures. Nonetheless, a direct order must be obeyed.

Impossibility of Resigning

Your enlistment may be for two, three, four, or six years—but whatever it is, you must serve it out; unlike private employment, you can't just quit. At present, volunteers who can't take the physical or psychological demands of army life may be dropped with honorable discharge (although without veterans' benefits), usually within six months of enlisting. However, this is strictly at the option of the service. *They* may decide to drop *you,* but you can't make the decision for yourself.

Nonetheless, this particular restriction sometimes turns out to be an advantage. Often a young person will join the Armed Forces after trying his hand at a dozen or more different things. Once in the service, he is forced to keep at his job long enough to learn it thoroughly and experience the rewards of success. Military discipline may be designed to benefit the service, but it often benefits the individual as well.

Frequent Transfer

A common complaint of servicemen is that no sooner do they get used to one post of duty than they're transferred to another. If you're in the service for any length of time, you may find yourself moving more often than you like. If you have a family, they'll have to move with you. Location options guarantee you'll stay in one area for a specified length of time, but not indefinitely; sooner or later, you must expect to move. Of course, moving expenses are paid and suitable new living quarters made available. Nonetheless, the pattern of constantly being uprooted can be very disturbing.

Lack of Privacy

Privacy is virtually unknown in the Armed Forces. You live and work with your own squad, eat and sleep with them. Each recruit usually has free time to spend as he pleases, but only rarely can he find a place where he can close the door and be alone for an hour or two.

Minimum Individual Activity

Teamwork is critical in the service. You do your share alongside others who do theirs. You must accept the give-and-take of a team; you must get along with people some of whom you may not even like. On the other hand, this can work out very well for the person who tends to be shy or introverted. The living and working arrangements of the service throw people together as in a very large family. They deal with each other at their best and their worst, and often come to understand each other very well.

THE DAILY ROUTINE

The above lists of advantages and disadvantages are no more than statements of facts. Only you can evaluate the facts in terms of your own temperament and needs, and decide whether the plusses outweigh the minuses. However, before you make up your mind, you might do well to consider the actual pattern of peacetime military life—the typical daily routine.

Reveille—getting-up time—is usually at five in the morning. You make your bed, tidy your immediate area, dress, and go to breakfast. There's a lot of griping about military food, but it's usually plentiful, varied, and at least as good as that in the average restaurant. After breakfast you may be assigned to an hour of group physical exercise. Then you attend appropriate classes or report for work on your assigned task. You break for lunch in the mess hall, return to duty, and stand retreat (formation and a short ceremony of lowering the flag) at about 4:30. Dinner follows, and you're probably free for the rest of the day. Typically, you join in the various activities on base—athletics of all kinds, gym, swimming, and lounges where you can watch TV, play cards or chess, or just take it easy. There are activity rooms for hobbies and crafts, and on larger posts there may be such elaborate recreational facilities as a pottery kiln or photographic darkroom. Lectures, movies and concerts may also be on the schedule. Or, if you prefer, you may leave the post—after you get permission; you're under military discipline and do not leave without a pass. Married servicemen live with their families, either on the base or nearby; they go home after work, just as they would in civilian life.

If your duties leave you free on weekends, you may spend them as you like. Weekend passes are easily arranged, but you may find yourself asking for them less often than you expected; there's usually plenty to do on the post. Emergency furloughs are obtainable if necessary, and of course in time of peace, your vacations are your own.

REQUIREMENTS FOR JOINING THE ARMED FORCES
Age

You must be at least 18 years old (17 with parents' consent); the upper limit varies with the individual service and the kind of enlistment, but is usually no more than 25 to 30. Individuals over the age limit may be accepted if they have essential vocational skills.

Moral Character

All branches of the service demand a good moral character. A police record of any kind may limit your eligibility. However, minor infractions may be acceptable; to make sure check with your local enlistment officer.

Aptitude Test

While the service does not demand graduation from high school, it does require a certain level of competency in reading, reasoning, and arithmetic. All applicants must pass a general aptitude test; the passing grade varies according to the branch of the service. More information about the aptitude test, including sample questions, can be obtained from the appropriate recruitment office.

Physical Examination

Every applicant must pass a physical examination which indicates whether he's capable of handling the strenuous training and physical demands of the service. Of course, the requirements vary not only with the branch of the service, but also with the anticipated type of training. If you wear glasses, you may find yourself excluded from some assignments, but plenty of others will be open to you.

VOCATIONAL TRAINING

As noted, when you apply for enlistment in any branch of the service, you will be given an extensive test. This gives the personnel officers an idea of your chances for success in any of hundreds of available jobs. We've already seen that certain minimum levels are required in reading, reasoning, and arithmetic. Beyond that, job categories are classified according to the minimum score necessary in each part of the test to do the job well. So the training options available to you are determined by your own scores and how well they match those necessary for the job. You may take this screening test without obligation of any kind, simply to find out the types of training for which you would qualify.

The Armed Forces aren't interested in challenging you or substantially enlarging your potential. All they care about is your ability to do a basic, necessary job. Ideally, you're assigned to the most demanding training you can handle—no more and no less. Don't expect them to provide you with training just a little beyond your reach.

Nonetheless, you'll have many opportunities to move ahead, either through the quality of your job performance or through readily available promotional opportunity tests. These tests cover material necessary for the next job step. The Army doesn't care where you learned it, whether in Army or civilian life, in school or on the job. If you feel you know it, that's enough; you may take the test and receive credit if you pass.

Available Jobs

Although exact job titles, or "ratings," differ from one branch of the service to another, many vocational fields are available to men and women in all of them. The following list gives you some idea of the tremendous range of jobs you can learn—most of them directly transferable to civilian life when you leave the service.

Administrative and Personnel
Bookkeeping
Court Reporter
Journalism
Machine Accounting Clerk
Legal Services Assistant
Medical Records Clerk
Personnel Interviewing & Testing
Stenographer

Communications
Radio Operator
Audio Specialist
Aerial Photographer
Code & Cipher Operator
Cryptographer
Motion Picture Cameraman
Photographer
Telephone and Teletype Operator

Aviation Group
Air Traffic Controlman
Aviation Electrician
Aviation Machinist
Aviation Electronics
Maintenance Administration
Structural Mechanic

Construction Specialties
Carpenter
Electrician
Heating & Cooling System Specialist
Mason
Plumber

Data Processing
Computer Operator
Computer Repair Technician
Keypunch Operator
Programmer

Drafting & Cartography
Construction Drafting
General Draftsman
Illustrator
Map Compiler

Electronics & Precision Instruments
Electronics Technician
Radarman
Aviation Electronics
Ship Electronics
Radio Repairman
Missile Electronics
Camera Repair
Instrument Repair (all fields)

Food Service
Cook
Baker
Butcher
Diet Cook

General Mechanical Skills
Bricklayer
Boilermaker
Fireman
Painter
Pipefitter
Sheetmetal Worker
Steamfitter
Welder
Woodworker

General Skills
Intelligence Specialist
Weather Observer
Optical Instruments
Prosthetic Appliance Specialist
Dental Technician Specialist

Heavy Equipment Operation and Maintenance
Asphalt Equipment Operator
Concrete Paving Equipment Specialist
Crane Operator
Crawler Tractor Operator
Equipment Repairman
Grader Operator

Medical and Dental
E.K.G. & E.E.G. Specialist
Laboratory Specialist
Medical Aide
Operating Room Assistant
Pharmacy Assistant
Psychiatric Technician
Social Work Assistant
X-Ray Operator

Merchandising
Disbursing Clerk
Commissaryman
Shoe Repairman
Storekeeper
Textile and Leather Repair

Printing
Lithographer
Platemaker
Pressman
Silk Screen Printer

Transportation
Driver (various vehicles)
Dispatcher
Mechanic (various vehicles)

Extensive as this list may seem, it only hints at the possibilities; there are hundreds more. Of course, each category is not always open as an option. Given your qualifications, you would have to check with your local recruiting officers to determine what is available to you at a given time. If your specific field is not available, he may be able to suggest a related job, or you may be allowed to go through basic training uncommitted and choose from what's available when you're done. Most of the services will guarantee a general occupational area, even if they can't guarantee a specific occupation.

These options are all very well for the person who has a fairly clear idea of what he wants to do. However, the Armed Services also provided advantages for the one who's undecided. Such a person will, of course, be placed in an area appropriate to his qualifications. However, if he later decides on some other field he can prepare for it in his free time, take a test, and possibly enter it. He'll be given every opportunity for study, including books, 75% tuition payment for evening courses, and access to both military and civilian instructional facilities. That first work experience may not be a total loss; sometimes it's an essential preliminary to more serious decision-making. At the very least, it points out something you definitely don't want to do!

WOMEN IN THE SERVICE

Every branch of the Armed Forces offers exciting opportunities for women to grow in maturity, responsibility and experience. A girl in the Armed Forces often gets the chance to learn far more interesting tasks and assume far greater responsibilities than her counterpart in the civilian work world.

In the U.S. Army all training and service options open to men are open to women, except for actual combat service. In the Navy, women can take advantage of virtually all options available to the male sailor except for sea duty and work considered too physically strenuous—and the seagoing restriction has already been challenged! In the Air Force, Marines and Coast Guard, the options open to women are more restricted, but all include personnel work, administration, medical aid opportunities, communications and data processing. In most branches, broadcasting, photography and intelligence service are other fields usually open to women.

Opportunities for travel and overseas duty are among the guaranteed options for women as well as men. This applies to all branches of the service.

While the Armed Forces will not accept a married woman for enlistment, she can continue if she marries while in the service.

For a young woman, with her generally restricted opportunities for travel and varied experiences, the Armed Forces provides unusual social exposure. She gets to meet men from all over the country at varying levels of authority, on a footing of camaraderie and shared interests hardly possible elsewhere.

While the proportion of women in the Armed Services is still low, more and more girls are becoming aware of the tremendous advantages to be derived from enlistment. Since active combat duty is barred to women, the gravest disadvantage to men—the danger of active warfare—doesn't apply. For the girl adventurous enough to leave home and cope with a new and demanding environment, enlistment can provide an unforgettable and rewarding experience.

BRANCHES OF THE ARMED FORCES

There are five branches of the Armed Forces—Air Force, Army, Coast Guard, Marines, and Navy—and you must make your choice even before you volunteer, so it's a good idea to learn something about each of them.

U.S. Air Force

The Air Force is the flying branch of the Armed Forces. It is concerned with operation and maintenance of aircraft, aerial reconnaissance, and the like. Standards are relatively high, and at present pilots must be commissioned officers.

U.S. Army

This is the largest branch of the service. It is involved with ground defense operations, including all kinds of weaponry, artillery, transportation, and engineering activities. Tanks, half-tracks, and all other equipment for infantry operations are basically within Army jurisdiction. The Army also has some flying activities, primarily of helicopters and small planes.

U.S. Coast Guard

This relatively small branch of the service differs from the others in one important respect: while all the rest operate under the Department of Defense, in time of peace the Coast Guard operates under the Department of Transportation. Its peacetime activities include patrolling all coastlines (including those of the Great Lakes) and serving civilian shipping and recreational boating. The Coast Guard is famous for its ship rescue operations; less well known are its ecological and oceanographic studies and similar peacetime activities. In time of war, the Coast Guard is under the jurisdiction of the U.S. Navy and engages in active military duty.

U.S. Marines

This is a combat-ready branch of the service, trained for action on land or sea. Much has been said and sung about the Marines, and its is generally conceded that the training is physically more demanding and the discipline more stringent than in other services. The Marines are used as a quick task force in emergency situations. They are also responsible for guarding U.S. embassies throughout the world, so a Marine assignment can take you almost anywhere.

U.S. Navy

This is the ocean-going branch of the service, concerned with operation and maintenance of cruisers, battleships, submarines, naval aircraft, and the like. For men, all Navy service includes a tour of duty aboard ship, and may involve a fair amount of international travel by sea. However, there is also a good deal of land-based activity.

What would lead you to choose one branch of the service over another? Perhaps information and impressions picked up from people with service experience, perhaps nothing more than the movies and television shows you happened to see. Or you may be following up on a long-standing interest. For example, if you've been involved with small craft for years, you may want to join in the work of the Coast Guard. If you pride yourself on physical endurance, the image of the tough Marine may inspire you. The prospect of a long tour of duty in Germany, with access to European capitals, may make the Army your choice.

If you're still undecided, factors like the following may be important considerations.

Length of Enlistment

Enlistment terms in the Armed Forces are usually for three or four years. However, the Army has a special two-year enlistment option, not available in the other services. The Navy offers a six-year hitch. Special programs involving extensive education, such as community college programs or four-year degree programs, are available only with the longer enlistments.

Available Training

If your big concern is preparing for a career, you'll want to join the service that offers the training you're after. Remember, it's not enough to see "Automotive Technician" or "Construction Mechanic" listed in a recruiting brochure; make sure there's an opening at the time you apply. Discuss your needs with recruiters from all branches of the service, not just one or two. With luck, you may find exactly what you're looking for. Or you may have to compromise, weighing the advantages of the precise training you want against such disadvantages as an uncongenial location or longer term of enlistment.

Specific Options

Often, some particular option offered by one branch of the service and not another can be a deciding factor. Special options available throughout the Armed Forces have already been noted. Here are some others, more restricted in their scope.

Location Options

In the U.S. Army, the young man who enlists in the infantry, armored divisions, or artillery can elect to serve in Europe, Hawaii, Panama, Alaska or Korea. He is guaranteed 16 months of service in the area of his choice, once he has completed basic training. Women can also request these stations after their training.

In the Navy, most men travel the seas extensively. However, both men and women may request service at ports in Spain, Italy, Australia, England, Japan or Hawaii.

In the Air Force, both men and women may ask for service in England, Japan, Spain, Turkey, Greenland or Panama.

Unit of Choice Options

The Army offers considerable choice of unit within the United States; for each unit, there is some choice of location. The units include Infantry, Armor, Cavalry, Military Police, Airborne, Engineer, and Air Defense Command. Locations include: Fort Hood, Texas; Fort Riley, Kansas; Fort

Carson, Colorado; Fort Lewis, Washington; Fort Bragg, North Carolina; Fort Campbell, Kentucky; Fort Meade, Maryland; Fort Dix, New Jersey; Fort Sill, Oklahoma; Fort Benning, Georgia; Fort Ord, California; and Colorado Springs, Colorado. If for any reason you prefer to be stationed in any of these locations, the option is open to you.

In the Navy, recruits can request stationing on either the East or West Coast on completion of training.

Exact choice of location within the United States is not available in the other services.

Hospital Enlistment Option

For enlistees seeking medical training, the Army offers a choice of Army hospitals in Texas, Colorado, California, Washington, Pennsylvania, Washington, D.C., and Georgia. While each of the services offers a wide range of medical training, this location option is available only in the Army.

Overseas Buddy Option

We have already mentioned the buddy option, whereby friends may remain together during basic training. The Army extends this option; friends joining up together will be assigned to units in the same general overseas area, if they qualify for the Overseas Option.

Flight Training

The Armed Forces are probably the best way to learn to fly. Flight training is available in all branches of the service, but only in the Army is it available to anyone except a commissioned officer. In this service, such training is also available to warrant officers—a category different from that of the regular commissioned officer. If a young man has at least a high school diploma, but preferably two or more years of college, he may be enrolled in this special flight training program. At present, unfortunately, flight training is not available to women in any branch of the service.

Language Option

In the Army, a high school graduate who shows great aptitude for foreign languages may choose to study any language taught at the Defense Language Institute facilities, subject to the needs of the Army.

Other Special Army Options

The Army permits you to request any of the following assignments: Airborne Service (paratroopers), Rangers, Army Security, Army Intelligence, and Army Band. In each case, you must qualify for the option.

Other Special Navy Options

The Navy offers special options in the Nuclear Surface Navy, the Submarine Service, and the U.D.T./SEAL teams, a special group performing unusual sea assignments, including scuba diving. The Navy also seeks qualified musicians for its bands.

These are only a few of the considerations that might lead a recruit to choose one branch of the service over another. However, do not make a final choice on the basis of the above information. The Armed Forces changes day by day. New options may be added or old ones withdrawn at any time. Before you make a definite commitment, speak to representatives of all branches. Only they can bring you up to date on regulations, requirements, and the availability of specific training opportunities.

GETTING MORE INFORMATION

In everything said so far, we've come back to one idea: get more information. Where can you get it?

As in any job, start with yourself. Have you the temperament for the Armed Forces? Can you give up your own autonomy and work with a team? Are you willing to subordinate yourself to those above you in rank —whatever your private opinion of them? Can you live in close proximity to other people 24 hours a day? Are you ready to make a commitment that will tie you down for the next two years or more?

Discuss the prospects with parents, teachers, and friends. Some won't help you at all; many people find the very notion of enlisting so preposterous, they can't see the strengths and weaknesses. However, others will take you seriously, and help you evaluate the idea on its own merits. Don't bypass your parents; they've lived through several waves of recruiting, and can point out things you may not have thought of. In any case, you'll need their permission to enlist if you're under 18.

Meanwhile, start listening to recruiters. Even if you already prefer one branch of the service, contact them all; you may find reasons to change your mind. As in any job, try to pinpoint the type of training you want; you'll find it much easier to ask sensible questions and evaluate the answers. If your town doesn't maintain a recruiting station, your high school guidance counselor or local postmaster can help you. (The Armed Forces routinely send information to local post offices.) Or write to the separate branches of the service. You'll find their addresses in the telephone directory of the nearest large city; look first under "United States Government," and then separately under "Air Force," "Army," and so on.

However, don't depend solely on information from official recruiting sources; you can be sure they'll paint a rosy picture. Talk to people already in the service. If you don't know any, your high school can probably supply the names and addresses of former students who have signed up. If possible, visit a military installation. Even if you never expect to be assigned there, you'll absorb some of the flavor of military life.

EXHIBIT 14-1

Considerations in Joining the Armed Forces

A. Advantages of the Armed Forces
1. Excellent pay
2. Excellent training
3. Travel opportunities
4. Liberal vacations
5. Opportunities to meet people
6. PX privileges
7. Education
8. Family Benefits
9. Opportunities for promotion
10. Special options (buddy option, vocational school option, medical skills option, delayed entry option)
11. Special bonuses
12. Veterans' benefits
13. Retirement benefits
14. Knowing yourself

B. Disadvantages of the Armed Forces
1. Risk in time of war
2. Regimentation
3. Subordination to authority
4. Impossibility of resigning
5. Frequent transfer
6. Lack of privacy
7. Minimum individual activity

C. Requirements for Joining the Armed Forces
1. Age: 18 to 25, with some exceptions
2. Good moral character
3. Aptitude test
4. Physical examination

D. Branches of the Armed Forces
1. Air Force
2. Army
3. Coast Guard
4. Marines
5. Navy

E. Factors in Choosing a Branch of the Service
1. Long-standing interest
2. Length of enlistment
3. Available training
4. Specific options (location, choice of unit, etc.)

If you do enlist, give careful consideration to every option. Many recruits sign up simply to escape their old surroundings. They don't care what they do, they'll tell you, as long as they get away. These are the same people who often end up grumbling about their miserable assignments. So no matter how eager you are, don't throw away your options. They're among the newest and most valuable features of enlistment; make the most of them. If you like, ask your parents or guidance office to help you. The recruiting officer may have some suggestions, too. Listen to them, evaluate them, but don't swallow them whole. The recruiter works for the Armed Forces, and may understandably be putting their needs ahead of your own.

This chapter has presented a good deal of information about the Armed Forces; some of it is summarized in Exhibit 14–1 on page 197. If you're serious about signing up, go through it, point by point, as carefully as you can. Thousands upon thousands of young people have sampled the military life and been glad of it. You may be among them.

15

Combination Packages

So far we've been discussing alternatives as if you were being forced to make a hard-and-fast choice among them: work *or* school, vocational education *or* starting a business of your own. The fact is, no such choice is necessary. You're perfectly free to take a little of this and a little of that, and put together a combination package tailor-made to suit your own individual needs. It might include a few hours a day of work plus an afternoon or two of volunteer work, plus a course at school. Or the serious study of, say, music, combined with a small, manageable free-lance typing service on the side. Combinations like these are altogether feasible, and for some people they may be the best solution possible.

Let's see who might benefit from a "package" like this.

COMBINATION PACKAGES AND YOU

First, it makes sense if you aren't yet prepared to commit yourself full-time to any one thing. For example, you may not be ready to dismiss college, but neither do you want to give it all your energies. Or you need to work, but you're reluctant to choose a field and devote yourself to it, nine to five, day after day.

Second, you can't wait to graduate from high school and immerse yourself in the adult world. You want to move in grown-up circles, do grown-up things and put your adolescence behind you once and for all. For you, a part-time job, plus some volunteer work (perhaps with a political group), plus an adult educational course at the local "Y" might provide the perfect answer.

Third, a package makes sense if your primary, overwhelming commitment is to some branch of the arts. If so, you may have noticed we haven't said much about you until now. We've assumed that if you're cut out for music, painting, drama, ballet, or professional ice-skating, you know it without being told. Your own unshakeable sense of dedication guides you.

199

You know how much you'll have to give up, how hard you'll have to work. You even know that the odds against you may be overwhelming, but you're going ahead all the same. For years to come, your specialty will demand a major portion of your time and energy. Still, you want to keep in touch with the world—and you must earn money, if only to cover the cost of your lessons. In such a case, the combination package is not only reasonable, it's practically inescapable.

Finally, there's the person interested in marriage. This, too, is a subject we haven't discussed very much; as suggested earlier, no one gets married because he read about it in a book. Now, marriage certainly takes time. Adjusting to another person takes time, housekeeping takes time, establishing a home of your own takes time. Nonetheless, the typical young woman without children doesn't usually regard marriage in itself as a full-time responsibility. More often, both husband and wife continue to work, go to school, and pursue hobbies and other interests often on a part-time basis.

Of the various pursuits considered so far, several lend themselves particularly well to a part-time commitment. These include:

Work
Volunteer work
Starting a *small-scale* business of your own
Study of all kinds: academic, professional, occupational, or cultural

However, before we examine them in detail, a few general remarks are in order.

SOME WORDS OF WARNING

A combination of responsibilities turns out best if you're well organized by nature. You'll have to keep your activities separate, avoid conflicts in hours, allow time for travel and meals. It also helps if you're inclined to get your work done a day early rather than an hour late; then, if emergencies arise, you won't be burdened with a backlog of conflicting duties competing for your attention.

For some people, a combination package entails a certain confusion of identity. At one moment you're a student or budding pianist; then suddenly you become a cashier; later on, you're a hospital volunteer, pushing a book cart. It's not surprising if you're unsettled by this psychological shifting of gears. Called upon to play such a variety of roles, you may feel you're losing sight of the person you really are. In that case, simplify the package; work out a schedule that provides greater continuity from one hour to the next.

Keep sight of your priorities. In each part of your package, the person you deal with—teacher, employer, client, or whatever—will see himself as

"Number One." If you're taking classes, your instructor will expect you to give top priority to your studies. At the same time, your boss will feel (and you can't blame him!) that as long as he's paying you, he wants first claim on your energies. If you're doing volunteer work, your supervisor will be quick to point out that you didn't have to volunteer in the first place, but having done so, you should be giving your very best. Among conflicting pressures like these, it becomes your personal responsibility to decide what matters most to you, and let your other activities be relatively routine.

There's another way of looking at this problem. Some commitments start and finish on schedule, make predictable demands, and that's it. But others seem to be open-ended. They soak up your time; getting them done to your own satisfaction seems to be a never-ending job.

Here's an example. Suppose you work in a retail store, four evenings a week, five to nine. You punch in at five, put in your hours, and you're done. No one expects you to come early; no one expects you to stay late. It's a nice, manageable job.

Suppose, on the other hand, that your part-time selling job takes you door-to-door. Your income comes entirely from commissions; the more you sell, the more you make. When nine o'clock comes around, there's always the temptation to ring one more bell. If you've done badly, you want to make up for it. If you've done well, you want to continue your lucky streak. Unless something compelling requires your attention, there's always the urge to keep working a little longer.

Here's another example. You're taking a Spanish course, six to eight, two nights a week. At five to eight, the teacher packs up his notes and the class is over. You finish your assignment within a day or two. At the next class meeting, your conscience is clear; you've done everything that can be done.

Now imagine you're taking a course in charcoal drawing. You're good, but nowhere near as good as you'd like to be. The one way to improve is to work: the harder you work, the more you'll improve.

The class starts at six, but you get there early and show your teacher some sketches you made at home. From six to eight, the time flies. You're still glowing with inspiration when you get home. You set up a still life on the kitchen table and try to recapture the special illumination of the studio; by midnight you're still drawing. Do you see what we mean by activities which are manageable, and those which are open-ended?

The point is this: if you're putting together a package of separate commitments, be careful about which of them are open-ended. They should be those which are directly involved with your own long-range interests and goals. If all your commitments are open-ended, you run the risk of being squeezed from every direction, with nothing turning out really well. If the wrong ones are open-ended, you may find that somewhere, in all the confusion, you've short-changed yourself. So when you assemble the package, put first things first; choose your priorities and reflect them in the allocation of your time.

With these admonitions out of the way, let's get back to the four types of activity mentioned earlier: work, volunteer work, starting a business of your own, and study. Since work figures in almost everybody's plans, we'll start there.

PART-TIME WORK

In recent years the part-time job has begun to achieve a new respectability. Adults, seasoned professionals, men as well as women, are turning to it as one way out of the relentless nine-to-five rat-race. As a result, more and more corporations are hiring part-time workers, not only in the lower echelons, but for serious executive or creative posts. This having been said, the fact remains that you, as a young and relatively inexperienced applicant, may have to do some compromising in your choice of part-time job. The field you choose may be of relatively little interest. Responsibilities may be limited and opportunities for advancement minimal. Promotions, if offered at all, may be contingent upon your switching to full-time work. And your salary is pretty sure to remain near the low end of the scale.

Nonetheless, part-time work has some unexpected rewards of its own. Because you're usually hired for peak business hours, the time goes quickly; you don't stand around being bored. Meanwhile your part-time job may provide a sympathetic insight into an occupation you would never have experienced otherwise; anyone who's ever waited tables, driven a cab or sold ice cream in the playground can never feel neutral about that line of work again. Finally, there's always the chance that your job may absorb you in spite of yourself; what began as a stop-gap may end up as a career.

Before we go into detail about part-time work, it makes sense to ask, "Which part of the time?" One part-time job may mean Monday through Friday, but only several hours a day. Another may entail a full eight-hour day, but only once or twice a week. We can go a step further: you could work one hectic week a month, perhaps in a bank or real estate office. Or you might be doing seasonal work, as in a resort, amusement park or garden supply store; you push yourself for a few busy months, save your money, and then take it easy until the next season.

All the above schedules have one thing in common: they assume a steady job. Apart from these is the large category of temporary work. Often this is a matter of filling in for absent or vacationing employees, or helping with unexpected peak loads. For example, some employment agencies specialize in providing office help on a day-to-day basis. Similar agencies provide waiters, waitresses, and other restaurant help. If you have the necessary skills, you can register with such an agency, and wait each morning for a possible call. If you're licensed to drive a cab, you may get a day's work by calling the garage; an idle cab doesn't earn money for anyone, and owners are often grateful to find a driver on short notice. One drawback of all these temporary jobs is that you never know whether you'll be working or for how long. This can snarl up your other commitments. (Of course, you can always refuse an assignment, but each refusal lowers your chances of being called again.) However, if your schedule is flexible, temporary work may be just the thing for you.

This takes us to a related subject. Some jobs, while technically full-time, allow plenty of free time on the job. For example, the owner of a small business may hire a clerk simply to cover the office while he's in the field. The clerk's duties would include answering the phone, filing, billing, a little typing, and the like; as long as she's in the office and completes her chores on schedule, no one cares what else she does with her time. Some baby-sitting jobs are of the same type; you're paid merely to be alert, dependable, and on the job. Obviously, work like this won't command much of a salary; the demands are too small. But it does leave great blocks of time in which to pursue such interests as writing, sketching or studying.

Finally, there is the intriguing subject of night work. Professional training, particularly in the arts, often requires that you be free during the day. You might be expected to attend classes, rehearse, practice an instrument, or whatever. Under such circumstances, the number of hours you work is secondary; the critical thing is that they dovetail with the rest of your schedule. This is where the night job comes in. Particularly in large cities, an incredible variety of work is done at night. To start, we can mention restaurant, hotel, hospital and theater jobs. Airports, train stations and bus terminals often operate round the clock. So do telephone answering services and computer installations. Banks and brokerages sometimes use the night shift to catch up on their paperwork. Guards, watchmen, cabdrivers, factory workers—any one of them could be working at night.

Some night jobs are every bit as taxing as the same work done by day. Others—hotel clerks, for example—are like the office jobs described above; you can do them full justice and still have time to yourself on the job. So if you're trying to put together a combination package around your own needs and interests, don't overlook the night job. However, a word of caution is in order. Just because you're working at night doesn't mean you have sixteen glorious daytime hours to fill as you please. Somewhere in there you must allow a time for sleep. Catnaps and coffee may keep you going for a day or two, but if you continue in that way, you'll soon be of no use to yourself or anyone else. If you work at night, you get your sleep by day—but you still get your sleep.

Where do you look for part-time or off-hours work? In a fair-sized city, a good place to start is the want-ad section of the newspaper. Under the heading, "Part-time," the Sunday edition of one major newspaper listed jobs in all the following categories: typist, stenographer, bookkeeper, teller, cashier, salesperson, credit collector, microfilm clerk, sales manager, phone interviewer, receptionist, inventory clerk, distributor (circulars), stock clerk, researcher, security guard, office supervisor, telephone answering clerk, driver, check processing clerk, restaurant helper, economics major, and crafts instructor. The hours included almost every conceivable time slot, including one from 3 A.M. to 7 A.M.! Additional part-time listings appeared under "Waiter/Waitress," "Sales," and "Domestic Help Wanted." Under "Temporary," there were innumerable ads for office workers (many from employment agencies), as well as requests for plumbers, electricians, and public contact work.

However, if your local paper doesn't offer what you want, you'll have to track down your own job. It helps to know which businesses depend on part-time help. These include:

Luncheonettes, Diners, and Restaurants

Here the need is continuous for employees who will work part-time or irregular hours. Workers include waiters and waitresses, busboys, hostesses, cashiers, checkers, kitchen and maintenance help, cooks, and even book-keepers, musicians, and hat-check personnel. You may work one meal (usually lunch or dinner), or a "split shift": lunch from about 11:30 A.M. to 2:30 P.M., dinner from 5:30 P.M. to 8:30 P.M.; the three-hour after-noon break is yours to use as you see fit. If you'd rather leave early, con-sider the breakfast-lunch shift, from about 6 A.M. to 2:30 in the afternoon. For night work, apply to a restaurant that's open 24 hours a day, And bear in mind that many restaurants hire extra help for peak hours like Friday and Saturday nights or weekends. Depending on their location, they may also need additional staff during holidays or at the Christmas season.

Retail Stores

Here the work includes selling, wrapping, cashiering, and stockroom work. As in restaurants, it is available on a dozen different part-time and temporary schedules. People are hired for peak hours (lunchtime and evenings), for peak days (Saturdays and sometimes Sundays) and for peak seasons. These may include not only Christmas and Easter, but also graduation, late spring and summer, and the start of school in the fall, depending on the type of store. Large stores have a variety of standard part-time schedules, while smaller ones may work out a schedule to meet your own needs. Either way, if you're interested, see the manager and talk it over.

Part-time selling may also include door-to-door canvassing, telephone sales, vending of ice cream, and other variations. In work like this, your income is usually from commissions; since the owner has little or nothing to lose, he's often willing to give you a try on whatever schedule you like.

Resorts

If you've ever been in a busy resort hotel, you're familiar with the vast range of work that gets done. To begin, there are usually several restaurants and dining rooms, requiring all the categories of restaurant help mentioned earlier. Sports pros, caddies, lifeguards, entertainers and a social staff are on hand to keep the guests busy and amused. There may be a day camp for the children, and special classes in such areas as dancing, bridge, chess, photography, and even foreign languages. Bellhops, chambermaids and porters are always in abundant supply. Less prominent are truck and bus drivers, maintenance personnel, and the usual contingent of clerical help. The work is usually full-time (you live on the premises) and intensive; in season, you may work a twelve-hour day, six-day week. However, the money comes in fast, and it tends to accumulate; you have neither time nor opportunity to spend it.

Child Care

As long as child care is needed 24 hours a day, seven days a week, you have a good chance of working on whatever schedule you like. You may register with a baby-sitting agency or acquire some clients of your own. You can canvass schools, particularly nurseries and private schools, to see if supplementary part-time help is needed (unless you have some sort of credentials, you probably won't be given major responsibility for the care of children). If you want all-day work, try a Saturday children's group, or start one of your own. For seasonal work, apply to summer camps; remember that apart from counsellors, these camps need people for food preparation, clerical work, maintenance of grounds and pool, and so on.

Delivery and Messenger Services

Many businesses, including photographic services, dental and medical laboratories, florists and newspapers, often require part-time messengers and delivery staff to make the daily rounds. This may entail work before and after normal business hours. Somewhat related are the private mail and messenger services often found in large cities. In this type of work, you keep moving and meet a lot of people, although rather superficially. If it sounds interesting, check the listings under "Delivery," "Messenger" or "Mail" in your classified directory.

Theaters

Every city with a reasonable number of movies, theaters, and concert halls has a continuing demand for part-time ushers, candy-sellers, matrons, and the like. You can apply directly to the theater manager. Bear in mind that the work usually involves getting home rather late.

Telephone Solicitations and Surveys

Here the demand is for people with an agreeable telephone voice who will work while others are at home: mornings, late afternoons, evenings and weekends.

Demonstrators

If you have particular skills in such fields as needlecraft, leathercraft, knitting, model-building or indoor plant cultivation, you may be able to create your own job teaching or demonstrating on a part-time basis. Stores selling the appropriate supplies and equipment might be interested in your services, or you can approach the adult education centers in your community.

In addition to the above, many types of business operate on an irregular schedule and therefore offer work at odd hours. These include: computer centers; telephone answering services; veterinarians and animal hospitals; medical centers; banks and brokerages; printing plants; post office; cab, bus, and truck drivers; dispatchers for cabs, tow trucks, etc.; office building maintenance; amusement parks; sports arenas, and hotels. In a separate category we have seasonal work, such as gardening, pool maintenance, snow removal, golf caddying, and moving.

Of course, the above lists don't begin to exhaust all possible sources of part-time or off-hours work; they include only a few of the more common choices. Apart from these, you're always free to inaugurate a job-hunting campaign of your own. For example, you might decide you'd like to work in a garage. Find a couple that have daily fluctuations, perhaps after a weekend or during the morning and evening rush. Decide which hours you'd like to work, and try to do a selling job on the owners. The challenge here is twofold: you must not only sell your own vocational skills, but you must also persuade the boss that part-time employment is a good idea. The following arguments may help you.

He'll save the salary he would otherwise be paying you during relatively idle periods of the day.

He won't be paying you for lunch hours or coffee breaks; overtime, if any, will be at your hourly rate, rather than the usual time-and-a-half.

Depending on the regulations in your state, he may save money on unemployment insurance, social security and workmen's compensation.

While your hours and salary may be part-time, he'll have the full-time benefit of your ideas and suggestions. You won't stop thinking about the job merely because you happen to be elsewhere.

You may represent a higher level of intelligence and responsibility than he could normally expect in this type of work.

In the event of employee absence or unexpected rush periods, you could upon occasion fill in. However, unless this job has top priority in your combination package, don't promise anything along these lines. Remember, the reason you want part-time work is precisely because you have other interests and commitments.

VOLUNTEER WORK

Since volunteer work is usually planned as a part-time activity, you should have no difficulty fitting it into a combination package. However, two points should be kept in mind.

First, don't confuse a fixed schedule, however short, with one which is flexible. If your assignment is feeding lunch to incapacitated patients from 11 A.M. to 1 P.M. on Tuesdays, then you're expected to make your appearance at that time of that day; report an hour early or late and you're of no use to anyone. Don't bother explaining that your other duties include a dog-walking job earlier in the day, and the dogs were a little late this morning. Nobody cares. The important thing is that you were due at a certain hour, and a lot depended on it. If you plan to combine volunteer work with other, open-ended activities which might make a fixed schedule impossible, ask for a more flexible assignment, where you can come in unexpected and unannounced, and still make your contribution.

Second, beware of letting small volunteer assignments turn into big ones. Volunteer work often expands to fill time; once people see that you're willing to pitch in and do a job, they'll find more and more jobs for you to do. This is particularly true of informal, idealistic groups concerned with political or community goals. Your heart is in the right place, you believe in the work, by cutting corners you can make the time—and before you know it, you're up to your ears in promises and responsibilities. Of course, if the volunteer assignment does in fact have top priority then no harm is done. But if you wanted a manageable volunteer job that could be combined with other interests, don't let it snowball until everything else is squeezed out. Insist from the start on a fixed, limited assignment with an unequivocal beginning and end.

GOING INTO BUSINESS FOR YOURSELF

As was pointed out in Chapter 12, going into business for yourself is nothing to be undertaken casually. As a rule, it's a major, full-time commitment, demanding every ounce of your mental and physical energies. However, certain simple, limited businesses can be attempted on a part-time basis. If you're a skilled artist, you can try your hand at occasional free-lance lettering or sign painting. Musicians and other entertainers can earn money at dances, weddings, children's parties, and the like; small bands are particularly in demand. Or, if you have no skills in areas like these, you can try setting up a typing or baby-sitting service.

However, there are several cautions. First, you'll be competing with serious, career-minded professionals. Unless you can deliver the same calibre of work at competitive prices, you'll be out of the running. Second, be careful of over-expansion. If you intend your business to be no more than a part-time commitment, don't solicit more work than you can manage. Of course, you can refuse the extra work, but at the risk of losing that customer for good. It's probably preferable to have some assistants on tap to handle the job, even if it eats up your profits. But then you find yourself an entrepreneur, with several people working for you, and you're back in the over-expansion trap.

Finally, in terms of the time required, a business of your own must be viewed as an open-ended operation. You can never completely control the volume of day-to-day business; you must be flexible enough to take it as it comes. If you fence yourself in with other, fixed commitments, you're in danger of neglecting your clients—which means that in short order you won't have any. If you intend to combine a small business with other activities, give yourself as much latitude as possible. For example, if you want to take a course or two, choose subjects in which an occasional absence will not destroy the continuity of the material. If you plan to study a foreign language, avoid classes at fixed times; instead, consider a private school where individual lessons can be scheduled at your own convenience. In short, recognize in advance that your business may crowd out your other interests, and build in the necessary safeguards.

If your business does thrive, you'll probably turn it into a full-time job and love every minute of it. In that case, congratulations and good luck!

PART-TIME STUDY

Along with work, part-time study is probably the most important part of the typical combination package. However, study means different things to different people. We will consider five types:

- Professional training in the arts
- Part-time college attendance as a matriculated student
- Part-time college attendance as a nonmatriculated student
- Occupational education
- Adult education courses

In addition, we'll look into a miscellaneous category, including correspondence schools, programs of independent study, and the like.

Professional Training in the Arts

The critical thing about training like this is not the area of study, but your own degree of interest. Suppose, for example, your field is ballet. Plenty of people study ballet once or twice a week, for recreation or exercise. The difference is that you've been working at it for the last decade, you give it hours of practice every day, and you regard it as the central force of your life. (Similar remarks could be made about art, photography, music, drama, gymnastics or ice-skating.) Your own compelling interest has led you to the field, you already have a fair degree of training, and you are prepared to give it years of your life. Under these circumstances, there isn't much we can tell you about professional training. You undoubtedly have your own teachers, to whom you are devoted and who in turn take a marked interest in you. School is the central activity of your schedule; other commitments, however interesting or unavoidable, play a clearly subordinate role.

Part-time College Attendance as a Matriculated Student

Matriculation, of course, means that you've met the college's entrance requirements and intend to pursue a program leading to a degree. It's a good idea if you're not quite ready to turn your back on college, but aren't inclined to make it a full-time commitment. To be sure, some colleges don't allow matriculated students to attend only part-time, or discourage the practice by setting prices prohibitively high. (For example, they will charge the same substantial tuition for any number of credits up to twelve.) However, matriculation as a part-time student is usually possible in municipal and state colleges, at least in evening session. Matriculation has at least two drawbacks; you must meet the school's entrance requirements, and you must take whatever required courses they specify for the degree, in English, mathematics, foreign languages or any other area. On the other hand, if you think you'll want a degree sooner or later, then even a few credits will bring you that much closer.

If you're interested in matriculating on a part-time basis, make every effort to talk things over with an adviser provided by the college. Don't hesitate to avail yourself of the adviser's time; it's what he's paid for. Spell out your interests, your reasons for attending part-time, your other commitments. The more the adviser understands of your outlook and goals, the more he can do for you—and it can be a great deal. In particular, he can help set up a program that will dovetail with your other responsibilities instead of conflicting with them.

Part-time College Attendance as a Nonmatriculated Student

If you want just a taste of college study, without being tied down in any way, you might sign up for a course or two as a nonmatriculated student.

You pay your money, attend classes, and learn for the sheer joy of learning. Theoretically, you may take whatever you like. In practice, the matriculated students usually register first and often fill up the more popular classes; this may not leave very much to choose from.

As we suggested, taking courses as a nonmatriculated student has several advantages. It's casual, it's carefree, you take only what you like and concern yourself with no one's standards but your own. On the other hand, there are a number of drawbacks. To begin, not all colleges allow nonmatriculants. When they do, the fees are usually higher than for matriculated students. As noted, you're the last to register, so the courses you want may already be closed. And finally, the fact is that you're not making progress toward a degree; if you ever decide to matriculate, you may still have to start at the very beginning. (In some colleges, the credits earned as a nonmatriculant can be applied toward a degree, provided you did the assignments and passed the tests like an ordinary matriculated student. Talk it over in advance with a college adviser.)

One more warning: as a nonmatriculated student, you may be allowed to register for relatively advanced courses, on the grounds that it's your own time and money you'll be wasting. Make sure you're ready for them. If in doubt, ask the chairman of the appropriate department.

Occupational Education

Occupational education students usually complete their studies as quickly as possible, so they can start earning money in their chosen fields. However, schools recognize that not everyone can attend on a full-time basis, particularly if the student also has to work. Consequently, many of them offer evening or other part-time programs which allow you to combine your occupational schooling with other activities. If you'd like to attend an occupational school on a part-time basis, discuss it with someone in the admissions office.

However, you'll still want to take all the steps outlined in Chapter 9 to make sure the occupation in question is the right one for you. Occupational training is narrow, specific, and very practical; it will help you earn a living, but it's not likely to provide intellectual stimulation or give you a sweeping new outlook on life.

Adult Education Courses

These are the courses you may have been looking for all your life; the ones you take for no reason in the world except that you feel like it. They cover everything from aviation to zoology. Some, like stenography, will help you get a job; others may teach a practical skill like carpentry, or a hobby like weaving; still others are designed to satisfy your intellectual concern about the universe, yourself, and everything in between. You may never get credit for them; even when sponsored by regular colleges, adult education courses are rarely applicable toward a degree. What you will get is fun, challenge, new ideas and skills, and the chance to meet other enthusiastic adults with interests akin to your own.

The range of subjects offered in adult education courses dazzles the imagination. New York University's School of Continuing Education, one of the oldest and largest of such schools, lists over 2,000 courses, attracting more than 40,000 registrations a year. The contents—to sample just one letter from the alphabetical listing—include ecology, editing, emergency management, emotional awareness, encounter techniques, English, environmental theater, experimental theater, and evolution. Occasionally, the material appears to overlap conventional academic areas. In such cases, the instructor can be counted on to stress ideas rather than details and techniques. He is well aware that you don't intend to make a career of the subject, and encourages you to explore it from a cultural and conceptual point of view.

Most adult education courses are offered after work or on weekends, when an employed adult can spare the time. They can be found in high schools, colleges, YMCA's and similar institutions, libraries, museums, churches, community centers, and dozens of other places. Fees may range from nothing at all to substantial sums, comparable to the fees of local colleges. If you want more information about these courses, check with your librarian; she may maintain a file of all the courses in your community.

Incidentally, adult education courses are traditionally an admirable place to meet people. Every school has its own body of legends about all the couples who met and married there—or are going steady, at the very least. Of course, you choose your courses for their intrinsic interest, but if making friends is one of the fringe benefits, don't turn your back on it!

Other Types of Study

Apart from the forms of study already described, various other types lend themselves to being combined with additional part-time commitments. Correspondence courses are returning to fashion; they enable you to take almost anything you wish on a schedule of your own choosing. A few colleges offer external degree programs requiring as little as three weeks' residence; all the rest of the work is done independently, off campus. The schools include the University of Oklahoma, Syracuse University in New York, Goddard College in Vermont, and the University of South Florida. New York goes them one step better; its Regents External Degree Program allows the student to obtain a degree without any residence requirement whatever. Details of these and similar programs are given in the next chapter. Keep them in mind if you plan to incorporate part-time study into a combination package.

* * *

The most important thing about a combination package is that you design it to suit yourself. No one knows better than you just what you're interested in, what you want to do, where you're headed. For this reason, no one is better qualified to plan the package that meets your needs. The suggestions given in this chapter are not hard-and-fast rules; they're intended merely as guidelines. Accept, reject, or modify them as freely as you please. Plan carefully and you'll end up with an arrangement that's exactly right for you.

16

College Reconsidered

Evidence accumulated over the past few years suggests that the great college boom is tapering off at last. In part this is due to a sharp decrease in the birth rate, but there are at least two other factors: changing attitudes toward the need for higher education, and publicity about lack of employment opportunities. The United States Office of Education has reported that in the fall of 1973, part-time college enrollment of both men and women climbed, but full-time enrollment of both groups actually dropped. And in May 1974 the New York State Board of Regents cautioned the state's colleges against over-expansion, pointing out the downward projections on future college needs, based on "a decline in the live birth rate and a leveling off of the projection of high school graduates seeking post-secondary education."

Yet a mass movement away from college would be as deplorable as a mass movement in the reverse direction. The answer does not lie in mass movements of any kind. It lies in considered individual evaluations, based on individual requirements and goals. If one million freshmen enter college next year, let us hope it will be the result of one million separate, personal decisions made by one million human beings.

This having been said, it is clear that there can be no quick characterization of the person for whom college would be right or wrong. Yet we can hint at a single broad principle. If you find yourself asking questions— whether intellectual, practical, or personal—which can be answered within the formal academic structure of college, then think seriously of attending. If you have no questions, if you're considering college only for lack of anything better to do, then see whether there isn't some more productive way to fill the time.

Notice that nowhere have we said anything about academic ability. The truth is that given some skill in handling the printed word, in expressing oneself in speech and writing, and in coping with the rudiments of arithmetic and algebra, it doesn't take extraordinary academic ability to benefit from college. What it does take is purpose. College faculty have suspected this for years, and with the advent of large-scale open enrollment policies (under which every high school graduate can claim a place in college), their hunches have been confirmed. Admittedly, thousands of open enrollment students are seriously underprepared. That many drop out is not surprising; even in the most prestigious private colleges half the students drop out! More significant is the number who stay. They may not make the Dean's list, but they remain, graduate, and achieve their professional and personal goals. There are honor students who would be better off almost anywhere than in college; there are C and C— students for whom college is exactly right.

ALTERNATIVES WITHIN COLLEGE

However, the decision to attend college is no longer as clear-cut as it used to be. In recent years, higher education has seen so many changes that college attendance can mean a hundred different things. You may choose a residential college, a commuting college, or one of the new external degree programs in which you need never set foot on campus at all! You may enter directly after high school or wait awhile—and for that matter, many colleges will admit qualified high school students immediately after the junior year. You may attend full- or part-time. Once you begin, you may attend consecutively or drop out for a year or so. You may rush through your studies in as few as three years, or stretch them out to five, six, or even more. You may go to formal classes or depend on one form or another of independent study. In short, there appear to be as many alternatives within college as there are outside it! In the book *Campus 1980*, a collection of essays published under the auspices of the Academy for Educational Development, educator Lewis Mayhew paints the following picture of the future college student:

During his first year he will do an independent study project, take a course on Western civilization and another on the philosophy of science and religion. He will acquire intellectual skills through individual effort expended with the guidance of a faculty member who serves as his adviser. The next summer he will go to South America to live in a village where he will spend his time helping the villagers adapt new technology to old ways of doing things. Intrigued, he could elect to stay for another year but will have been in conference with his colleges advisers so that he could work on an anthropological study of the village. The needed resource materials he will receive from the nearest Latin-American university via electronic transmission from the library of his home institution. After returning from 18 months in Latin America, this student will take a year-long course in mathematics, one in psychology, and will do an independent study survey of the history of China. The following year he will marry a fellow student and move into a married-students apartment. He and his wife will form a research team for a joint project of teaching preschool children in a nearby community and will at the same time take courses in religion and theology.

. . . During the next year, as their first child will be born, the student couple may decide to drop out of school for a year. To insure adequate income as well as to continue educational progress, the husband will accept a year's work-study experience in an electronics firm where he will be taught the skills of advanced programming. As both he and his wife want to gain some understanding of sociology, a friend will have tape-recorded all lectures given in the subject and they will play and discuss them during the evening. So successful will this experiment be that they each will take and pass a comprehensive examination, and hence be awarded full academic credit. Finally, during the next year they may decide to receive their bachelor's degree . . . after graduation the husband may accept a position with an airline company as an aircraft controller. His first six months he will spend receiving training and then begin to fill his full shift.

While the overall picture presented here may still be very far from realization, isolated features are available already. It is not too soon for interested students to weigh choices like these:

- Traditional or Non-Traditional Studies
- Part- or Full-time Attendance
- Immediate or Deferred Admission
- Duration of Undergraduate Studies.

Let's consider these alternatives in more detail.

TRADITIONAL OR NON-TRADITIONAL STUDIES

What is meant by "non-traditional studies"? Think of the conventional four-year college, with its trappings of classrooms, lectures, credits, examinations, requirements, assignments, majors, minors, and all the rest. Non-traditional studies could mean everything else. Samuel Gould, former chancellor of the State University of New York, has this to say of it:

Non-traditional study is more an attitude than a system. . . . This attitude puts the student first and the institution second, concentrates more on the former's need than the latter's convenience, encourages diversity of individual opportunity rather than uniform prescription, and deemphasizes time, space, and even course requirements in favor of competence and, where applicable, performance. It has concern for the learner of any age and circumstance, for the degree aspirant as well at the person who finds sufficient reward in enriching life through constant, periodic, or occasional study. This attitude is not new; it is simply more prevalent than it used to be. It can stimulate exciting and high-quality educational progress; it can also, unless great care is taken to protect the freedom it offers, be the unwitting means to a lessening af academic rigor and even to charlatanism.

Non-traditional education can, and does, take a hundred different forms. There is the University Without Walls, an organization of 20 colleges offering students educational opportunities defined by the students themselves —at work, at home, through interneships or, for that matter, in actual attendance at one or more of the schools. (Participating schools are Antioch, Bard, Chicago State, Friends World, Goddard, Loretto Heights, Morgan State, Northeastern, Illinois State, Roger Williams, Skidmore, Staten Island Community, Stephens, New College at Sarasota, Florida, the Universities of Massachusetts, Minnesota, South Carolina, and Howard and Shaw Universities.) There is New York's Empire State College, where each student develops his own courses with the help of an adviser. There is Minnesota's Metropolitan State College, which uses the entire city as its campus and which exists for one purpose only: to educate those over the age of 20 who, for whatever reason, never made it through college. These three programs are only a sample; the number is growing every day. Instruction can take place almost anywhere; in religious institutions, government agencies, museums and galleries, YMCA's and the like, performing art studios, or theaters—plus, of course, conventional academic institutions. It may be offered through employers, industry, self-study, tutors, recreational and sports groups, or proprietary and correspondence schools. The forms of instruction may include lectures and classes; on-the-job training; short term conferences, institutes and workshops; individual lessons from a private teacher; discussion groups; independent informal study; travel-study programs; community projects; television or video cassettes; radio, records, or audio cassettes; computer-assisted instruction; even talk-back telephone instruction! However, in all discussion of non-traditional education, four approaches recur: independent study, recognition for experience, credit by examination, and external degrees.

Independent Study

Imagine you're a serious, hard worker who functions best on your own. You may or may not be in school, but even if you are, you feel the classes don't always treat the right subjects in the right way; their net effect is often to hold you back. If this describes you, you're a natural candidate for independent study. You begin with a theme, build a plan of study around it, and discuss your ideas with an adviser or teacher. The two of you agree upon a deadline, some tangible evidence of your work—often a written report—and an appropriate number of credits. You may even formalize your agreement in a written contract. You then dig in on your own. If you need advice, guidance, or answers to specific questions, you check back with your supervisor. When the time is up, you deliver the agreed-upon evidence of your work, your adviser evaluates it, and if it is acceptable you collect the credits as promised.

This is independent study. Its potential is almost limitless. It can take place on a conventional campus or on your own. It may represent all of your academic load, or only part. You may see your adviser regularly, intermittently, or not at all. The only essential ingredients, apart from yourself, are a qualified person to evaluate your work and an agency to accredit it.

Recognition for Experience

The recognition in question here—usually in the form of college credits —is based on the fact that employed people, in connection with their work, often learn material which is normally covered in college-level courses. For example, a stock salesman may acquire a background in economics; a computer operator may complete the equivalent of a beginning college math class; a housewife learns as much about nutrition as is taught in the typical first-year course. It is important to note that credit is *not* given merely for having led a purposeful or rewarding life. In his book, *How to Change Colleges*, educator Harold Taylor cautions that "a distinction has to be made at some point between what people ordinarily do from day to day and what they should do if they are members of a college student body. There are many things that are beneficial to personal development —marriage, raising children, running a rock band—but not necessarily as part of the college curriculum." The credit is reserved for clearly defined college work, learned on the job.

Credit by Examination

However you've acquired your educational background—independent study, experience, on-the-job training, or whatever—someone must decide whether, in quantity and quality, it merits acceptance as college-level work. One convenient way to make the decision is simply to give a test. Many colleges have been doing this for years. If you think you know as much philosophy, or calculus, or Sanskrit as is taught in one of their courses, you take an appropriate examination; if you pass, the credit is yours.

On a larger scale, the College-Level Examination Program (CLEP), sponsored by the College Entrance Examination Board, achieves the same results. CLEP examinations are standardized tests given throughout the United States at colleges, at test centers administered by the Educational Testing Service, and to service personnel through the auspices of the United States Armed Forces Institute. The tests are of two types. One consists of general examinations in mathematics, natural science, English composition, and the social sciences. The other deals with more specific areas such as psychology, geology, statistics, and introductory sociology. At present, more than 1,100 colleges and universities have agreed to utilize CLEP to some degree.

Credit by examination is also available through other standardized tests. The College Proficiency Examination Program (CPEP), developed for residents of New York State, is comparable to CLEP but has been used on a smaller scale. And most students are familiar with the Advanced Placement Tests which sometimes allow college credit to well-prepared high school seniors.

External Degree Programs

We've been saying a lot about collecting credits in one way or another. However, if these credits are to be applied toward a degree, they must be evaluated and consolidated, and the degree must be awarded by some suitable recognized agency. To appreciate the problems this may pose, consider the case of Nina. When Nina was still in high school, she earned six advanced placement credits for work in English and French. She then attended college, amassing 40 more credits before deciding to leave. During all this time her hobby was history; by now, she believes, she's learned the equivalent of two or three college courses. Moreover, in her job as a bookkeeper, she's picked up some knowledge of accounting. Nina would like somehow to apply all this work toward a degree, completing the remaining credits either on her own or at a small private college nearby.

This is where an external degree program comes in. It is administered by a degree-granting organization—frequently a college—which will keep track of your credits, see to it that they're properly evaluated, and ultimately award you a degree. Some programs go much further; they may include such features as classes, workshops, independent study programs, correspondence courses, taped courses, and even computer-assisted instruction. The program may require attendance on campus for at least a few weeks a year, or—like the Regents External Degree Program in New York State—it may have no such restrictions at all. When it comes to the details of the program, there can be as many variations as there are students enrolled. Formal coursework, Army courses, independent study, on-the-job training, correspondence and occupational courses, and more can be combined in whatever proportions the student pleases. However, there is one unifying factor: at the end of the rainbow is a college degree.

The four programs outlined above by no means exhaust the possibilities of non-traditional education. In one place or another, it will embrace work-study programs, community projects, Army and VISTA service, and dozens of other experiences. In fact, there are schools that let you design your own program; just decide what you want to do, obtain their approval, and you're on your way! However, these four approaches are among those most frequently encountered.

For the individualistic young high school graduate, tired of being told what to do and how to do it, the prospect of non-traditional education seems to fire the imagination. The very name holds out new hope. This makes it all the more important to point out several potential drawbacks.

First, it puts a heavy burden of motivation and initiative on the individual student. It's up to you to keep working; no one else will do the job.

Second, the external degree program deprives the student of stimulating association with faculty and classmates. There is no doubt that such interaction is an important part of education; some authorities consider it the most important part. Whatever you may gain through independent work, it's well to be aware of what you will lose.

Finally, most non-traditional programs are so new, no one knows for sure how they'll be received. Will an external degree really carry as much weight as one earned in an established college? Will a program composed largely of independent study be as impressive as one of conventional classes? And, with such a proliferation of experiments, can college standards really be maintained, or will the non-traditional degree smack of the watered-down, the second-rate?

If, after you've weighed these objections, non-traditional education still seems like a good idea, you'll need to pin down a program of interest to you. A number of programs are outlined in the following two books:

Coyne, John and Hebert, Tom. *This Way Out: A Guide to Alternatives to Traditional College Education in the United States, Europe, and the Third World.* New York: E. P. Dutton & Co., Inc., 1972.
Houle, Cyril O. *The External Degree.* San Francisco: Jossey-Bass Publishers, 1973.

However, the field is expanding so rapidly that new programs are being introduced and older ones dropped every day. For the most recent information, try the following:

- Speak to the guidance counselor in your high school. She often receives announcements of experimental new college programs.
- Check with your local library. It may include a file of educational offerings.
- If you've narrowed down your colleges to two or three, write asking about opportunities for non-traditional study. Be as specific as possible; indicate your field of interest, the approach you prefer, and why you feel that non-traditional study will serve you better than the more conventional methods. Address your letter to the appropriate department or to the Office of Academic Advising.
- If you're planning to attend a state college, write to the Office of Higher Education in your own state. They should know about the non-traditional programs in the system. Again, provide them with as much information about yourself as you can. If you don't know the exact address, send your letter to the Office of Higher Education, Department of Education, in your state capital. It will get into the right hands.

If you do obtain any information, share it with others—including the college advisers in your own school. The picture is changing so fast that even for professionals, it's all but impossible to keep abreast of the field.

PART- OR FULL-TIME STUDY

Some aspects of part-time college study have already been considered in Chapter 15. Traditionally, the part-timers had no choice—financial or personal responsibilities ruled out the possibility of going to school full-time. More recently, however, part-time study has become attractive in its own right. It represents a workable compromise between pursuit of a degree and total commitment to undergraduate study.

Today, part-time students account for whatever increase is taking place in college enrollments. In some colleges close to half the student body attend on a part-time basis, and the proportion is expected to grow. As college costs soar, and as older people return to school, the investment in time and money for full-time higher education may become more and more of a luxury.

If you're considering part-time study, find out which of the schools you're interested in accept part-time matriculated students, whether the courses are in the day or evening, and what you can expect in the way of residence, scholarships, and other arrangements. As a rule, part-time students are rarely considered for financial aid. However this may change; as colleges recognize their responsibility to the part-timers, so they must acknowledge that it should include all benefits available to full-time students.

If you're interested in part-time degree programs on a broader scale, write to the National University Extension Association, 1 DuPont Circle, Washington, D.C., requesting their publication, *Guide to Part-Time Degree Programs.*

IMMEDIATE OR DEFERRED ADMISSION

The point has been made that when college graduates were interviewed ten years after receiving the degree, 60 percent felt they would have profited from an interruption in their studies. The preferred time for this interruption was the period between high school and college. This idea is reflected in the current practice of deferred admission, the college's policy of allowing an incoming student to wait a year before beginning his studies. Some colleges grant deferment routinely; others want to be told how the student plans to use his time. At least one, Brown University, actually encourages the incoming freshman to wait a year before starting college. The idea is clearly taking hold that an extra year outside the academic framework will pay for itself in terms of increased experience and maturity.

The same viewpoint is seeping into the high schools. More and more high schools—and not only the "progressive" ones—are encouraging seniors to combine studies with a program of paid or volunteer work outside the school. New York City's Hunter College High School, a special school for gifted students, offers its seniors a program known as the Inter-College Year. In this program, the students are allowed to cut their academic load to as little as one course, supplemented by independent study, community service, or work, either volunteer or paid. Work done by the seniors may be, and often is, quite routine; the school has found that a high school senior can learn a great deal, even from a fairly boring job. This confirms a finding cited by psychologist Goodwin Watson: "Most people who experienced both college education and employment rated their learning on a new full-time job above what they had learned in their most productive year spent entirely in college classes."

If you're going to college, should you plan on deferred admission? It depends on you. If you are a little older than the average freshman, if you have a fair amount of work experience, if you're planning a career that will take quite a few years of study, then you may be eager to get started. On the other hand, if you are relatively young, if your background consists mostly of schooling or, for that matter, if another year's savings would strengthen your financial position, then deferred admission is a reasonable course of action.

If you're interested in deferred admission and have already received your college acceptance, write to the Admissions Office outlining your plans. Remember that deferred admission is a privilege, not a right, so spell out your case in some detail. If you haven't yet applied to college, you can simply put it off until you yourself are ready to begin. (However, talk it over with your high school guidance counselor; whenever you decide to apply, you'll need his cooperation and advice.) Don't worry about how college administrators will react to that unexplained year; they're getting used to the idea.

A word of caution is in order. In a few fields—mathematics and physics come to mind—youth seems to be something of an asset. Prodigies are not uncommon, and a surprising amount of serious work is done by people under 25. It is significant that in Russia, where for a while all teen-agers were required to work in factories or agriculture as part of the growing-up process, math and physics students were exempted from the regulation. If you are interested in one of these fields, there is the possibility that deferred admission will represent an academic loss in the long run. This doesn't mean that you must rule it out; the loss may be offset by a corresponding gain. But you might do well to discuss your plans with your high school adviser or someone in the field you plan to enter.

DURATION OF UNDERGRADUATE STUDIES

Traditionally, the completion of a Bachelor's Degree in the United States takes four years. However, there is nothing sacred about this number; it goes back to British custom of the early seventeenth century, and ironically, the British universities themselves long ago cut the time period from four years to three. There have always been students who required more than four years, and there has always been a handful who needed less. Right now, the four-year span is being seriously challenged, and students who prefer to move at a different pace are being accommodated to an increasing extent.

At one extreme, we find the student who intends to earn the degree in three or three and a half years. From the financial point of view, at least, the advantages are indisputable; if we keep in mind the price tag of $5000 or more a year for full-time private undergraduate education, the saving of even a semester makes a real dollars-and-cents difference. Academically, the picture is somewhat different. Dr. Joan Stark, assistant dean at Goucher College, studied a special group of well-prepared young women who were given the opportunity to complete college in three years. She found that the girls who actually did the job differed from those who did not in three important respects: first, they had clearly defined career goals and were anxious to get started as soon as possible; second, they were planning on extensive graduate study; and third, they were interested in escaping the educational scene. Dr. Stark found that some of the most serious students abandoned the plan in midstream; they found that three years were simply not enough to build up the intellectual and cultural background they wanted.

In schools with a trimester system, early completion is routine; by signing up for all three trimesters each year, you are in effect completing your studies in two-thirds the traditional time. (A similar remark applies to schools on the quarter system.) Even if your school is on a conventional schedule, the combination of carrying a heavier-than-average load and attending summer school should enable you to save a semester or two. However, many colleges do not offer summer school, and a few will not transfer summer credits from other institutions.

A second form of acceleration is the combined B.A.-M.A. program. Under this plan, you still attend for the conventional four years, but you graduate with a Master's degree instead of a Bachelor's. As a rule, such programs are offered only in universities with a graduate program. In any case, not all departments offer a combined degree, and it is usually restricted to gifted, or at least proficient students. If you are interested, write to the appropriate department in the college of your choice.

As we have seen, the mere fact that acceleration is possible does not necessarily make it a good idea. It always presupposes that you are a better-than-average student, capable of handling the pressures of an increased academic load. It also requires a measure of maturity; to receive your degree at, say, twenty, and move directly into the competitive adult world can be something of a shock. If you are entering college fairly young —seventeen or younger—further acceleration should be weighed very carefully, regardless of your academic ability. In any case, talk over your plans with a college adviser early in the proceedings; the adviser may know of obstacles you never even considered.

At the other end of the spectrum, we have the option of completing college in more than four years. This can be done in dozens of different ways. One student used a device that worked very well—for her, anyway. After her sophomore year, she signed up each semester for the conventional five courses, tried them all, and dropped the one that seemed least rewarding. The extra time allowed her to do ample justice to each of her remaining classes, and to carry a part-time job besides. The plan required staying in college an extra half-year, but she felt the benefits were well worth it.

More common is the practice of extending the period of time by taking a leave of absence somewhere along the way. This approach, once considered rather eccentric, is gaining wider and wider acceptance; the final report of the Carnegie Commission on Higher Education urges "greater opportunities for all people to drop in and out of learning situations." A recent study by Nancy S. Lindsay of Harvard University shows that of 200 Harvard and Radcliffe undergraduates who dropped out in this way, most thought they had benefited from the experience. Eighty-two percent of the group worked during at least some of their leave, and 75 percent did some travelling. Not only did they report a relaxation of the inner tensions which had contributed to their leaving, but they got more out of college upon their return to studies.

Incidentally, while all these options may be very exciting, it is not usually necessary to decide among them ahead of time. If you think you might like to finish college in less than four years, keep the possibility in the back of your mind and see how things go. If you feel you might benefit from a leave of absence, that's fine too; thousands of students are doing the same thing. However, be sure to arrange it through the registrar's office. Don't just disappear, or your place may not be waiting when you want to come back.

Some students are held back from temporarily dropping out by one lurking fear. "What if I never return? What if I never get the degree at all?"

These questions can be answered in two different ways. First, at what point in your life can you claim you're never going back? You can return to college at 25, at 30, at 50, if you like. College is not an obstacle course, to be put behind you as soon as possible. It is an experience that can reward you at any time of life. Professor Ronald Gross of New York University's School of Continuing Education has expressed the hope that "through the gradual erosion of those constraints of place, time, age and mode of learning which now define schooling, it will gradually become impossible to tell where school begins and life stops." Nor is this a remote pipe-dream. On the contrary, the colleges are sure to cooperate—not only because of snowballing demand, but because with the decreasing pool of 18- to 23-year-olds, they will have to find new markets if they are to stay in business.

But suppose you're right; suppose you never get the bachelor's degree at all. What of it? Your way of life will still be as rewarding—personally and professionally—as anything else you might do. The choice is yours.

Bibliography

Allen, Louis L. *Starting and Succeeding in Your Own Small Business.* New York: Grosset and Dunlap, Inc., 1967.

Astin, Alexander and Panos, Robert J. *The Educational and Vocational Development of College Students.* Washington, D.C.: The American Council on Education, 1969.

Belitsky, A. Harvey. *Private Vocational Schools and Their Students.* Cambridge, Mass.: Schenkman Publishing Co., Inc., 1969.

Berg, Ivar. *Education and Jobs: The Great Training Robbery,* Boston: Beacon Press, 1971.

—————. "Education and Performance: Some Problems." *Journal of Higher Education* 43 (1972): 192–202.

Bettelheim, Bruno. "The Student Revolt." *Vital Speeches* 35 (1969): 405–410.

Blank, Blanche. "Degrees: Who Needs Them?" *AAUP Bulletin* 58 (1972): 261–266.

Carnegie Commission on Higher Education. *Less Time, More Options.* New York: McGraw-Hill, Inc., 1971.

"The College Graduate—1980 Job Prospects." *Occupational Outlook Quarterly* 14 (1970): 4–5.

"The Colleges Want Them . . . But Do They Want the Colleges?" *The New York Times,* June 29, 1971, page 42.

"Columbia President-Elect Finds Widespread Alienation of Youth." *The New York Times,* August 4, 1970, page 13.

Denty, Ralph E. "Vocations and the Universe." *Vocational Guidance Quarterly* 20 (1972): 163–164.

Dictionary of Occupational Titles, third edition. Washington, D.C.: United States Department of Labor, 1965.

Dole, Arthur A. "Stability of Reasons for Going to College." *Journal of Educational Research* 63 (1970): 373–378.

Dun & Bradstreet. *Patterns for Success in Managing a Business.* New York: Thomas Y. Crowell Company, 1967.

Eurich, Alvin, ed. *Campus 1980.* New York: Delacorte Press, 1968.

Folger, John. "The Job Market for College Graduates." *Journal of Higher Education* 43 (1972): 202–222.

Furniss, W. Todd, ed. *Higher Education for Everybody? Issues and Implications.* Washington, D.C.: American Council on Education, 1971.

"Fourth Annual Gallup Poll of Public Attitudes Toward Education, 1972." *Phi Delta Kappan* 54 (1972): 33–46.

Gould, Samuel B. And Cross, K. Patricia. *Explorations in Non-Traditional Education.* San Francisco: Jossey-Bass, Inc., Publishers, 1972.

Gross, Ronald. "From Innovations to Alternatives." *Phi Delta Kappan* 53 (1971): 22–24.

"Harvard Study Finds Some Benefits in Temporarily Dropping Out of College." *The New York Times,* April 30, 1974, page 21.

"The Job Gap for College Graduates in the '70's." *Business Week,* September 23, 1972, pages 48–58.

Jencks, Christopher et al. *Inequality: A Reassessment of the Effect of Family and Schooling in America.* New York: Basic Books, Inc., Publishers, 1972.

Kinsey, Douglas K. "Critics Distort Views about NCVA." *Voluntary Action News* 4 (March–April, 1973): 11.

Kursh, Harry. *Apprenticeships in America.* New York: W. W. Norton & Company, Inc., 1965.

Lass, Abraham and Wilson, Eugene S. *The College Student's Handbook.* New York: David White Company, 1970.

Little, J. Kenneth. *Review and Synthesis of Research on the Placement and Follow-Up of Vocational Education Students.* Research Series No. 49 VTO 10175. Columbus, Ohio: ERIC Clearing House on Vocational and Technical Education, 1970.

Livingston, J. Sterling. "Myth of the Well-Educated Manager." *Harvard Business Review* 49 (1971): 79–89.

Novak, Michael. "Do Students Want Education?" *Commonweal* 92 (March 13, 1970): 10–13.

Occupational Outlook Handbook. (U.S. Bureau of Labor Statistics.) Bulletin no. 1650.

Perrella, Vera C. "Employment of Recent College Graduates." *Monthly Labor Review* 96 (1973): 41–50.

President's Science Advisory Committee, Panel on Youth. *Youth; Transition to Adulthood.* Washington, D.C.: U.S. Government Printing Office, 1973.

Quey, Richard L. "Structure of Work as Purposeful Activity." *Vocational Guidance Quarterly* 19 (1971): 258–265.

Rosenbloom, Paul. "Vocation Education for a Changing World." In Rosenberg, Jerry M., ed. *New Conception of Vocational and Technical Education.* New York: Teachers College Press, n.d.

Schindler-Rainman, Eva and Lippitt, Ronald. *The Volunteer Community: Creative Use of Human Resources.* Washington, D.C.: Learning Resources, 1971.

"Special Report on Youth." *Fortune,* 79: (June, 1969): 73–74.

Stark, Joan. "Three-Year B.A. Who Will Choose It? Who Will Benefit?" *Journal of Higher Education* 44 (1973): 703–715.

Strachan, Margaret P. *Volunteering: A Practical Guide for Teen-Agers.* New York: David McKay Co., Inc., 1971.

Taubman, Paul and Wales, Terence. "Higher Education, Mental Ability and Screening." *Journal of Political Economy* 81 (1973): 28–55.

Taylor, Harold. *How to Change Colleges.* New York: Holt, Rinehart and Winston, Inc., 1971.

"Top Dartmouth Graduate Voices Despair." *The New York Times,* June 14, 1971, page 40.

Trent, James W. and Metzger, Leland L. *Beyond High School.* San Francisco: Jossey-Bass, Inc., Publishers, 1968.

Waterman, Alan and Waterman, Caroline. "A Cross-Institutional Study of Variables Relating to Satisfaction with College." *Journal of Educational Research* 65 (1971): 132–136.

————. "Relation between Ego Identity Status and Satisfaction with College." *Journal of Educational Research* 64: (1970): 165–168.

Withey, Steven B. *A Degree and What Else?* New York: McGraw-Hill, Inc., 1971.